Gregmears

Language Fundamentals

GRADE 5

D1264741

Editorial Development: Bonnie Brook
Communications
Content Editing: Marilyn Evans
Leslie Sorg
Copy Editing: Sonny Bennett
Art Direction: Cheryl Puckett
Cover Design: Liliana Potigian
Illustration: Mary Rojas
Design/Production: Arynne Elfenbein
Marcia Smith

EMC 2755

Helping Children Learn since 1979

Congratulations on your purchase of some of the finest teaching materials in the world.

Correlated to State Standards

For information about other Evan-Moor products, call 1-800-777-4362, fax 1-800-777-4332, or visit our Web site, www.evan-moor.com.
Entire contents © 2007 EVAN-MOOR CORP.
18 Lower Ragsdale Drive, Monterey, CA 93940-5746. Printed in USA.

Visit *teaching-standards.com* to view a correlation of this book's activities to your state's standards. This is a free service.

CPSIA: Bang Printing, 6080 Triangle Drive, City of Commerce, CA USA. 90040 [7/2011]

Table of Contents

Language Fundamentals • EMC 2755 • © Evan-Moor Corp.

Adverbs

Prepositions

Sentences

Mechanics

Capitalization

Abbreviations

Punctuation

What's in *Language Fundamentals*?

Language Fundamentals is your comprehensive resource for grade-level grammar, mechanics, usage, and vocabulary practice. The broad scope of language skills and the range in difficulty of the activity pages enable you to precisely target those skills that each student needs to practice.

Targeted Skill Practice

The core of *Language Fundamentals* is the 160-plus pages of student-friendly skill activities.

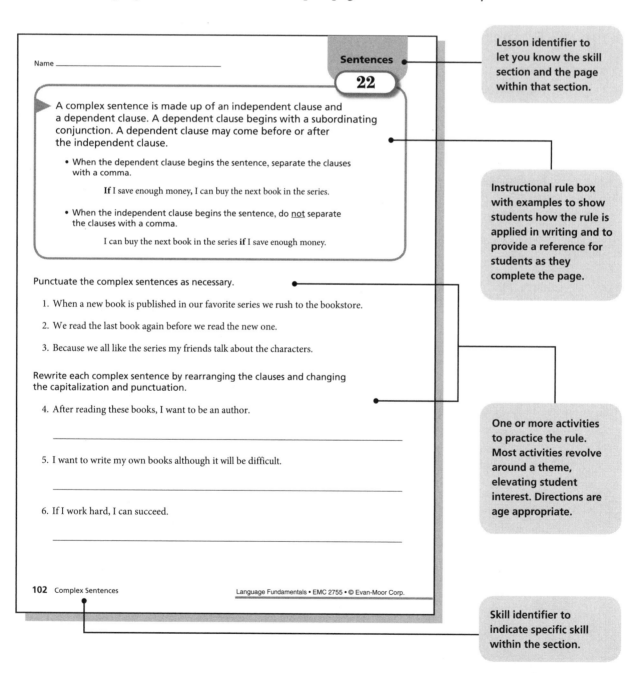

Name _____

Sentences

22

A complex sentence is made up of an independent clause and a dependent clause. A dependent clause begins with a subordinating conjunction. A dependent clause may come before or after the independent clause.

- When the dependent clause begins the sentence, separate the clauses with a comma.

    If I save enough money, I can buy the next book in the series.

- When the independent clause begins the sentence, do <u>not</u> separate the clauses with a comma.

    I can buy the next book in the series **if** I save enough money.

Punctuate the complex sentences as necessary.

1. When a new book is published in our favorite series we rush to the bookstore.

2. We read the last book again before we read the new one.

3. Because we all like the series my friends talk about the characters.

Rewrite each complex sentence by rearranging the clauses and changing the capitalization and punctuation.

4. After reading these books, I want to be an author.

    _____

5. I want to write my own books although it will be difficult.

    _____

6. If I work hard, I can succeed.

    _____

102 Complex Sentences   Language Fundamentals • EMC 2755 • © Evan-Moor Corp.

Lesson identifier to let you know the skill section and the page within that section.

Instructional rule box with examples to show students how the rule is applied in writing and to provide a reference for students as they complete the page.

One or more activities to practice the rule. Most activities revolve around a theme, elevating student interest. Directions are age appropriate.

Skill identifier to indicate specific skill within the section.

Review Pages

There are 31 review pages presented in multiple-choice test format to provide test-prep practice. Each review covers a small subset of skills and may be used as an assessment of student skill acquisition.

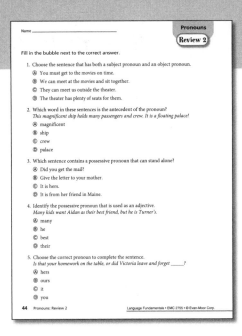

Paragraph Editing

These pages provide students with an opportunity to edit and correct paragraphs containing errors commonly made at this grade level. Each page is tied to specific skills addressed in the Targeted Skill Practice pages. After practicing a skill, students can use the corresponding pages in this section to transfer the skill to the context of writing.

A reproducible chart of proofreading marks is provided on page 183. Students can refer to this chart when editing those pages that direct students to use proofreading marks.

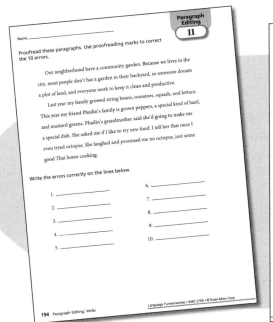

As a supplement to your core language arts program

What if....

- you've finished the material on a particular skill in your core program and your students still don't seem to get it?

- there is an objective in your state standards that is not covered in the core program?

- you need homework materials to reinforce the core program lessons?

- you have a new student who missed a number of vital language lessons?

- you want to provide a resource teacher, after-school program, or tutor with language practice that connects with class work?

- you want to provide ongoing test prep exercises as you move through your language program?

> *Language Fundamentals* can meet all these needs.

As an at-the-ready resource for those teachable moments

What if....

- your students do not understand comma placement in complex sentences?

- you begin a short story assignment and suddenly realize your students do not understand comma and quotation mark placement in dialogue?

- you are grading vocabulary quizzes and realize that some students have little transference of affix meaning from a known word to an unfamiliar word?

> *Language Fundamentals* has practice to address these skill needs.

As the perfect companion to Evan-Moor's *Daily Language Review*

Thousands of grade 1 through 6 classrooms use *Daily Language Review* for focused practice and review. Multiple studies show that this type of distributed, or spaced, practice is a powerful strategy for achieving proficiency and retention of skills.

Student responses on the weekly *Daily Language Review* units will indicate those skills needing further reinforcement. *Language Fundamentals* can then be used to provide the reteaching and additional practice. For example:

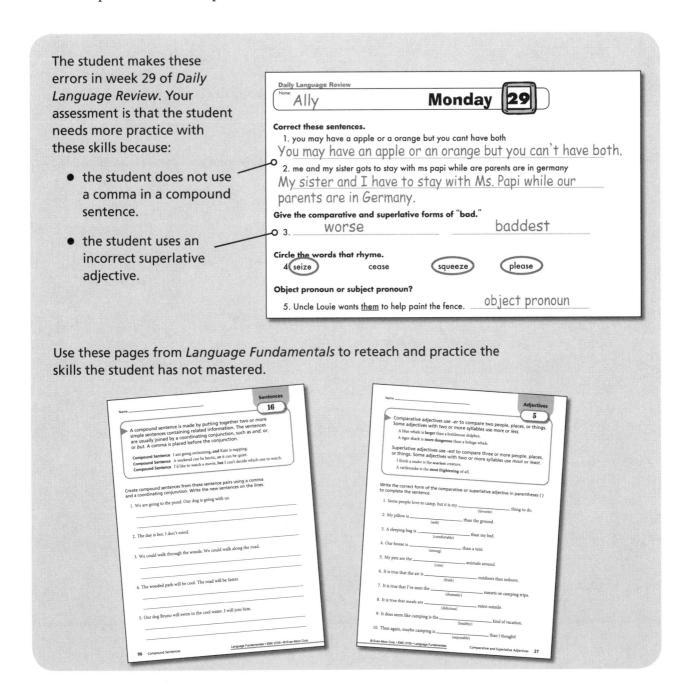

The student makes these errors in week 29 of *Daily Language Review*. Your assessment is that the student needs more practice with these skills because:

- the student does not use a comma in a compound sentence.

- the student uses an incorrect superlative adjective.

Use these pages from *Language Fundamentals* to reteach and practice the skills the student has not mastered.

Name _____

A noun names a person, place, thing, or idea.

Person	Place	Thing	Idea
leader	colony	flag	independence
pioneer	wilderness	plow	change
inventor	laboratory	invention	progress

Underline all the nouns in the sentences. Write *person, place, thing,* or *idea* below each noun.

1. Imagine being an explorer who leaves his country to search the world.

2. You are the captain of a ship sailing on a wide ocean.

3. You are a sailor with a map and only one bright star to follow in the sky.

4. Your goal is to find gold for your king or queen.

5. The discovery of a new continent could make you a hero.

6. You could also run out of food, or your boat might sink in a bad storm.

7. You could be swept into the water by a wave and attacked by a shark.

8. Exploration is dangerous. It takes courage to sail to an unknown land.

> A noun can be singular or plural.
>
> - A singular noun names one person, place, thing, or idea.
>
> - A plural noun names more than one.
>
> - Add *s* to most nouns to make them plural.
>
> | Singular | Plural |
> | --- | --- |
> | pioneer | pioneer**s** |
> | desert | desert**s** |
> | wheel | wheel**s** |
> | thought | thought**s** |

Circle the singular nouns. Underline the plural nouns.

1. Many settlers left their homes and traveled across the country.

2. They followed their dreams and headed for new places.

3. They had a belief that they could build farms and start new towns.

4. They packed wagons pulled by horses or other animals for the trip.

5. Often they could take only a few special objects, like a chair or a clock.

6. Sometimes grandparents, aunts, and uncles were left behind.

7. Kids could usually bring their pets and maybe a small toy.

8. Kids helped their parents along the way to their new home.

9. They would help cook meals, tend the animals, and watch for danger.

10. Sometimes a man, woman, or child kept a diary of events.

11. Many journals describe accidents and deaths along the way.

12. Today we can read those tales in books to learn about those experiences.

   Language Fundamentals • EMC 2755 • © Evan-Moor Corp.

> Add *es* to singular nouns that end in *sh, ch, x, s,* and *z* to form the plural.

Singular	Plural
brush	brushes
bunch	bunches
tax	taxes
pass	passes
klutz	klutzes

Complete each sentence. Choose a word from the word box.
Write it in plural form on the line.

> porch   dress   bench   waltz   dish   ax   lynx   bush   ranch   wish

1. Every pioneer family needed tools, such as _____.

2. There might be trees and _____ to cut down.

3. There were small cabins or bigger homes with _____ to build.

4. Over time, some small farms expanded into huge cattle or sheep _____.

5. There was often danger from wolves and wildcats, such as _____.

6. Pioneers grew their own food and made the shirts and _____ they wore.

7. They made all of their furniture, such as tables and _____.

8. Kids had to pitch in on more chores than just doing the _____.

9. They might have other _____, but they were needed as workers.

10. For fun, a family might go to a barn dance with square dancing and _____.

> To form the plural of nouns that end in a consonant and *y*, change the *y* to *i* and add *es*.

Singular	Plural
library	librar**ies**
story	stor**ies**

If a noun ends in a vowel and *y*, just add *s*.

Singular	Plural
alley	alley**s**
boy	boy**s**

Complete each sentence. Choose a word from the word box.
Write it in plural form on each line.

> holiday   family   bakery   balcony   cherry   tray   city   berry   joy

1. Early in the morning, _____ open to sell fresh bread.

2. In small towns, there may be one store, but in _____ there are many.

3. Along with bread, there are _____ of rolls and cookies for sale.

4. There are always fresh pies filled with _____ or _____.

5. There are often special baked goods made just for the _____.

6. Food is one way that people celebrate the _____ of every season.

7. Long ago, those businesses were all run by _____.

8. They lived upstairs and might be seen relaxing at night on their _____.

Name _____

> Some nouns have irregular forms with special spellings.

Singular	Plural
mouse	**mice**
goose	**geese**
ox	**oxen**
tooth	**teeth**
foot	**feet**
person	**people**
child	**children**
woman	**women**
man	**men**

Read each clue. Write the word in the correct singular or plural form on the line.

1. I walk on my two _____.

2. _____ head south for the winter.

3. The _____ wore tuxedos for the wedding.

4. I lost my first _____ when I was six years old.

5. The _____ run on the playground.

6. _____ have kept animals as pets for many years.

7. I use my _____ to chew my food.

8. Early settlers used _____ for plowing.

9. My friend screams when she sees _____.

10. The _____ made quilts that told stories.

Name _____

Some nouns have the same spelling in the singular and the plural form. Use the context of a sentence to tell if the noun is singular or plural.

sheep   deer   moose   buffalo   fish   trout   aircraft

Singular   I see one **aircraft** coming in to land.
Plural   There are many **aircraft** on the deck of the ship.

For each word in bold, circle *singular* or *plural* to tell how it is used. If it is singular, write a sentence using the plural form. If it is plural, write a sentence using the singular form.

1. Once there were thousands of **buffalo** on the prairie.   singular   plural

   _____

2. In most places, it is still easy to see lots of **deer** around.   singular   plural

   _____

3. It is more unusual to see a **moose** in the wild.   singular   plural

   _____

4. **Sheep** are still raised on many farms and ranches.   singular   plural

   _____

5. Some people would rather catch a **fish** than eat it.   singular   plural

   _____

6. One big **trout** makes a very tasty meal.   singular   plural

   _____

Fill in the bubble next to the correct answer.

1. What kinds of nouns are included in this sentence?
   Look at a painting to see how an artist uses imagination.
   Ⓐ person, place, and thing
   Ⓑ person, place, and idea
   Ⓒ person, thing, and idea
   Ⓓ person, place, thing, and idea

2. Which sentence has plural nouns correctly made with *s* and *es*?
   Ⓐ They used axes to cut down the trees and branchs.
   Ⓑ There were birds, such as finches, living in the trees.
   Ⓒ There are still low bushs where the foxes like to hide.
   Ⓓ The baby foxs hide behind their mothers.

3. Which sentence has the correct plural form for the word that ends in *y*?
   Ⓐ George Washington is said to have cut down a tree with cherris.
   Ⓑ Ben Franklin founded one of the first librarys.
   Ⓒ Sam Adams was a leader for independence in the colonies.
   Ⓓ There are many storys about Abe Lincoln and his honesty.

4. How many plural words are found in this sentence?
   The oxen pulled the wagon with the woman and children while the man walked.
   Ⓐ two
   Ⓑ three
   Ⓒ four
   Ⓓ five

5. Which sentence uses *sheep* in the singular form?
   Ⓐ Sheep give wool for making cloth.
   Ⓑ The lost sheep is back in the pen.
   Ⓒ The sheep are grazing in the meadow.
   Ⓓ The shepherd and his dog bring in all the sheep.

> A possessive noun shows ownership. For singular nouns, add an apostrophe and s ('s) to form the possessive.
>
> the king**'s** soldiers
> the state**'s** capital
> the flag**'s** stars

Read each sentence. Circle the possessive noun.

1. Each student's project is to research one colony.

2. The school library's resources will be a place to start.

3. I will use my family's computer to find more information.

4. I need to identify the colony's founder or key leader.

5. I need to know this person's name and background.

Circle the noun that should be possessive. Write each possessive noun correctly on the line.

6. I want to find the ship name, like *The Mayflower*. _____

7. I'll draw a map with each important settlement location. _____

8. I need to figure out a scale so the map size is accurate. _____

9. I can make a diorama to show a typical colonist home. _____

10. I can use pictures of food to show a farmer typical crops. _____

11. I want to find out about a child life in the colony. _____

12. I want my report to hold each classmate attention. _____

A possessive noun can be singular or plural.

- For plural nouns that end in s, add an apostrophe after the s (s').

    the student**s'** observations

    the field**s'** crops

    the cloud**s'** shapes

- Form the possessive of irregular plurals by adding an apostrophe and s ('s).

    the **women's** gardens

    the **mice's** babies

    the **fish's** tails

Read the sentences. Circle each noun that should be possessive, and then write each noun correctly on the line.

1. The trees flowers are in bloom. _____

2. The flowers wonderful scent fills the air. _____

3. The bees hive is always buzzing now. _____

4. Other insects peeps and clicks can be heard. _____

5. Some families picnics are being joined by ants. _____

6. Some frogs croaks signal that they are out and about. _____

7. The deers fawns hide beside their mothers. _____

8. Robins nests are filled with blue eggs waiting to hatch. _____

9. Children shouts in the park mean a ballgame is in progress. _____

10. Spring days sights, sounds, and fun are always the best! _____

A proper noun names a specific person, place, thing, or idea.

- A proper noun begins with a capital letter.
- A common noun names any person, place, thing, or idea. It does not start with a capital.

Proper Noun	Common Noun
George Washington	president
Central Park	park
St. Patrick's Day Parade	parade
Independence Day	holiday

Underline the common nouns. For the proper nouns, circle the letters that should be capitalized.

1. My family is visiting new york city in july.

2. We will drive across the george washington bridge to get to the city.

3. We can leave our car in the garage at our hotel on columbus avenue.

4. We will take the subway to visit chinatown on mott street.

5. I want to have lunch at a restaurant before we go to the statue of liberty.

6. We'll take a ferry to ellis island to see exhibits about immigrants to america.

7. I hope we can take a boat that sails under the brooklyn bridge.

8. I know the bridge was built by john roebling and his son, washington.

9. We can ride a big elevator to the top floor of the empire state building.

10. I also want to go to broadway or times square to see a play or a musical.

11. We can take a carriage pulled by a horse to see central park.

12. Best of all will be the fireworks over the hudson river on independence day!

Language Fundamentals • EMC 2755 • © Evan-Moor Corp.

Fill in the bubble next to the correct answer.

1. Which sentence has a singular possessive noun?

    Ⓐ The museum has some dinosaurs' skeletons on display.

    Ⓑ A dinosaur had hundreds of bones in its body.

    Ⓒ Experts' knowledge is needed to put each skeleton together.

    Ⓓ The museum's experts are the best in the world.

2. Which sentence has the most plural possessive nouns?

    Ⓐ Each student's ticket must be stamped with today's date.

    Ⓑ The children's teams are carrying their schools' banners.

    Ⓒ The women's races are popular events today.

    Ⓓ One team's fans cheer louder than the rest!

3. Which sentence has the correct plural possessive for *aircraft*?

    Ⓐ Several aircraft's pilots were on the deck of the ship.

    Ⓑ The aircrafts' pilots were tired from hours of flying.

    Ⓒ The aircraftes' wings were all damaged in the storm.

    Ⓓ The aircrafts mechanics were needed to fix the wings.

4. Which sentence has only proper nouns?

    Ⓐ Italy is shaped like a boot on a map of Europe.

    Ⓑ The English Channel is a big body of water.

    Ⓒ Holland is also called the Netherlands.

    Ⓓ France's largest neighbors are Spain and Germany.

5. Which sentence has one common noun and one proper noun?

    Ⓐ Tourists love to visit the Grand Canyon.

    Ⓑ The Grand Canyon is in Arizona.

    Ⓒ The OK Corral in Tombstone is popular.

    Ⓓ Tucson is also a popular city with tourists.

Name _____

> An adjective describes a noun or a pronoun. Adjectives can come
> before the nouns they are modifying, or they can follow linking verbs.
>
> The **first** movies were **silent**.
>
> - *First* is an adjective that comes before the noun *movies.*
>
> - *Silent* is also an adjective that describes movies, but it follows
>   the linking verb *were.*

Underline the adjectives in the sentences.

1. Imagine going to a big cinema.

2. You find a comfortable seat and watch the dark screen turn bright.

3. You expect the movie to be exciting.

4. It stars a handsome actor and a beautiful actress who are famous.

5. But when you see them on the huge screen, you do not hear human voices.

6. Silent movies explained the story with printed words on the screen.

7. As movies became popular, talking pictures were invented.

8. You had to be a good reader who was fast to watch a silent film.

9. Watching a foreign film from another country is a similar experience.

10. You read English words on the screen as the actors speak a different language.

 Language Fundamentals • EMC 2755 • © Evan-Moor Corp.

> Adjectives describe the sight, sound, smell, touch, or taste of a noun.

	Adjective	Noun
Sight	green	plant
Sound	gruff	voice
Smell	fragrant	garden
Touch	soft	fur
Taste	delicious	meal

Read the sentence and the type of adjective identified in the parentheses ( ).
Circle the correct adjective to complete the sentence.

1. The morning dew is _____.
   (sight)   wet   sparkling   cold

2. The _____ sunlight dries everything quickly.   bright   yellow   warm
   (touch)

3. A breeze blows the _____ air from the ocean.   fresh   freezing   moist
   (smell)

4. _____ insects awaken in the grass.   Humming   Big   Colorful
   (sound)

5. They jump and buzz around the _____ flowers.   pretty   sweet   sticky
   (taste)

6. My _____ nose tells me that spring is here.   red   stinky   itchy
   (touch)

7. The air is _____, but my nose knows it is there. thick   odorless   clear
   (smell)

8. The _____ pollen in the air makes me sneeze!   invisible   silent   strong
   (sight)

Adjectives can tell how many and what kind.

How Many	What Kind
ten friends	**pure** gold
more supplies	**fresh** air
fewer choices	**new** books
several advantages	**old** furniture

Write adjectives from the word box to complete the sentences. On the line below each sentence, explain what the adjective tells. The first one has been done for you.

> dozens   broken   ancient   brilliant   thousand   multiple

1. Archaeologists who dig for buried objects must have ___**brilliant**___ imaginations.

   Brilliant tells what kind of imagination.

2. They have to take a _____ piece of pottery and imagine a whole pot or jar.

   _____

3. It must be very exciting when they discover _____ of objects in one place.

   _____

4. It's fascinating to visit a museum and see _____ displays of all kinds of artifacts.

   _____

5. It's amazing to think of _____ objects in the ground for a

   _____ years!

   _____

Fill in the bubble next to the correct answer.

1. Which sentence has one adjective?

   Ⓐ The black clouds are rumbling.

   Ⓑ The white lightning is flashing.

   Ⓒ The cold raindrops hit the tin roof.

   Ⓓ The freezing rain turns to ice.

2. Which word is an adjective in this sentence?
   A bear can be dangerous if you stand too close to her cubs.

   Ⓐ bear

   Ⓑ dangerous

   Ⓒ too

   Ⓓ close

3. Complete the sentence with an adjective that describes *taste*.
   The _____ drink was refreshing.

   Ⓐ cool

   Ⓑ tall

   Ⓒ lemon

   Ⓓ slushy

4. Complete the sentence with the adjective that describes *how many*.
   _____ kids want to try out for our team this year.

   Ⓐ Fewer

   Ⓑ New

   Ⓒ Lazy

   Ⓓ Talented

5. Complete the sentence with the adjective that describes *what kind*.
   The _____ bracelets were an unusual gift.

   Ⓐ five

   Ⓑ many

   Ⓒ chipped

   Ⓓ numerous

Adjectives are used to make comparisons.

- Comparative adjectives with *–er* compare a noun to another noun.

   The new knife is **sharper** than the old one.

   sharp + **er** = sharper

- Superlative adjectives with *–est* compare a noun with two or more other nouns.

   We could take a train or a bus, but an airplane is the **fastest** way to go.

   fast + **est** = fastest

Circle the correct form of the adjective to complete each sentence. Then write *C* for *comparative* or *S* for *superlative* in the sentence to tell what kind of adjective is needed.

1. Our first train trip was _____ than the second.   longer   longest

2. On the second trip, we made our _____ mistake ever.   bigger   biggest

3. We got the _____ tickets we could buy.   cheaper   cheapest

4. We got to the station _____ than we planned.   later   latest

5. Other passengers got there _____ and took all the seats.   earlier   earliest

6. The floor is the _____ place to sit on a train!   harder   hardest

7. Soon one family member was _____ than the next.   grumpier   grumpiest

8. Our dog on his leash was _____ of all.   crankier   crankiest

9. Mom looked on the map and saw a _____ town to visit.   closer   closest

10. It was the _____ decision to cut short our trip!   wiser   wisest

    Language Fundamentals • EMC 2755 • © Evan-Moor Corp.

> Comparative adjectives use *–er* to compare two people, places, or things. Some adjectives with two or more syllables use *more* or *less.*
>
> A blue whale is **larger** than a bottlenose dolphin.
>
> A tiger shark is **more dangerous** than a beluga whale.
>
> Superlative adjectives use *–est* to compare three or more people, places, or things. Some adjectives with two or more syllables use *most* or *least.*
>
> I think a snake is the **scariest** creature.
>
> A rattlesnake is the **most frightening** of all.

Write the correct form of the comparative or superlative adjective in parentheses ( ) to complete the sentence.

1. Some people love to camp, but it is my _____ thing to do.
   (favorite)

2. My pillow is _____ than the ground.
   (soft)

3. A sleeping bag is _____ than my bed.
   (comfortable)

4. Our house is _____ than a tent.
   (strong)

5. My pets are the _____ animals around.
   (cute)

6. It is true that the air is _____ outdoors than indoors.
   (fresh)

7. It is true that I've seen the _____ sunsets on camping trips.
   (dramatic)

8. It is true that meals are _____ eaten outside.
   (delicious)

9. It does seem like camping is the _____ kind of vacation.
   (healthy)

10. Then again, maybe camping is _____ than I thought!
    (enjoyable)

> Some adjectives have irregular comparative and superlative forms.

Adjective	Comparative	Superlative
many	more	most
good	better	best
bad	worse	worst
some	fewer	least

The blue team has **many** wins.

The green team has **more** wins.

Our red team has the **most** wins.

Circle the correct adjective to complete the sentence. Write it on the line.

1. Our team is _____ this week than last week.
   (good, better, worst)

2. We have _____ players that are trying harder.
   (most, best, more)

3. There were _____ mistakes on the field than before.
   (fewer, least, some)

4. We have _____ reasons to be proud of our improvement.
   (most, many, least)

5. I predict we will play our _____ game ever today.
   (good, better, best)

6. But if we lose, it will not be the _____ thing that could happen!
   (bad, worse, worst)

Fill in the bubble next to the correct answer.

1. Complete the sentence with the correct form of the adjective.
   The city lights are _____ on a clear night than a misty one.
   - Ⓐ least bright
   - Ⓑ more bright
   - Ⓒ brighter
   - Ⓓ brightest

2. Which sentence has two superlative adjectives?
   - Ⓐ The darkest color will be good on that chair.
   - Ⓑ She has the reddest hair of the family.
   - Ⓒ The larger dog has the longest tail I have seen.
   - Ⓓ The greenest frogs live in the most tropical places.

3. Which adjective could be used to compare two friends?
   - Ⓐ taller
   - Ⓑ shortest
   - Ⓒ some
   - Ⓓ least

4. Choose the correct adjective for the comparison.
   A football player is _____ than a ballet dancer.
   - Ⓐ less graceful
   - Ⓑ strongest
   - Ⓒ more heavier
   - Ⓓ more quick

5. What is the rule for using *less, least, more,* and *most* with an adjective?
   - Ⓐ if the adjective comes before the noun
   - Ⓑ if the adjective comes after the noun
   - Ⓒ always when the adjective has two or more syllables
   - Ⓓ sometimes when the adjective has two or more syllables

Proper adjectives are made from some proper nouns.
Proper adjectives begin with a capital letter.

We speak the **English** language because we were once a colony of **England.**

Proper Noun	Proper Adjective	Proper Noun	Proper Adjective
Japan	**Japanese**	Belgium	**Belgian**
Egypt	**Egyptian**	Hawaii	**Hawaiian**
Ireland	**Irish**	Argentina	**Argentinean**
Pakistan	**Pakistani**	France	**French**
Switzerland	**Swiss**	Poland	**Polish**
Vietnam	**Vietnamese**	Thailand	**Thai**
Hungary	**Hungarian**		

Underline the proper adjective in the sentence. Then write the proper noun
it comes from on the line.

1. The Hawaiian Islands are found in the Pacific Ocean. _____

2. The Australian continent is located in the Pacific, too. _____

3. The Chinese people have one of the oldest cultures. _____

4. Russia is the European country with the most land. _____

5. The Swiss Alps are among the most famous mountains. _____

6. The Rhine is a famous German river. _____

7. Warsaw is a famous Polish city. _____

8. Hanoi is a well-known Vietnamese city. _____

9. You don't need to fly to Bangkok for Thai food. _____

10. You don't need to visit Budapest for Hungarian goulash. _____

Language Fundamentals • EMC 2755 • © Evan-Moor Corp.

The words *a, an,* and *the* are called articles.

- Use *a* before singular nouns or other adjectives that start with a consonant.
- Use *an* before singular nouns or other adjectives that start with a vowel.
- Use *the* with singular or plural nouns.

> **A** good friend is coming to visit. She is **an** aunt.
> **The** boys are forming a team and **the** coach is pleased.

Demonstrative adjectives tell which one. The words *this, that, these,* and *those* are demonstrative adjectives when they are used before a noun.

- Use *this* and *that* before singular nouns.
- Use *these* and *those* before plural nouns.

> **This** book is new. **That** book is old.
> **These** sandwiches are fresh. **Those** sandwiches are stale.

This, that, these, and *those* are pronouns when they stand alone and do not come before a noun.

Underline each article once and each demonstrative adjective twice.
For each demonstrative adjective, circle the specific noun being pointed out.
For each article, circle the noun or adjective that determines the choice of article.

1. This contest will be easy to win for an experienced baker like me.

2. I start with these carrots and use a gadget to shred them.

3. The grated carrots go in this bowl.

4. I will chop those walnuts and sprinkle them in a pan.

5. An optional ingredient is raisins in this particular recipe.

6. The batter goes in that round pan and into an oven to bake.

7. Did I remember to add the soda that makes the cake rise?

8. Maybe those other bakers in the contest have a chance to win after all!

Fill in the bubble next to the correct answer.

1. Which word is a proper adjective?

   (A) Irelandian

   (B) Indiana

   (C) Italian

   (D) India

2. Which rule for using proper adjectives is correct?

   (A) A proper adjective always ends in a vowel.

   (B) A proper adjective always begins with a capital letter.

   (C) A proper adjective always follows a proper noun.

   (D) A proper adjective always comes before a proper noun.

3. Which sentence correctly uses the articles *a* and *an?*

   (A) An letter is addressed to a author.

   (B) A author is writing an book about elephants.

   (C) We can look for a book to read about an elephant.

   (D) Here are an book and a article that you and I would like.

4. Which sentence correctly uses a demonstrative adjective?

   (A) This trip will be easier if we have a map.

   (B) That maps are too old to use.

   (C) We can find our way with a good compass.

   (D) Look in the atlas for the map we need.

5. Together, how many articles and demonstrative adjectives are in this sentence?
   These dead leaves and the branches are from those trees.

   (A) one

   (B) two

   (C) three

   (D) four

   Language Fundamentals • EMC 2755 • © Evan-Moor Corp.

Pronouns are used in place of nouns. Pronouns can be singular or plural.

I   you   he   she   it   they   we   me   him   her   them   us

Lydia is in fifth grade. **She** is in our class.

David is in our class. **He** is in fifth grade.

Lydia and David are new students. **They** are both friendly.

Jenny and I sit next to **Lydia and David. We** like them.

Underline the pronoun in each pair of sentences. On the line, write the noun that the pronoun replaced.

1. The bus is coming. It is late.   _____

2. Mr. Jefferson is the driver. He is usually on time.   _____

3. Isaiah and Felicia are laughing. They love a joke.   _____

4. Carmen is laughing. She is usually reading quietly.   _____

5. Tony sits next to Carlos. Tony is grinning at him.   _____

6. Carlos is looking at Rosa. Carlos is smiling at her.   _____

7. Why are the kids laughing? What happened to them?   _____

8. My brother and I want to know. We missed something!   _____

9. Tony tells my brother and me. Tony looks at us.   _____

10. My brother and I grin. We laugh, too.   _____

> Pronouns are used in place of nouns. Use pronouns to avoid repeating names, words in a sentence, or words in a group of sentences.
>
> **I   me   you   he   she   him   her   it   they   them   we   us**
>
> Josh knows there is a fire siren blaring because **Josh** can hear **the siren**.
>
> Josh knows there is a fire siren blaring because **he** can hear **it**.
>
> The fire was put out quickly. **It** was in an empty lot. Fortunately, **it** did not spread.

Read the paragraphs. Write the correct pronouns above the underlined words.

The firefighters are visiting our school today. <u>The firefighters</u> are bringing one of their big trucks. The truck has a tall ladder on <u>the truck</u>. Jamal says <u>Jamal</u> would like to climb the ladder. Dora will, too, if <u>Dora</u> gets the chance. <u>Jamal and Dora</u> both like high places. Trang and I have decided that <u>Trang and I</u> are not like <u>Jamal and Dora</u>. <u>Trang and I</u> like to stay on the ground!

The firefighters discuss fire safety. <u>The firefighters</u> asked <u>Jamal, Dora, Trang, and me</u> some questions. Jamal is always the first to answer. Fire safety is important to <u>Jamal</u>. There was a fire in the apartment building where <u>Jamal</u> lives. <u>The fire</u> started in the kitchen of a neighbor, Mrs. Chan. <u>Mrs. Chan</u> had some papers too close to the stove. <u>The papers</u> caught fire. Everyone got out safely, including Mrs. Chan. Now Jamal is an expert on fire safety. <u>Jamal</u> told <u>Dora, Trang, and me</u> that <u>Dora, Trang, and I</u> should be, too!

> The antecedent is the noun or nouns that the pronoun refers to or replaces.

<u>Elizabeth</u> wants to babysit, but <u>**she**</u> is too young.
Antecedent   **Pronoun**

- The antecedent can be in a different sentence.

<u>Tom</u> would like to do yardwork. **He** should ask if anyone needs help.
Antecedent   **Pronoun**

- Make sure that the pronoun agrees with the antecedent in gender (male or female) and number (singular or plural).

Mr. Perez will hire **the children**. **He** will ask **them** to start work tomorrow.

Complete each sentence with the correct pronoun to match the underlined antecedent.

1. <u>Dr. Marcia Goodfriend</u> is the local veterinarian. _____ needs an assistant.

2. It would be interesting to work with <u>animals</u> and help _____ get well.

3. <u>Veterinarians</u> need lots of experience. _____ have patients that can't talk to _____.

4. Everyone calls her <u>Dr. Marcia</u>. _____ lets me call _____ that, too.

5. My dog <u>Max</u> is a new patient of Dr. Goodfriend. _____ is a good boy.

6. <u>My mother</u> was afraid Max would make a mess, but _____ is very pleased.

7. Max behaves better than other <u>puppies</u>. _____ can get into a lot of trouble.

8. Dr. Marcia says <u>Max and I</u> are a good pair, and _____ are lucky to have each other!

> The antecedent is the noun or nouns the pronoun refers to or replaces.
>
> If a pronoun can refer to more than one noun, the antecedent may be unclear. When this happens, rewrite the sentence to fix the unclear antecedent.
>
> | | |
> |---|---|
> | **Unclear** | The boys have plans for vacation, and **they** are ready. |
> | **Explanation** | It is not clear whether *they* refers to *the boys* or *plans*. |
> | **Clear** | **The boys** are ready for vacation. **They** have plans. |

Explain why each sentence is unclear. Rewrite each sentence correctly.

1. The friends are renting sailboats, and they are fast.

    Explanation: _____

    _____

    Rewrite: _____

    _____

2. There are sharks around, and now they can't go in the water!

    Explanation: _____

    _____

    Rewrite: _____

    _____

A singular pronoun takes the place of one person, place, thing, or idea.

I   you   he   she   it   me   him   her

My mother is a pilot.   **My father** is a pilot.
She is a pilot.   **He** is a pilot.

The airport is nearby.   **Flying** is fun.
It is nearby.   **It** is fun.

Circle the singular pronouns that can replace the underlined words.

1. Daphne is flying on the airplane.
   (She, You)   (him, it)

2. California is a long way for Daphne to travel alone.
   (She, It)   (she, her)

3. This flight is the first one for Daphne.
   (It, Him)   (she, her)

4. Daphne asked Dwayne, "Can Daphne visit Dwayne during the flight?"
                          (she, I)   (I, you)

5. Why isn't Dwayne sitting with Daphne?
      (him, he)   (she, her)

6. Dwayne is flying the plane!
   (He, Him)   (he, it)

A plural pronoun takes the place of more than one person, place, thing, or idea.

they   we   them   us   you

The computers are working.   **Michael and I** are doing research.
They are working.   **We** are doing research.

Maria and you will be next.   Finding **facts** takes time.
You will be next.   Finding **them** takes time.

Replace each underlined noun with the correct plural pronoun.
Write the pronoun on the line.

1. <u>Our teachers</u> are planning a science competition.

   _____ are planning a science competition.

2. <u>Our class</u> will challenge <u>other classes</u>.

   _____ will challenge _____.

3. I hope I can be on a team with <u>Lee and Bena</u>.

   I hope I can be on a team with _____.

4. <u>Adrianne and Lian</u> would also make good partners for <u>Lee and me</u>.

   _____ would also make good partners for _____.

5. If <u>you and Bena</u> work together, <u>our teams</u> can share ideas.

   If _____ work together, _____ can share ideas.

6. <u>The teachers</u> suggested a building competition for <u>our classes</u>.

   _____ suggested a building competition for _____.

Fill in the bubble next to the correct answer.

1. Which one tells something accurate about pronouns?

   Ⓐ Writers use pronouns mainly to write shorter sentences.

   Ⓑ Writers use pronouns only to replace people's names.

   Ⓒ Writers use pronouns to avoid repeating names or words.

   Ⓓ Writers should rarely use pronouns.

2. Choose the correct pronoun to complete this sentence.
   The cats are under the bed, and now _____ will not come out.

   Ⓐ them

   Ⓑ they

   Ⓒ we

   Ⓓ it

3. How many singular pronouns are in this sentence?
   If they ask me, then it will work out perfectly for us.

   Ⓐ one

   Ⓑ two

   Ⓒ three

   Ⓓ four

4. Which sentence has only plural pronouns?

   Ⓐ She will dress up for the party.

   Ⓑ You and I need costumes to wear.

   Ⓒ They have masks we can borrow.

   Ⓓ We should wear a costume with ears on it.

5. Which pair of sentences does <u>not</u> have a clear antecedent?

   Ⓐ The children went to the zoo. They saw giraffes.

   Ⓑ I met my friends at the mall. We went shopping.

   Ⓒ John and Susan went to the playground. He pushed her in the swing.

   Ⓓ The mother took her daughter to the museum. She had fun.

A subject pronoun replaces a noun that is the subject of a sentence.

I you he she it we they

The team members are having a party.   **Hannah and I** are cooking.
They are having a party.   **We** are cooking.

Greg will clean up.   **The party** is on Saturday.
He will clean up.   **It** is on Saturday.

Write the correct subject pronoun in each sentence for the word in parentheses.

1. _____ does not want a party for her birthday. (My mother)

2. _____ tried to get backstage. (My cousin and I)

3. _____ sailed into the bay. (The boat)

4. _____ are both working late. (Our parents)

5. _____ skateboards every afternoon. (My brother)

6. _____ like to put on plays for our family. (My sister and I)

7. _____ accidentally spilled soup on the rug! (You and my brother)

8. _____ used her allowance to buy a new CD. (My sister)

9. _____ need a new pair of ballet slippers. (Myself)

Write a sentence with a subject pronoun about your family.

10. _____

_____

> An object pronoun follows an action verb or a preposition (words such as *about, at, for, of, to,* and *with*).
>
> **me   you   him   her   it   us   them**
>
> This book is just right **for me**. I'll **read it**. Then I'll **give it to her.**

Circle the object pronouns in the sentences.

1. We had a guest speaker today who talked to us about poetry.

2. He read some poems, and then some students asked him questions.

3. I liked the poems and wanted to know how the poet wrote them.

4. He said that writing takes time, so don't try to do it quickly.

5. Then he read my poem, and the class really liked it.

6. You said there was a woman artist who spoke to you about painting.

7. You should show her your drawings from art class.

8. She could talk to you about how to express different ideas.

9. With help, we could collaborate on a book about us.

10. You could draw pictures of me, and I could write about you!

11. Our friends could be in it.

12. Everyone would know us!

> A possessive pronoun shows ownership. A possessive pronoun does <u>not</u> need an apostrophe. Some possessive pronouns are used before a noun and serve as adjectives.
>
> **her   his   its   my   our   their   your**
>
> The tree has **its leaves**. The flowers have **their petals**. The wind has **your hat**.

Underline the possessive pronouns. Circle the noun modified by each possessive pronoun.

1. Nature can be powerful and show its force in different ways.

2. Hurricanes are known for their high winds and for their names, too.

3. A hurricane gets a person's name, so it could be your name or my name.

4. Kids in our class knew about tornadoes and their destruction from the movies.

5. A tornado sends Dorothy on her imaginary journey in *The Wizard of Oz*.

6. Storm chasers do their dangerous work in *Twister*.

7. That movie inspired my brother to decorate his room with weather maps!

8. Most people recognize a tornado by its unique funnel shape.

9. Your weather depends on where you live, and our area rarely gets tornadoes.

10. My uncle lives in an earthquake zone, and a big quake is his biggest worry.

11. My aunt lives by a large river, and her concern is flooding.

12. We get blizzards that nearly bury our whole house, but we like our snowy winters!

Language Fundamentals • EMC 2755 • © Evan-Moor Corp.

Name _____

> A possessive pronoun shows ownership. A possessive pronoun does <u>not</u> need an apostrophe. Some possessive pronouns can stand alone.
>
> **his   hers   mine   ours   yours   theirs**
>
> Did Dylan say the canary is **his?** Andrew and Alexis claimed the snake is **theirs.**

Complete each sentence with a possessive pronoun from the list above.

1. All of my friends have pets, and today I will get _____.

2. I like your dog, but I don't want one just like _____.

3. The neighbors have a dog, but I think _____ is too ferocious for me.

4. I like cuddly pets and want _____ to be a little shy.

5. Rachel has a cat, but I have not seen _____.

6. She says her cat is bigger than Jack's cat and stronger than _____.

7. My sister is also getting a pet, so she'll have _____ and I'll have _____.

8. She wants a puppy and says if I get one, then _____ can play together.

Write two sentences about a pet that include possessive pronouns that stand alone.

9. _____

_____

10. _____

_____

Name _____

Fill in the bubble next to the correct answer.

1. Choose the sentence that has both a subject pronoun and an object pronoun.

   Ⓐ You must get to the movies on time.

   Ⓑ We can meet at the movies and sit together.

   Ⓒ They can meet us outside the theater.

   Ⓓ The theater has plenty of seats for them.

2. Which word in these sentences is the antecedent of the pronoun?
   This magnificent ship holds many passengers and crew. It is a floating palace!

   Ⓐ magnificent

   Ⓑ ship

   Ⓒ crew

   Ⓓ palace

3. Which sentence contains a possessive pronoun that can stand alone?

   Ⓐ Did you get the mail?

   Ⓑ Give the letter to your mother.

   Ⓒ It is hers.

   Ⓓ It is from her friend in Maine.

4. Identify the possessive pronoun that is used as an adjective.
   Many kids want Aidan as their best friend, but he is Turner's.

   Ⓐ many

   Ⓑ he

   Ⓒ best

   Ⓓ their

5. Choose the correct pronoun to complete the sentence.
   Is that your homework on the table, or did Victoria leave and forget _____?

   Ⓐ hers

   Ⓑ ours

   Ⓒ it

   Ⓓ you

   Language Fundamentals • EMC 2755 • © Evan-Moor Corp.

Name _____

> A verb is a word that tells what a noun does or is.
>
> Mollie **makes** beautiful scrapbooks.
>
> Her scrapbooks **are** colorful.
>
> Mollie **pasted** a party invitation onto a page.
>
> She **will take** photos at the party.

Underline the verb in each sentence.

1. Mollie goes to the craft store for supplies.

2. Today she will choose some bright pink paper.

3. Last Saturday, she cut yellow paper into fancy shapes.

4. Scrapbooks are popular.

5. Mollie's friend taught her about this great hobby.

6. At the craft store, colorful beads sparkle in bins and jars.

7. Mollie buys beads, ribbons, and paper for her scrapbook.

Write three sentences about one of your favorite things to do.
Circle the verbs.

8. _____

_____

9. _____

_____

10. _____

_____

> An action verb tells what a noun does, did, or will do.
>
> - Most action verbs express an action that can be seen or heard.
>
>   Sean and his parents **ride** the train into the city.
>   The train's wheels **clicked** on the track.
>
> - Other action verbs express an action that cannot be either seen or heard.
>
>   The family **likes** train travel.
>   Sean **will enjoy** a city adventure.

Write the action verb in each sentence.

1. Sean watches the scenery from his seat by the window.   _____

2. His dad points to the city's skyline.   _____

3. At the train station, the family looks at a map.   _____

4. First, they will visit the Empire State Building.   _____

5. That elevator flew to the top floor!   _____

Underline the action verb in each sentence. Circle *yes* if the action can be seen or heard and *no* if it cannot be seen or heard.

6. Sean wants a sandwich for lunch.   yes   no

7. The family walks to a sandwich shop.   yes   no

8. His dad dreams of a giant corned beef sandwich.   yes   no

9. After lunch, the family rode the subway.   yes   no

10. They arrived at the theater just in time for the show.   yes   no

> A linking verb connects the subject of a sentence to a word or words in the predicate that name or describe the subject. Linking verbs do <u>not</u> show action.
>
> **am   is   are   was   were   will be**
>
> Hamsters **are** popular pets.
>
> A hamster **will be** a good pet for our family.
>
> This hamster **is** the cutest one at the pet store.

Circle the linking verb in each sentence.

1. The fur of a hamster is very soft.

2. Hamsters are awake at night and asleep during the day.

3. I am a real fan of hamsters!

4. My mom's first pet was a hamster.

5. My hamster will be happy with his new wheel.

Circle the linking verb in each sentence. Underline the subject and the words linked to it by the linking verb.

6. The little hamster is so sweet!

7. Pete the hamster will be asleep in the afternoon.

8. His cheeks are round.

9. My little brother was afraid of the hamster.

10. They are best friends now!

> A linking verb connects the subject of a sentence to a word or words in the predicate that name or describe the subject. Linking verbs do <u>not</u> show action.
>
> **appear   become   feel   look   seem   smell   sound   taste**
>
> The cooking students **appear** nervous.
>
> The soup **smells** delicious.

First, write the linking verb. Then, write the word or words connected to the subject by the linking verb.

1. In the cooking school, the air always smells good. _____ _____

2. The kitchens sound full of life. _____ _____

3. The students look busy. _____ _____

4. Today, they seem very worried. _____ _____

5. The teachers appear strict. _____ _____

6. If the students pass the test, they become chefs. _____ _____

7. That pudding tastes too sweet. _____ _____

8. The sauce looks lumpy. _____ _____

9. The meat seems undercooked. _____ _____

10. I feel a little sick. _____ _____

Choose the best answer to each question.

1. Which of these is the correct definition of a verb?

   Ⓐ a word that names a person, place, or thing

   Ⓑ a word that describes a noun

   Ⓒ a word that tells what a noun is or does

   Ⓓ a word that takes the place of a noun

2. Which sentence contains an action verb?

   Ⓐ The athlete lifts the weights.

   Ⓑ She is strong.

   Ⓒ The weights feel heavy.

   Ⓓ Good health is important.

3. Which sentence contains a linking verb?

   Ⓐ My cousin studies yoga.

   Ⓑ Yoga is a kind of exercise.

   Ⓒ I read about it in the encyclopedia.

   Ⓓ My cousin practices every day.

4. Which sentence contains a linking verb?

   Ⓐ I work out with my cousin.

   Ⓑ That exercise looks difficult.

   Ⓒ My cousin walks the balance beam.

   Ⓓ He raises his arms for balance.

5. Which sentence contains a linking verb and an action verb?

   Ⓐ How do you exercise?

   Ⓑ Jose practices judo.

   Ⓒ Karen's favorite sport is rock climbing.

   Ⓓ I feel better when I swim.

> The tense of a verb tells when the action takes place.
>
> • When the action is happening now, the verb is in the present tense.
>
> • When the action has already happened, the verb is in the past tense.
>
> • When the action is going to happen, the verb is in the future tense.
>
> **Present Tense** The pony **paws** the ground.
> **Past Tense** He **pulled** the cart around the lake.
> **Future Tense** More tourists **will ride** in the pony's cart tomorrow.

Decide whether the action is happening in the present, happened in the past, or will happen in the future. Underline the verb and circle the tense.

1. We will go to Ireland in the spring.   present   past   future

2. The grass is very green there.   present   past   future

3. My dad calls Ireland the "Emerald Isle."   present   past   future

4. Last year, we rode in a pony cart around some lakes.   present   past   future

5. It rained most of the time.   present   past   future

6. I will take a better raincoat this trip.   present   past   future

7. Nobody minds the rain there.   present   past   future

8. A man at the inn called a rainy day "soft."   present   past   future

9. We will visit old castles on this trip.   present   past   future

10. It will rain again!   present   past   future

A present tense verb tells that the action:

Is Happening Now The quarterback **makes** a touchdown.
Happens Regularly My dad **watches** our favorite team every week.

Underline the present tense verbs. Then write whether the action is happening now or happens regularly.

1. Every Sunday, my dad and I relax in front of the television. _____

2. We sit on the couch and wear our team hats. _____

3. Today our team plays an important game. _____

4. They are playing their biggest rival. _____

5. I am eating popcorn for a snack. _____

6. During every game, I call the plays like a professional announcer. _____

7. The quarterback fumbles that ball! _____

8. The coach looks pretty upset! _____

9. The coach throws his hat whenever he is mad. _____

10. For the second time today, the kicker makes the extra point. _____

11. That wraps it up! _____

12. We love football. _____

Write two sentences in the present tense about sports.

13. Now: _____

14. Regularly:_____

> A past tense verb tells that an action took place in the past and is over.
>
> The class **elected** a new president yesterday.
>
> Susan **won** the election.
>
> Most of our class **voted** for her.

**Underline the sentence in each pair that has a past tense verb.
Circle the past tense verb.**

1. The class has an election every year. Yesterday we put our ballots in the box.

2. I lost the election. Susan is our new class president.

3. My friends feel sorry for me. I worked hard in the campaign.

4. I am happy for Susan. She ran a fair campaign.

5. Our class made a good choice. I will support President Susan.

Rewrite each sentence in the past tense.

6. I design a poster for my presidential campaign.

_____

7. My sister helps me color in the letters.

_____

8. I write some good speeches.

_____

The past tense of most regular verbs is formed by adding *ed*. Some regular verbs require spelling changes before the *ed* ending is added.

- When a regular verb ends in a silent *e*, drop the silent *e* and add *ed*.

  Present use   share   bake
  Past us**ed**   shar**ed**   bak**ed**

- When a regular verb ends in a consonant followed by a *y*, change the *y* to *i* and add *ed*.

  Present bury   study   worry
  Past bur**ied**   stud**ied**   worr**ied**

- When a regular verb ends in a single vowel followed by a single consonant, double the final consonant and add *ed*.

  Present stop   beg   wrap
  Past sto**pped**   be**gged**   wra**pped**

Write the past tense of each regular verb.

1. trap   _____

2. cry   _____

3. roast   _____

4. hope   _____

5. want   _____

6. turn   _____

Fill in the blank with the past tense of the verb in parentheses ( ).

7. Brianna _____ the cards.
   (shuffle**)**

8. Keli _____ a turn to make snacks for everyone.
   (skip)

9. The next player _____ the dice.
   (roll)

10. He _____ to move his game piece three spaces to win.
    (hurry)

Irregular verbs have special forms to show that an action has taken place in the past.

Present Tense Ms. Albert **drives** a delivery truck. She **eats** lunch here every day.

Past Tense She **drove** a school bus last year. She **ate** in the cafeteria sometimes.

Complete each sentence with the past tense of the irregular verb in parentheses ( ). Use the word box below.

drank	froze	knew	shone	slid
found	heard	saw	slept	told

1. The rain _____ on the roads yesterday.
   (freeze)

2. Cars and trucks _____ on the slippery surfaces.
   (slide)

3. My mom _____ on the radio that schools were closed.
   (hear)

4. I _____ my little sister that we could stay home.
   (tell)

5. We _____ hot chocolate.
   (drink)

6. I _____ a good book.
   (find)

7. My little sister _____ under blankets on the couch.
   (sleep)

8. Finally, the sun _____ on our frozen town.
   (shine)

9. We _____ the ice melting.
   (see)

10. I _____ that we would go to school tomorrow.
    (know)

Name _____

> Many verbs have an irregular past tense. There are no rules for forming the past tense of these irregular verbs.

Present Tense	Past Tense
I **sing** in the choir.	I **sang** in the choir.
You **ring** the bells.	You **rang** the bells.
She **blows** the trumpet.	She **blew** the trumpet.
The notes **grow** louder and louder.	The notes **grew** louder and louder.
I **wear** a choir robe.	I **wore** a choir robe.
You **tear** the sheet of music.	You **tore** the sheet of music.

Write the past tense form of each irregular verb. Use a dictionary if necessary.

Present	Irregular Past		Present	Irregular Past
1. write	_____		10. spend	_____
2. freeze	_____		11. send	_____
3. shake	_____		12. ring	_____
4. take	_____		13. rise	_____
5. steal	_____		14. ride	_____
6. sell	_____		15. swim	_____
7. teach	_____		16. begin	_____
8. bring	_____		17. draw	_____
9. stick	_____		18. know	_____

Fill in the bubble next to the correct answer.

1. Which sentence is in the present tense?
   Ⓐ We learned about the Civil War.
   Ⓑ I will read a book about President Lincoln tomorrow.
   Ⓒ I found the book at the library.
   Ⓓ American history is interesting.

2. Which sentence is about an action that happens regularly?
   Ⓐ Fifth-graders have art class on Thursdays.
   Ⓑ Now we go to gym class.
   Ⓒ Our gym teacher is nice.
   Ⓓ Steve takes his turn on the mat.

3. Which one is the correct past tense of the verb *cry*?
   Ⓐ cryed
   Ⓑ cryyed
   Ⓒ cried
   Ⓓ crieed

4. Which one is the correct past tense of the verb *hop*?
   Ⓐ hoped
   Ⓑ hopped
   Ⓒ hooped
   Ⓓ hopeed

5. In which sentence is the past tense of the irregular verb correct?
   Ⓐ The girl <u>buyed</u> a vanilla ice-cream cone.
   Ⓑ The store <u>selled</u> many cones that hot day.
   Ⓒ She <u>standed</u> in the shade of a big tree.
   Ⓓ Later the girl <u>bought</u> a chocolate ice-cream cone.

> In some sentences, a main verb and a helping verb form a verb phrase.
>
> The main verb shows action. The helping verb works with the main verb to express time or something more about the action.

am	was	be	has	must
are	will	being	had	can
is	be	been	have	could

Sentence	Helping Verb	Main Verb
Maria **can take** a taxi to the airport.	can	take
She **will arrive** at the airport on time.	will	arrive
Maria **must pack** her suitcase now.	must	pack

Write the helping verb and the main verb in the correct column.

	Helping Verb	**Main Verb**
1. Everyone at the airport is hurrying.	_____	_____
2. The lines at the counters are getting longer.	_____	_____
3. I have slipped our tickets into this envelope.	_____	_____
4. I must remember that!	_____	_____
5. We could eat lunch now.	_____	_____
6. Everyone will board the plane soon.	_____	_____
7. Dad has brought a magazine for the flight.	_____	_____
8. Mom and I will read our books.	_____	_____
9. The plane is lifting off the runway.	_____	_____
10. I can see our house from up here!	_____	_____

Name _____

> A verb in the future tense tells what is going to happen. To form the future tense of a main verb, use the helping verb *will.*
>
> **Present Tense** We **learn** about the ocean in school. I **study** hard.
> **Future Tense** We **will learn** about sharks tomorrow. I **will study** this book.

Write the future tense of each verb.

1. swim   _____   4. sink   _____

2. eat   _____   5. rock   _____

3. float   _____   6. follow   _____

Rewrite each sentence in the future tense and underline the future tense verb.

7. Dr. Brown travels to the Ocean Institute in the summer.

_____

_____

8. He searches for a special kind of shark.

_____

9. The scientists from the institute live on a boat for weeks.

_____

_____

10. They dive into the ocean in a special cage.

_____

> The present progressive tense of a verb shows that an action is in progress. The action is happening now and will continue for a period of time.

Subject	Helping Verb	Main Verb
I	**am**	talking.
You	**are**	talking.
He	**is**	talking.
We	**are**	talking.
They	**are**	talking.

Underline the present progressive verb in each sentence.

1. My friends and I are forming a reading club.

2. We are choosing a book for our first meeting.

3. Arlene is reading a book about a girl named Alice.

4. I am suggesting a book about a horse.

5. All of our members are going to the library tomorrow.

Fill in the blank with the present progressive form of the verb in parentheses ( ).

6. I _____ the pages quickly. (turn)

7. The beautiful horse _____ from a horse thief. (run)

8. The sheriff _____ the thief. (chase)

9. We _____ the story with great excitement. (follow)

10. The reading club _____ the end of the story. (discuss)

> Choose the correct tense for the verb to indicate when the action happens.
>
> - **Present Tense** is happening now or happens regularly.
>
>   I **rake** leaves every autumn.
>
> - **Present Progressive Tense** is happening now and is continuing for a time.
>
>   The leaves **are falling** from the trees.
>
> - **Past Tense** has happened before now and is over.
>
>   I **watched** a squirrel bury an acorn yesterday.
>
> - **Future Tense** will happen sometime after now.
>
>   After school, my little brother **will jump** into the pile of leaves.

Complete each sentence with the correct form of the verb in parentheses ( ).
Write the name of the tense.

Tense

1. Yesterday, I _____ my cider with a cinnamon stick.   _____
   (stir)

2. My mom _____ homemade donuts later today.   _____
   (make)

3. Warm donuts always _____ good on a cold day.   _____
   (taste)

4. I _____ about those donuts now!   _____
   (think)

Complete each sentence with a verb in the indicated tense.

5. Every day, _____ . (Present)

6. Yesterday, _____ . (Past)

7. Still, _____ . (Present Progressive)

8. Tomorrow, _____ . (Future)

> It is important to use the same tense in every sentence unless there is a good reason to change tenses.

Incorrect	My aunt **teaches** in the new school. She **taught** kindergarten there.
Correct	My aunt **teaches** in the new school. She **teaches** kindergarten there.
Incorrect	She **sings** with the kids every day. **Yesterday,** she **teaches** a new song.
Correct	She **sings** with the kids every day. **Yesterday,** she **taught** a new song.

Write the correct form of the verb in parentheses ( ).

1. The kindergartners recited the alphabet. Tomorrow, they _____ at picture books.
   (look)

2. They like to draw pictures. Ms. Lee _____ the pictures around the room.
   (hang)

3. Little Timmy is pounding on the drums. Yesterday, Katie _____ the cymbals.
   (bang)

4. The children will enjoy show-and-tell. Cara _____ her pet mouse.
   (bring)

Write two sentences in each tense. Make sure that both sentences are in the same tense when necessary.

5. Present Tense: _____

   _____

6. Past Tense: _____

   _____

7. Future Tense: _____

   _____

8. Present Progressive: _____

   _____

Fill in the bubble next to the correct answer.

1. In which sentence is the main verb underlined?

   Ⓐ Calvin <u>can</u> climb the tree in his yard.

   Ⓑ He <u>has</u> climbed it many times.

   Ⓒ The branches have <u>grown</u> thick and strong.

   Ⓓ Calvin <u>has</u> grown strong, too!

2. In which sentence is the helping verb underlined?

   Ⓐ Soon the female <u>will</u> lay her eggs.

   Ⓑ One bird is <u>carrying</u> more twigs to the nest.

   Ⓒ Birds have <u>made</u> a nest in the top of the tree.

   Ⓓ The birds have <u>built</u> a cozy nest.

3. Which sentence is in the present progressive tense?

   Ⓐ By noon, the day has grown quite hot.

   Ⓑ Calvin would like a cold drink.

   Ⓒ His dad is making lemonade in the kitchen.

   Ⓓ He will carry a pitcher of lemonade to his son.

4. In which sentence is the verb in the correct tense?

   Ⓐ Yesterday, the sun shines all day.

   Ⓑ On hot days, I am going to the beach.

   Ⓒ Last week, I will go to the beach every day.

   Ⓓ I play in the house when it rains.

5. In which pair of sentences are the verbs in the same tense?

   Ⓐ The rain falls on our backyard. It made the grass green.

   Ⓑ The birds sing as the rain falls. They find worms in the lawn.

   Ⓒ The adult birds fed the worms to their babies. The babies will chirp.

   Ⓓ The rain will fall all day. The air smells fresh.

Name _____

> A verb must agree in number with the subject.

Singular	Plural
Roberto **travels** to Oregon.	Ian and Brian **travel** there, too.
Chris **goes** to the desert.	We **go** to the seashore.
He **is** anxious to leave.	They **are** excited as well.

Complete each sentence with the present tense form of the verb in parentheses ( ).
Be sure that the verb agrees in number with the subject. Watch out for spelling changes.

1. We _____ the Ash Meadows National Wildlife Refuge.
   (visit)

2. Chris _____ the list of endangered animals.
   (study)

3. He _____ us the story of the endangered Warm Springs pupfish.
   (read)

4. Many kinds of fish, birds, and mammals _____ in this refuge.
   (live)

5. The bald eagle _____ the refuge as a migration stopover.
   (use)

6. You sometimes _____ desert bighorn sheep.
   (see)

7. The ranger _____ to a place in the distance.
   (point)

8. Snakes _____ nocturnal in the hottest weather.
   (become)

9. The Mojave Desert _____ this wildlife refuge.
   (surround)

10. In the refuge, springs _____ warm pools.
    (form)

11. A bird-watcher _____ her binoculars on a distant spot.
    (focus)

12. Chris _____ a jackrabbit with giant ears.
    (spot)

> A verb must agree in number with its subject.

Incorrect	Correct
Scuba divers needs special gear.	Scuba divers **need** special gear.
I is afraid of jellyfish.	I **am** afraid of jellyfish.
Paige and Carla dives off the boat.	Paige and Carla **dive** off the boat.

When a subject has two parts joined by *and*, it takes a plural verb.

Read each sentence. If the subject-verb agreement is correct, write *Correct* on the line. If the subject-verb agreement is <u>not</u> correct, rewrite the sentence.

1. I learns about the coral reefs.

   _____

2. Instructors teach us about jellyfish.

   _____

3. He and Carla swim well.

   _____

4. I pays attention to the instructor.

   _____

5. The instructor and the student jumps into the water.

   _____

6. She show us a special way to breathe.

   _____

Fill In the bubble next to the correct answer.

1. In which sentence do the subject and verb agree in number?

   Ⓐ Nina sprain her ankle.

   Ⓑ She limps along the sidewalk.

   Ⓒ The doctor give her a pair of crutches.

   Ⓓ Manny carry her books.

2. Which one is the correct rule for making a regular present tense verb agree with a singular subject?

   Ⓐ Change the *y* to *i* and add *ed.*

   Ⓑ Use the plural form of the verb.

   Ⓒ Make no change to the verb.

   Ⓓ Add *s* or *es* to the verb.

3. In which sentence do the subject and the verb agree in number?

   Ⓐ You dances well.

   Ⓑ I dances well, too.

   Ⓒ He dance well.

   Ⓓ She dances well, too.

4. In which sentence do the subject and the verb agree in number?

   Ⓐ Nina and Manny meets after school.

   Ⓑ They meet at the bus stop.

   Ⓒ Manny help Nina.

   Ⓓ He help her with her crutches.

5. In which sentence do the subject and the verb agree in number?

   Ⓐ Manny and Nina go to the library on Saturday.

   Ⓑ Eddie and Fran goes to the library, too.

   Ⓒ They meets their friends there.

   Ⓓ I sees them together at a table.

> Adverbs modify verbs, adjectives, and other adverbs. Adverbs can tell *when, where,* or *how.*
>
> **When:** then, yesterday, soon, later, now
>
> Our class took a field trip **yesterday** to the Monterey Bay Aquarium.
>
> **Where:** there, outside, nearby, here, home
>
> We took a bus **there.**
>
> **How:** quickly, loudly, happily, swiftly, quietly
>
> The bus roared **loudly** as it started up.

Circle the adverb in each sentence.

1. Soon we saw the aquarium.

2. We clapped and cheered loudly.

3. Someone was waiting for us outside.

4. We quickly left the bus.

Does the underlined adverb tell *when, where,* or *how?* Circle the correct answer.

5. We <u>quickly</u> walked to the entrance.	when	where	how
6. The otters swam <u>nearby</u>.	when	where	how
7. A guide <u>quietly</u> talked to us about otters.	when	where	how
8. <u>Then</u> it was feeding time.	when	where	how
9. They waited <u>patiently</u> for their supper.	when	where	how
10. They swam <u>happily</u> once they had eaten.	when	where	how

> You can make an adverb out of many adjectives by adding –*ly* to them. Most adverbs that end in –*ly* tell *how*.
>
> **quietly   quickly   impatiently   gloomily   swiftly**
>
> The golden retriever waited **impatiently** for someone to let him out.
>
> "He doesn't want to be inside," Trina responded **gloomily.**

In each sentence, circle the adverb that tells *how*.

1. Barkley jumps excitedly every time we go near the door.

2. He barks loudly because he wants us to open it.

3. "Be quiet, Barkley," I say sternly.

4. He wags his tail happily and barks some more.

Make an adverb by adding –*ly* to each adjective below.
Write a sentence using each word you made.

eager_____   slow_____   proud_____   correct_____

5. _____

_____

6. _____

_____

7. _____

_____

8. _____

_____

> Many adverbs do not end in *–ly.* These adverbs can tell *where* and *when* an action happens.
>
> **Where** Keisha ran **home** to tell her mother about her science project.
> **When** **Tomorrow** she and her lab partner will begin the project.

Circle the adverb that tells *where* or *when* in each sentence. Underline the word or words the adverb modifies.

1. Keisha and Hahn will complete their science project on the solar system soon.

2. They worked today to find the materials they need for the project.

3. They looked everywhere to find things they could use to make planets.

4. "Hahn, bring those tennis balls here," Keisha said.

5. "Tomorrow we can use them in our display," she continued.

Use an adverb from the word box to complete each sentence.

> there   Yesterday   nearby   tonight   home

6. _____, we had our science fair at school.

7. Many families were _____ to see the display of projects.

8. My little brother had to stay _____ because he had a cold.

9. We live _____, so my father could check on him and still see my project.

10. I won first prize, so _____ my family is going to celebrate!

Name _____

> Some adverbs can tell *how much*. These adverbs modify adjectives and other adverbs.
>
> **so   too   really   very   totally   quite**
>
> Mr. Mack takes his class on a **very unusual** field trip.
>
> The wagons move **too slowly** sometimes.

Underline the adverb that tells *how much* in each sentence. Draw an arrow to the word it modifies.

1. The place where the class camps is too far to walk, so we ride in wagons.

2. Everyone is so excited as the wagons start out.

3. The wagons move very slowly compared to cars.

4. The class doesn't mind because they know they'll get there quite soon.

5. Once the class arrives at the camp, they set things up really quickly.

6. Mr. Mack cooks chili that is so delicious!

7. Everyone is totally full by the time dinner is over.

8. By the time the sun has set, everyone is very tired.

9. At the end of the weekend, everyone is really dirty, but no one cares.

10. The class is quite glad to get home, but they can't wait until next year's trip.

> Use *more* or *less* with an adverb when comparing two nouns.
>
> Jake plays basketball **more often** than Eric does.
>
> Eric plays basketball **less often** than Jake does.
>
> Use *the most* or *the least* with an adverb when comparing three or more nouns.
>
> Eric plays golf **the most often** of anyone in his family.
>
> Eric's dad plays golf **the least often** of anyone in the family.

Use *more* or *the most* with the adverb in parentheses ( ) to correctly complete each sentence.

1. I run _____ than my brother.
   (swiftly)

2. He's on a track team, so he practices _____ than I do.
   (frequently)

3. His friend Antonio practices _____ of us all.
   (frequently)

4. No matter how much they practice, though, I still run _____
   of any of us! (swiftly)

Use *less* or *the least* with the adverb in parentheses ( ) to correctly complete each sentence.

5. The armadillo moves _____ than the deer.
   (noisy)

6. Angel plays _____ of the three of them.
   (noisy)

7. Michael is tardy _____ than Carl.
   (often)

8. Josh attends practice _____ of any member of the band.
   (often)

> Some adverbs have irregular forms for comparisons.

Kenya did **well** on the state test.
She did **better** than she did last year.
She hopes to do **the best** on next year's test.

Alain performed **badly** in the spelling bee this year.
He performed **worse** this year than last because he wasn't feeling well.
He performed **the worst** this year of the last three, but he knows he'll do better next year.

Write the correct form of the adverb in parentheses ( ) to complete the sentence.

1. I performed _____ in this year's spelling bee.
    (badly)

2. I know I performed _____ last year than I did this year.
    (well)

3. I performed _____ of anyone who was there.
    (badly)

4. I usually perform _____ of anyone, but I felt terrible.
    (well)

5. I coughed _____ the day before than today, but I thought I was okay.
    (badly)

6. Next year, I know I'll do _____!
    (well)

Write a sentence using the words in parentheses ( ).

7. (sing the best) _____

    _____

8. (act worse) _____

    _____

Negatives are words that mean *no* or *not*.

Paulo did **not** realize that it was his mother's birthday on Sunday.

He had **never** forgotten her birthday before.

He had **no** present to give to his mother.

The right present was **nowhere** to be found.

Write the correct word from the word box to complete each sentence.

> no   not   never   nowhere

1. Shirenda can _____ remember her sister's birthday.

2. She has _____ idea why it's so hard to remember.

3. We _____ forget Shauna's birthday.

4. We know that Shauna goes _____ on her birthday unless we take her.

5. There is _____ way we're going to let Shirenda forget again.

6. This year, Shirenda does _____ stand a chance!

7. We'll _____ let her rest until she has bought a card and a present.

8. This is _____ going to be like any other year for Shauna.

Write a sentence about a birthday using each of the words in parentheses ( ).

9. (not) _____

_____

10. (never) _____

_____

Fill in the bubble next to the correct answer.

1. Which underlined adverb tells *when?*

    Ⓐ She walked <u>home</u> all by herself.

    Ⓑ The team cheered <u>loudly</u> when they won.

    Ⓒ The trip was <u>very</u> exciting.

    Ⓓ The paper is due <u>tomorrow</u>.

2. Which underlined adverb tells *how?*

    Ⓐ Joti smiled <u>happily</u> as they called her name.

    Ⓑ Lori was going to turn in her paper <u>tomorrow</u>.

    Ⓒ Oscar had <u>never</u> been to that store.

    Ⓓ Michael ran <u>home</u> to tell his father about his grade.

3. Which underlined adverb tells *how much?*

    Ⓐ Jim reads stories <u>well</u>.

    Ⓑ He'll read <u>tomorrow</u> for Ms. Winters' first-grade class.

    Ⓒ He is <u>very</u> happy to read to them.

    Ⓓ The class sits <u>there</u> and listens to him quietly.

4. Which word in this sentence is a negative?
   I have never heard anything bad about him.

    Ⓐ have

    Ⓑ never

    Ⓒ anything

    Ⓓ heard

5. Which sentence is written correctly?

    Ⓐ Kim Lee is nowhere going to give up.

    Ⓑ Kim Lee is never going to give up.

    Ⓒ Kim Lee is no going to give up.

    Ⓓ Kim Lee is not never going to give up.

A preposition is used to show the relationship of a noun or pronoun to another word. Prepositions can show position, direction, or other relationships.

between	around	for	from	toward
across	during	through	to	inside
onto	over	before	in	under

I see a statue **on** the hill.

> *On* tells where the statue is.

It stands **beside** a plaque **with** information.

> *Beside* tells where the statue stands. *With* tells what the plaque has.

The field **behind** the statue is where a battle took place.

> *Behind* tells where the field is.

Underline the prepositions in the sentences.

1. The Revolutionary War was fought between the American colonies and England.

2. Many colonists felt that living under English rule was unfair.

3. The English king across the Atlantic Ocean did not agree.

4. The American colonies provided raw materials for English factories.

5. The colonists bought English goods and paid taxes to the king.

6. The king held onto the colonies and would not listen to their demands.

7. Over time, the desire for independence grew stronger inside the colonies.

8. During the years before the war, anger toward the king increased.

9. All through the colonies, patriot leaders rallied people around them.

10. Finally, in 1776 the colonies declared their independence from England.

A prepositional phrase is made up of a preposition, the noun or pronoun that comes after the preposition, and any words in between.

The noun or pronoun is called the object of the preposition.

between	around	for	from	toward
across	during	through	to	inside
onto	over	before	in	under

Prepositional
Phrase

There is a rider coming **down the road.**

Preposition   Object of the Preposition

Underline the prepositional phrase in each sentence. Then circle the object of the preposition in each phrase.

1. The patriots looked across the river.

2. They were watching for a very important signal.

3. They were counting the lights inside the Old North Church.

4. The tall steeple stood above other buildings.

5. They could not miss the signal from the church.

6. It flashed for only a short time, so the British did not notice.

7. Soon riders were dashing through the countryside.

8. Paul Revere was the most famous rider on that night.

9. He warned the colonists to get ready for the British soldiers.

10. The next day, the famous battle at Bunker Hill took place.

A prepositional phrase is made up of a preposition, the object of the preposition, and any words in between. Some prepositional phrases describe nouns.

Prepositional
Phrase

The view **from the window** is clear.
Noun

Prepositional
Phrase

The shed **behind the house** is empty.
Noun

Complete each prepositional phrase.

1. a nation with _____

2. the river between _____

3. the town beside _____

4. the house on _____

5. the bridge over _____

6. the volcano above _____

7. many strange fish below _____

8. I see the path through _____

9. the road across _____

10. the family inside _____

Bonus: Underline each preposition and circle the object in each prepositional phrase.

A prepositional phrase is made up of a preposition, the object of the preposition, and any words in between.

Some prepositional phrases describe verbs and adverbs. They tell *where, when,* or *how.*

Prepositional Phrase

Where: I can see **down the river.**
Verb

Prepositional Phrase

When: Late **in the night,** it started to rain.
Adverb

Prepositional Phrase

How: The water roars **with a powerful sound.**
Verb

Underline the prepositional phrase in each sentence. Draw an arrow from the prepositional phrase to the word it describes. Then circle *how, when,* or *where* to explain what the phrase tells.

1. The rain falls in buckets.	how	when	where
2. I hear the water rushing down the windows.	how	when	where
3. The lightning crackles before each thunderbolt.	how	when	where
4. I creep deeper under my quilt.	how	when	where
5. The house shakes after each jolt as the storm rages.	how	when	where
6. The wind screams loudly through the trees outside.	how	when	where
7. I worry that the roof might blow off the house.	how	when	where
8. I wonder if a twister is headed toward us!	how	when	where
9. Suddenly, my father is talking in a loud voice.	how	when	where
10. It's morning, and he's calling me down to the kitchen!	how	when	where

Name _____

Fill in the bubble next to the correct answer.

1. Which word is the preposition in the sentence?
   There is a cat with a black tail outside.

   Ⓐ there

   Ⓑ with

   Ⓒ tail

   Ⓓ outside

2. Identify the prepositional phrase in this sentence.
   The date for the class picnic is May 1.

   Ⓐ date for the class

   Ⓑ for the class picnic

   Ⓒ for the class

   Ⓓ the class picnic is May 1

3. Find the object of the preposition in this sentence.
   I can eat a snack before the game today.

   Ⓐ snack

   Ⓑ before

   Ⓒ game

   Ⓓ today

4. Which sentence has a prepositional phrase that describes a noun?

   Ⓐ Let's go after school.

   Ⓑ We can leave before dinner.

   Ⓒ We could enter through that gate.

   Ⓓ The gate across the street is closer.

5. Which sentence has a prepositional phrase that describes a verb?

   Ⓐ The green car on the bridge has stopped.

   Ⓑ The exit before ours is Number 50.

   Ⓒ The red car is behind us.

   Ⓓ The drive to town is very quick.

  Language Fundamentals • EMC 2755 • © Evan-Moor Corp.

Name _____

> A sentence is a group of words that expresses a complete thought. A declarative sentence states something and ends with a period (.). The declarative sentence is the most common kind of sentence.
>
> Rome is an ancient city.
>
> My ancestors came from Italy.
>
> Spaghetti with meatballs is my favorite dish.

Read each declarative sentence. Write a declarative sentence of your own about the topic in parentheses ( ).

1. Rome is near the Mediterranean Sea.

   (a city) _____

2. My family traveled there last year.

   (a trip) _____

3. I ate spaghetti almost every day.

   (a favorite food) _____

4. My great-grandmother came from Italy.

   (a relative) _____

5. We looked for her house in the countryside.

   (a house) _____

6. We saw many grapevines and olive trees.

   (a plant) _____

An interrogative sentence asks a question and ends with a question mark (**?**).

May I borrow that book**?**

Do you like detective stories**?**

Many interrogative sentences begin with one of these question words: *who, what, when, where, how,* or *why.*

Who wrote the Sherlock Holmes stories**?**

How many of the stories by Sir Arthur Conan Doyle have you read**?**

Which of the sentences are interrogative and which are declarative?
Place the proper mark of punctuation at the end of each sentence.

1. Sherlock Holmes was a detective in stories by Sir Arthur Conan Doyle___

2. Why are these stories about Sherlock Holmes so popular___

3. Have you ever read *The Hound of the Baskervilles*___

4. Sherlock Holmes solved all his mysteries by examining clues and thinking___

Write questions to go with the answers below.

5. Question: _____

   Answer: Doctor Watson is Sherlock Holmes's assistant.

6. Question: _____

   Answer: The stories take place in England.

7. Question: _____

   Answer: The stories take place more than one hundred years ago.

8. Question: _____

   Answer: Nancy Drew is my favorite fictional detective.

  Language Fundamentals • EMC 2755 • © Evan-Moor Corp.

> An exclamatory sentence expresses strong feeling and ends with an exclamation point (*!*).

>> That desert sun is hot!

>> What a terrific day!

>> How glad I am to see you!

> Sometimes an exclamatory sentence begins with the word *what* or the word *how.* Do not mistake such exclamations for a question.

Add the correct mark of punctuation to the end of each sentence. Then identify each sentence with an *e* for *exclamatory* or an *i* for *interrogative.*

1. The Painted Desert is beautiful_____   _____

2. How does the guide know where he is going_____   _____

3. It is so hard to wait_____   _____

4. What protects the dunes from erosion_____   _____

5. What incredible colors those are_____   _____

6. How exotic these desert creatures are_____   _____

7. How do they stand the heat_____   _____

Write an exclamatory sentence about the topic in parentheses ( ). Don't forget the exclamation point!

8. (a sudden storm) _____

9. (a beautiful day) _____

10. (an unexpected quiz) _____

Name _____

> An imperative sentence gives a command. It ends with a period (.).
>
> > Treat animals with kindness.
> > Tell your dog to sit.
> > Turn right at the corner.
>
> An imperative sentence may include the courtesy word *please.*
> An imperative sentence might also include the name of the person
> or animal being addressed.
>
> > **Please** close the door quietly.
> > Pay attention **please.**
> > Give me your paw, **Maggie.**

Look at the picture. Write three commands that you might hear at this place.

1. _____

2. _____

3. _____

Imagine that, as you are walking your dog, someone stops you to ask directions
to your school. Write three imperative sentences that give directions.

4. _____

5. _____

6. _____

Language Fundamentals • EMC 2755 • © Evan-Moor Corp.

A sentence is a group of words that expresses a complete thought. There are four kinds of sentences.

- A declarative sentence states something and ends with a period.

    Breakfast is the most important meal of the day.

- An interrogative sentence asks a question and ends with a question mark.

    Did you have breakfast this morning?

- An exclamatory sentence expresses a strong feeling and ends with an exclamation point.

    I sure did!

- An imperative sentence gives a command and ends with a period.

    Eat a healthy breakfast every day.

What kind of sentence is it? Label each sentence as declarative, interrogative, exclamatory, or imperative.

1. Whole grains are an important part of a balanced diet. _____

2. Try to avoid sugary drinks like sodas. _____

3. Have you ever eaten brussels sprouts? _____

4. Brussels sprouts are delicious! _____

Write one of each kind of sentence. Don't forget the correct punctuation mark.

5. Declarative: _____

6. Interrogative: _____

7. Exclamatory: _____

8. Imperative: _____

A sentence must express a complete thought. A group of words that does not express a complete thought is called a sentence fragment.

Sentence Fragment	New Zealand.
Complete Sentence	New Zealand is green and beautiful.
Sentence Fragment	On the map.
Complete Sentence	I found New Zealand on the map.

Write *sentence* if the group of words expresses a complete thought and *fragment* if the group of words does not express a complete thought.

1. Shaped by volcanoes. _____

2. Volcanoes formed New Zealand. _____

3. The ash and lava created interesting landforms. _____

4. With active volcanoes. _____

5. New Zealanders live with active volcanoes. _____

6. Live on ranches in New Zealand. _____

7. Millions of sheep live on ranches in New Zealand. _____

8. Rugby, a kind of football. _____

9. New Zealanders love to play rugby, a kind of football. _____

Write a sentence of your own about a place you would like to visit.

10. _____

_____

_____

> A complete sentence must have a subject and a predicate.
> A sentence fragment is missing a subject or a predicate or both.
>
> **Sentence Fragment** Our marching band. (missing predicate)
> **Complete Sentence** Our marching band practices on Tuesday.
>
> **Sentence Fragment** Polished their instruments. (missing subject)
> **Complete Sentence** The horn players polished their instruments.
>
> **Sentence Fragment** Onto the football field. (missing subject and predicate)
> **Complete Sentence** The band marched onto the football field.

Write *sentence* or *fragment* after each group of words.

1. The Jefferson School parade started early. _____

2. Later, the drill squad. _____

3. The band's lively tunes. _____

4. The tuba played the low notes. _____

5. Practiced hard every week. _____

6. The drum major wears a tall hat. _____

7. The honor guard carries the flags. _____

8. On the day of the game. _____

9. Everyone is excited. _____

Choose one of the fragments above and turn it into a complete sentence.

10. _____

_____

_____

Fill in the bubble next to the correct answer.

1. Which group of words expresses a complete thought?

   Ⓐ Skate in the competition.

   Ⓑ The best students in Ms. Boe's class.

   Ⓒ Lindsey laces her skates.

   Ⓓ Impresses the judges.

2. Which sentence is declarative?

   Ⓐ Dancing on roller skates is hard!

   Ⓑ The skaters move together around the rink.

   Ⓒ Did you make your own costume?

   Ⓓ Arrive on time for rehearsal.

3. Which sentence is interrogative?

   Ⓐ Many talented skaters are competing.

   Ⓑ Tony looks confident.

   Ⓒ Are those new skates?

   Ⓓ These judges are tough!

4. Which sentence is imperative?

   Ⓐ I can't skate to that music!

   Ⓑ Is it too fast?

   Ⓒ Listen closely.

   Ⓓ You should take the turn slowly.

5. Which sentence is exclamatory?

   Ⓐ What a great dance routine!

   Ⓑ Will they skate as a team?

   Ⓒ Isaac and Angelina always practice together.

   Ⓓ Watch them as they circle the rink.

Name _____

> Every sentence has two parts, a subject and a predicate.
>
> - The subject tells who or what the sentence is about.
> - The predicate tells what the subject is or does.
>
> | Subject | Predicate |
> |---|---|
> | Our old computer | crashed last week. |
> | This new keyboard | feels strange to me. |

Draw one line under the subject and two lines under the predicate in each sentence.

1. I opened a new file for my document.

2. My friend helped me.

3. We are working together on this project.

4. He downloads photographs.

5. I type the report.

Make the best match of subjects to predicates. Draw a line to connect each pair.

Subject	Predicate
6. Information ●	● are posted every day.
7. My friend ●	● is easy to find with a computer.
8. Online dictionaries ●	● do not always work right.
9. Weather reports ●	● tells me about great Web sites.
10. Computers ●	● help us with our spelling.

A complete sentence has two parts, a subject and a predicate.

- The subject names the person, place, or thing that the sentence is about.

- The predicate tells what the subject is or does.

Subject	Predicate
The city	is a lively place.
Drivers	honk their horns.
He	ran a red light.

Write the subject and predicate of each sentence.

1. Shoppers rush into the department store.

_____   _____
Subject   **Predicate**

2. This jacket is on sale!

_____   _____
Subject   **Predicate**

3. We will eat lunch in a restaurant.

_____   _____
Subject   **Predicate**

4. This juicy hamburger with pickles tastes good.

_____   _____
Subject   **Predicate**

Write one sentence about something you do on a Saturday. Divide it into subject and predicate.

5. _____

_____   _____
Subject   **Predicate**

    Language Fundamentals • EMC 2755 • © Evan-Moor Corp.

> In an imperative sentence, *you* is always the subject, even though it is not stated. We understand that the subject is *you*, so we say that the subject is "you, understood."
>
> **(You)** Raise the curtain.
>
> **(You)** Focus the spotlight on the star of the show.
>
> **(You)** Take a bow.

Write the subject of each sentence. When the sentence is an imperative sentence, write *you, understood.*

1. The stage is set.   _____

2. Programs have been printed.   _____

3. Hand a program to each person.   _____

4. Listen to the director.   _____

5. The audience takes their seats.   _____

6. Be quiet.   _____

Write four imperative sentences. Write the understood subject in the parentheses ( ).

7. (_____) _____

8. (_____) _____

9. (_____) _____

10. (_____) _____

> The complete subject of a sentence includes all the words that tell about the subject. The simple subject is the main noun or pronoun in the complete subject.

	Simple Subject
The people in my neighborhood are very friendly.	people
The kids on this street get along well.	kids
Laurie Perkins plays with everyone.	Laurie Perkins

Choose a noun from the word box that is the best simple subject for each sentence.

> poles   game   evening   backyard   kids

1. My favorite outdoor _____ is volleyball.

2. That family's large _____ gives us a perfect place to play.

3. Two metal _____ hold an old volleyball net.

4. The oldest _____ become team captains.

5. A warm summer _____ is the perfect time for a game.

Underline each complete subject. Circle the noun that is the simple subject.

6. Our next-door neighbor lent some tools to my parents.

7. The neighborhood children like to play kickball.

8. Our parents invited us to play in the backyard.

9. The youngest kids play in the sandbox.

10. My friend's parents are planning a neighborhood barbecue.

> The simple subject is the most important word in the complete subject.

- Sometimes the simple subject is the same as the complete subject.

    Readers value their public library.

    Complete Subject Readers
    Simple Subject Readers

- Sometimes the simple subject is made up of two or more words that name a person or a place.

    The Gordon Library in our town has very helpful librarians.

    Complete Subject The Gordon Library in our town
    Simple Subject Gordon Library

Underline the complete subject and circle the simple subject in each sentence.

1. The students in my class visit our school library almost every day.

2. The school librarian answers our questions.

3. My classmate is writing a report on an author.

4. Laura Ingalls Wilder wrote a series of popular books.

5. She wrote stories about her life on the prairie.

6. The helpful librarian found a biography of the author.

7. A nineteenth-century author is the subject of my report.

8. Robert Louis Stevenson's books are very exciting.

9. My time in the library is spent with his book *Treasure Island.*

10. I can't put that book down!

The complete predicate includes all the words in the predicate.
The simple predicate is the verb.

- The simple predicate may be only one word.

**Simple
Predicate**

My dad **likes** books about history.

Complete Predicate

- The simple predicate may be the main verb and a helping verb.

**Simple
Predicate**

I **am reading** a book by Virginia Hamilton.

Complete Predicate

The complete predicate is underlined. Write the simple predicate after the sentence.

Simple Predicate

1. Virginia Hamilton <u>wrote many books</u>. _____

2. Her grandmother <u>was a slave</u>. _____

3. Both of her parents <u>told amazing stories</u>. _____

4. The newspaper editor <u>has asked for a review</u>. _____

5. I <u>have picked a book by Virginia Hamilton</u>. _____

6. My class <u>is reading one of her books now</u>. _____

Write sentences about something you like to do.
Underline the complete predicate and circle the simple predicate.

7. _____

8. _____

   Language Fundamentals • EMC 2755 • © Evan-Moor Corp.

The complete predicate includes all the words in the predicate. The simple predicate is the verb. The simple predicate may be only one word, or it may be the main verb and a helping verb.

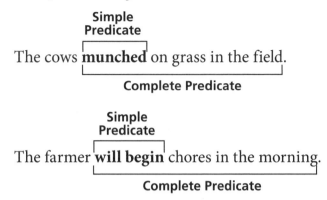

Simple Predicate

The cows **munched** on grass in the field.

Complete Predicate

Simple Predicate

The farmer **will begin** chores in the morning.

Complete Predicate

The complete predicate in each sentence is underlined. Circle the simple predicate.

1. Large modern dairy farms <u>have automatic milking machines</u>.

2. A farmer with a small farm <u>still milks the cows the old-fashioned way</u>.

3. That herd of cows <u>will return to the barn in the evening</u>.

4. The corn in the field <u>grows tall</u>.

5. Freshly picked corn <u>tastes so good</u>!

Choose a simple predicate from the word box to finish each sentence. Underline the complete predicate.

> are   Clean   comes   pass   is boiling

6. _____ the silk from the ears of corn.

7. A pot of water _____ on the stove.

8. That lettuce _____ from our garden.

9. Aunt Sally, please _____ the tomatoes.

10. They _____ juicy and delicious.

Name _____

Fill in the bubble next to the correct answer.

1. In which sentence is the complete subject underlined?
   Ⓐ The table tennis players <u>took</u> their places at the table.
   Ⓑ The <u>table tennis</u> players took their places at the table.
   Ⓒ The table tennis <u>players</u> took their places at the table.
   Ⓓ <u>The table tennis players</u> took their places at the table.

2. In which sentence is the simple subject underlined?
   Ⓐ The taller player <u>won</u> the last match.
   Ⓑ <u>The taller player</u> won the last match.
   Ⓒ The taller <u>player</u> won the last match.
   Ⓓ <u>The taller</u> player won the last match.

3. In which sentence is the complete predicate underlined?
   Ⓐ One player <u>will serve</u> the ball.
   Ⓑ One player <u>will serve</u> the ball.
   Ⓒ One player <u>will serve the ball</u>.
   Ⓓ <u>One player</u> will serve the ball.

4. In which sentence is the simple predicate underlined?
   Ⓐ <u>Mitch</u> is handling his paddle well.
   Ⓑ Mitch <u>is handling</u> his paddle well.
   Ⓒ Mitch is <u>handling</u> his paddle well.
   Ⓓ Mitch <u>is</u> handling his paddle well.

5. Which of these is the subject of every imperative sentence?
   Ⓐ the first word
   Ⓑ you, understood
   Ⓒ the first noun
   Ⓓ There is no subject.

Language Fundamentals • EMC 2755 • © Evan-Moor Corp.

> Some sentences have parts that are joined by connecting words called conjunctions.

- One kind of conjunction is a coordinating conjunction.

  and   but   or   so   yet

- A coordinating conjunction connects two words, two phrases, or two simple sentences.

  I would like a sandwich **and** milk.

  I would like a game to play **or** a book to read.

  We can find a restaurant, **and** you can buy lunch.

  We have plenty of games, **but** they have many books.

Circle the coordinating conjunction in each sentence.

1. Let's choose a place to eat and a movie to see.

2. I would like pizza, but I had pizza for lunch yesterday.

3. Emma thinks Mexican or Chinese food would be good.

4. Ella wants a hamburger, but she will eat anything.

5. Corey wants to get popcorn at the movies, so he won't eat much.

6. Tamara will only eat a salad, a sandwich, or fruit.

7. This is too complicated, so let's just go to a movie together.

8. We need to decide on a movie and a time to meet.

9. I want to see *Cartoon Movie*, but Matt wants to see *Food Fight*!

10. We're all good friends but can't agree on anything today!

> A compound sentence is made by putting together two or more simple sentences containing related information. The sentences are usually joined by a coordinating conjunction, such as *and, or,* or *but.* A comma is placed before the conjunction.
>
> **Compound Sentence** I am going swimming, **and** Kate is napping.
> **Compound Sentence** A weekend can be hectic, **or** it can be quiet.
> **Compound Sentence** I'd like to watch a movie, **but** I can't decide which one to watch.

Create compound sentences from these sentence pairs using a comma and a coordinating conjunction. Write the new sentences on the lines.

1. We are going to the pond. Our dog is going with us.

   _____

   _____

2. The day is hot. I don't mind.

   _____

3. We could walk through the woods. We could walk along the road.

   _____

   _____

4. The wooded path will be cool. The road will be faster.

   _____

   _____

5. Our dog Bruno will swim in the cool water. I will join him.

   _____

   _____

> A compound sentence is made by putting together two or more simple sentences containing related information. The sentences are usually joined by a coordinating conjunction, such as *so* or *yet*. A comma is placed before the conjunction.
>
> **Compound Sentence**   Many people like dinosaurs, **so** the museum displays a dinosaur skeleton.
>
> **Compound Sentence**   I know dinosaurs are extinct, **yet** they still scare me!

Create compound sentences from these sentence pairs using a comma and the coordinating conjunction *so* or *yet*. Write the new sentences on the lines.

1. Modern birds are related to dinosaurs. They don't look like lizards to me.

   _____

   _____

2. The T-Rex had powerful jaws and teeth. We know it was a carnivore.

   _____

   _____

3. I thought the T-Rex was fast. It only ran 10 or 12 miles per hour.

   _____

   _____

Complete each sentence with the correct coordinating conjunction.

(or   but   so)

4. Our class wanted a field trip, _____ we went to the Natural History Museum.

5. Our guide pointed out the oldest fossil in the museum, _____ it didn't look very old.

6. Our teacher said we could either give a report on the trip, _____ we could make a diorama.

A clause is a group of words with a subject and a predicate.

- An independent clause can stand alone as a complete sentence.
- A dependent clause <u>cannot</u> stand alone as a complete sentence.

Independent Clause	Dependent Clause
Lightning struck the old oak tree.	When lightning struck the old oak tree
A large branch crashed to the ground.	After a large branch crashed to the ground

Circle *independent* if the clause can stand alone as a complete sentence.
Circle *dependent* if the clause cannot stand alone as a complete sentence.

1. while we were sleeping one night   independent   dependent

2. a thunderstorm blew in from the north   independent   dependent

3. rain pelted the windows of my bedroom   independent   dependent

4. although I'm a sound sleeper   independent   dependent

5. I awoke with a start   independent   dependent

6. when I hear the first clap of thunder   independent   dependent

7. since I had left the window open   independent   dependent

8. my books on the windowsill are wet   independent   dependent

Write an independent and a dependent clause about a storm.

9. Independent: _____

_____

10. Dependent: _____

_____

Some sentences have parts that are joined together by connecting words called conjunctions.

- One kind of conjunction is a subordinating conjunction.

after	although	because	before	if	since	so
that	though	unless	until	when	where	while

- A subordinating conjunction connects an independent clause and a dependent clause to make what is called a complex sentence.

Complex Sentence

We can't meet the star player until the game ends.

|_____|_____|
Independent Clause   **Dependent Clause**

Complete each sentence with a subordinating conjunction from the word box. Use each word only once.

> so   because   unless   when   before   if   until   after

1. We can grow a garden this summer _____ there is rain.

2. Last year, the garden failed _____ it was so dry.

3. The sun parched the ground _____ it was just dust.

4. The dust filled the air _____ the wind blew.

5. It was too hot to be outside _____ you had a pool.

6. We spent most of our time outside _____ the sun went down.

7. I did read a lot of great books _____ the summer was over.

8. This summer, I hope it is cooler _____ we can do more.

A subordinating conjunction connects an independent clause and a dependent clause to make a complex sentence.

- The subordinating conjunction begins the dependent clause.

- When a subordinating conjunction starts the sentence, place a comma after the dependent clause.

  While the cookies bake, we can decorate for the party.

- When the subordinating conjunction is in the middle of the sentence, do not use a comma.

  We can decorate for the party **while** the cookies bake.

Circle the subordinating conjunction and underline the dependent clause in each sentence. Place a comma in the sentence if necessary.

after	although	because	before	if	since	so
that	though	unless	until	when	where	while

1. Before school ends today we have to decide on our social studies project.

2. Since we are a small group I think we should try to make something.

3. We could pretend to be Betsy Ross and make a flag if anyone can sew.

4. When the project is finished we can hang the flag in our classroom.

5. Although cloth would be better we could make the flag from paper.

6. I'm sure I can donate a white sheet to use after I ask my mother.

7. Because it is the first flag we only need cloth for thirteen stars.

8. The stars need to go on blue cloth that we do not have.

9. Until we get some red cloth we can't add the thirteen stripes on the flag.

10. Unless we find more supplies our flag project won't fly!

> A complex sentence contains one independent clause and one or more dependent clauses. Both clauses have a subject and a predicate, but a dependent clause does not express a complete thought and cannot stand alone.

Independent Clause	the people had little time to prepare
Dependent Clause	before the storm began
Complex Sentence	The people had little time to prepare before the storm began.

Independent Clause	the plows could not clear the roads
Dependent Clause	because the snow fell so fast
Complex Sentence	Because the snow fell so fast, the plows could not clear the roads.

Draw one line under the dependent clause and two lines under the independent clause in these complex sentences.

1. When a big snowstorm is forecast, we make a special trip to the grocery store.

2. The store is crowded because everyone has heard the weather forecast.

3. As my mom and dad shop for the important supplies, I look for marshmallows.

4. Marshmallows and hot chocolate make a nice treat when you are snowed in.

5. If the electricity goes off, we will need our flashlights and candles.

6. Unless the weather forecast is wrong, we will not have school the next day.

7. I like to help build a fire in the fireplace when there is a big storm.

8. We toast marshmallows in the fire until we go to bed.

9. As the snow falls, we watch the friendly flames dance.

10. Because it is cold, we all sleep by the fire.

> A complex sentence is made up of an independent clause and a dependent clause. A dependent clause begins with a subordinating conjunction. A dependent clause may come before or after the independent clause.
>
> - When the dependent clause begins the sentence, separate the clauses with a comma.
>
>   **If** I save enough money, I can buy the next book in the series.
>
> - When the independent clause begins the sentence, do <u>not</u> separate the clauses with a comma.
>
>   I can buy the next book in the series **if** I save enough money.

Punctuate the complex sentences as necessary.

1. When a new book is published in our favorite series we rush to the bookstore.

2. We read the last book again before we read the new one.

3. Because we all like the series my friends talk about the characters.

Rewrite each complex sentence by rearranging the clauses and changing the capitalization and punctuation.

4. After reading these books, I want to be an author.

   _____

5. I want to write my own books although it will be difficult.

   _____

6. If I work hard, I can succeed.

   _____

Fill in the bubble next to the correct answer.

1. Which sentence is a compound sentence?
   Ⓐ A good car mechanic is hard to find.
   Ⓑ My dad became a mechanic because he likes engines.
   Ⓒ He knows all about cars and trucks.
   Ⓓ His hands get dirty every day, but he likes his work.

2. Which word is a subordinating conjunction?
   Ⓐ but
   Ⓑ if
   Ⓒ or
   Ⓓ and

3. Which word is a coordinating conjunction?
   Ⓐ but
   Ⓑ after
   Ⓒ because
   Ⓓ since

4. Which sentence is a complex sentence?
   Ⓐ I am reading a book about a famous doctor.
   Ⓑ It is a long book, but I will be finished reading soon.
   Ⓒ Because I want to be a doctor, the book is interesting to me.
   Ⓓ The librarian showed me this book, and I checked it out with my library card.

5. Which complex sentence has the correct punctuation?
   Ⓐ When my brother plays football he always makes a touchdown.
   Ⓑ If he continues to play well, he'll get a college scholarship.
   Ⓒ He hopes to go to State University, because they have a great coach.
   Ⓓ Because it is a good school my parents want him to go there, too.

> Combine two short sentences to make your writing more interesting. One way to do this is to move key words and phrases from one sentence to another.

Two Sentences The aquarium is full of fish. It is **in our living room.**

Combined Sentence The aquarium **in our living room** is full of fish.

Two Sentences I chose all the fish. I chose them **by myself.**

Combined Sentence I chose all the fish **by myself.**

Underline the phrase in the combined sentence that has been moved.

1. Mark cleans the aquarium. He cleans it with a soft brush.

   Combined: Mark cleans the aquarium with a soft brush.

2. The water is being cleaned all the time. The water is cleaned by a filter.

   Combined: The water is being cleaned all the time by a filter.

Combine the two sentences by moving a phrase from the second sentence.

3. Mark and David go to Frank's Aquarium Store. They go on Saturdays.

   _____

4. Mark likes those angelfish. Those angelfish are in the tanks along the wall.

   _____

5. David watches brightly colored fish. They are in a saltwater tank.

   _____

6. Frank scoops a striped fish out of the tank. He scoops it with a net.

   _____

> You can combine sentences with related ideas to form compound and complex sentences.
>
> - Use a coordinating conjunction and a comma to build a compound sentence from simple sentences.
>
>> **Simple Sentences** This lake is very deep. The fish are plentiful.
>> **Compound Sentence** This lake is very deep, **and** the fish are plentiful.
>
> - Use a subordinating conjunction to build a complex sentence from simple sentences.
>
>> **Simple Sentences** I am excited. I see a dragonfly.
>> **Complex Sentence** I am excited **because** I see a dragonfly.

Combine each pair of simple sentences to build a compound sentence or a complex sentence. Connect the simple sentences with the conjunction in parentheses ( ).

1. Dragonflies live at the lake. I am hoping to see some today. (and)

   _____

   _____

2. They have been around for millions of years. They are threatened now. (but)

   _____

   _____

3. Their habitat is disappearing. People are moving into their territory. (because)

   _____

   _____

4. We should preserve the lake. Dragonflies need wetlands. (because)

   _____

   _____

> A run-on sentence is made up of two or more sentences that run together without punctuation or a connecting word.
>
> Cindy draws pictures she wants to draw a picture of me.
>
> - You can correct a run-on sentence by forming two sentences.
>
>   Cindy draws pictures. She wants to draw a picture of me.
>
> - You can also correct the run-on by making it into a compound sentence. Add a comma and a coordinating conjunction.
>
>   Cindy draws pictures, **and** she wants to draw a picture of me.

Write *run-on* or *correct* after each sentence.

1. Mary Cassatt painted pictures of mothers and children.   _____

2. Mary Cassatt was born in Pennsylvania she died in France.   _____

3. Her paintings hang in many museums I am going to see one.   _____

4. I will see her painting at the Metropolitan Museum of Art in New York. _____

Correct the run-on sentences from the exercise above. First, turn each run-on into two simple sentences. Then, turn each run-on into one compound sentence.

5. Simple sentences: _____

_____

Compound sentence: _____

_____

6. Simple sentences: _____

_____

Compound sentence: _____

_____

Language Fundamentals • EMC 2755 • © Evan-Moor Corp.

A run-on sentence can be corrected by turning it into a compound sentence. Use a coordinating conjunction.

Run-on   Susan broke her ankle she wears a soft cast.

Correction   Susan broke her ankle**, and** she wears a soft cast.

A run-on sentence can be corrected by turning it into a complex sentence. Use a subordinating conjunction.

Run-on   Susan broke her ankle she wears a soft cast.

Correction   **Because** Susan broke her ankle, she wears a soft cast.

Correct each run-on sentence by using the way suggested in parentheses ( ).

1. Face masks are good protection balls fly at a catcher's face. (complex sentence)

   _____

   _____

2. Astronauts walk in space special suits protect them. (complex sentence)

   _____

   _____

3. Al's fishing boots keep his pants dry they protect him from water. (compound sentence)

   _____

   _____

4. I wear rubber gloves for dishwashing I put on an apron, too. (compound sentence)

   _____

   _____

Fill in the bubble next to the correct answer.

1. Which sentence combines these short sentences by moving a phrase?
   The guitarist strums the strings. She strums them with her thumb.

   Ⓐ The guitarist strums the strings she strums them with her thumb.

   Ⓑ The guitarist strums the strings, and she strums them with her thumb.

   Ⓒ The guitarist strums the strings by strumming with her thumb.

   Ⓓ The guitarist strums the strings with her thumb.

2. Which sentence combines these sentences by forming a compound sentence?
   Steve plays the French horn. He wants to play the trumpet.

   Ⓐ Steve plays the French horn and the trumpet.

   Ⓑ Steve plays the French horn, and he wants to play the trumpet.

   Ⓒ Steve plays the French horn with the trumpet.

   Ⓓ Steve plays the French horn, although he wants to play the trumpet.

3. Which sentence combines these sentences by forming a complex sentence?
   Jeanine practices her solo. She wants to play perfectly.

   Ⓐ Jeanine practices her solo because she wants to play perfectly.

   Ⓑ Jeanine practices her solo, and she wants to play perfectly.

   Ⓒ Jeanine practices her solo, she wants to play perfectly.

   Ⓓ Jeanine practices her solo to play perfectly.

4. Which of these is a run-on sentence?

   Ⓐ The boys play well because they practice regularly.

   Ⓑ "Greensleeves" is my favorite song that they play.

   Ⓒ Ms. Walter's students will sing in a recital at the concert hall this weekend.

   Ⓓ Beatrice will sing a beautiful song it is by my favorite composer.

5. Which one corrects this run-on sentence?
   My brother plays in a rock band I like to listen to them practice.

   Ⓐ My brother plays in a rock band. I like to listen to them practice.

   Ⓑ My brother plays in a rock band and I like to listen to them practice.

   Ⓒ My brother plays, I like to listen to them practice.

   Ⓓ My brother plays in a rock band, I like to listen to them practice.

   Language Fundamentals • EMC 2755 • © Evan-Moor Corp.

> Capitalize the first word in a sentence.
>
> Too much junk food gave me a stomachache.
>
> If you write someone's exact words, capitalize the first word in the quotation.
>
> Maria said, "Drink some water, and take a rest."
>
> If there is a break in the sentence in a quotation, do <u>not</u> capitalize the word that starts the next part of the quotation.
>
> "Yes, get some sleep," said Mrs. Gomez, "and you will feel better in no time."

Read the sentences. Circle *yes* if the underlined word needs to be capitalized and *no* if it doesn't need to be capitalized.

1. <u>the</u> sleepover was planned for Friday night.   yes   no

2. "Let me know if you're going," said Bella, "<u>because</u> I'm not sure."   yes   no

3. "I'm always tired afterwards," said Bella, "<u>so</u> I have to think about it."   yes   no

4. "<u>so</u> am I, but we can always catch up on sleep on Saturday night," I said.   yes   no

Read the story. Circle the words that need to be capitalized.

my mother is a doctor. she works hard to help people stay healthy. one day, she had to take time off. we went to traffic court to challenge a parking ticket. "Dr. Franklin," the judge said, "what is your problem with this ticket?"

"well, Judge Morita," she answered, "I think that Officer Iyo made a mistake when he wrote the ticket."

"but it says you parked by a fire hydrant."

"yes, Judge," my mom said, "but there is no fire hydrant at the corner of Smith and Elm Streets."

the judge cried, "you're right, doctor! I'm parked there right now. Case dismissed!"

Capitalize the names of the days of the week.

Sunday, Monday, Tuesday

Capitalize the names of the months of the year.

January, February, March

Do not capitalize the names of the four seasons of the year.

spring, summer, fall or autumn, winter

Circle the words that should be capitalized in the schedule.

september 2007						
Sunday	**monday**	**Tuesday**	**Wednesday**	**thursday**	**Friday**	**saturday**
					1 Help Mom store summer clothes.	2 Call Tanitia to arrange sunday shopping date.
3 Buy Dad a new tie for his birthday in october.	4 Go to Ann's party.	5 School starts. Clear out locker from last june.	6 Start project on the climate in autumn.	7 Pick up winter coats from cleaners.	8 Plan next tuesday's meeting for kids who volunteer.	9 Reserve tickets for october concert.

Answer the following questions. Remember to capitalize the names of the days and months.

1. When is your birthday? _____

2. What is your favorite day of the week? _____

3. What is your favorite month of the year? _____

4. What is your favorite season? _____

> Capitalize the names of holidays.
>
> | Veterans Day | Fourth of July | Christmas | Hanukkah |
> |---|---|---|---|
> | Labor Day | Memorial Day | New Year's Eve | Kwanzaa |

Proofread the following paragraph. Write three lines under the first letter of any word that needs to be capitalized.

December is the most hectic month of the year. It seems as if we've just recovered from thanksgiving when the holiday season is upon us. Some people travel to see family members on christmas. The holiday hanukkah also takes place in December and lasts for eight days. Many people celebrate the seven days of kwanzaa starting on December 26. I love the holiday season. Sometimes in the middle of December though, I wish it were a slow month like May. Then, only memorial day interrupts our busy schedules.

Write a sentence about each holiday. Use the correct capitalization.

1. (valentine's day) _____

_____

2. (fourth of july) _____

_____

3. (halloween) _____

_____

4. (father's day) _____

_____

5. (memorial day) _____

_____

Fill in the bubble next to the correct answer.

1. Which sentence has the correct capitalization?

   Ⓐ this saturday is the first day of winter.

   Ⓑ This Saturday is the first day of winter.

   Ⓒ This Saturday is the first day of Winter.

   Ⓓ this Saturday is the first day of winter.

2. Which sentence has the correct capitalization?

   Ⓐ "the sky is cloudy," Jason said, "so it's probably going to rain."

   Ⓑ "The sky is cloudy," Jason said, "so it's probably going to rain."

   Ⓒ "the sky is cloudy," Said Jason, "So it's probably going to rain."

   Ⓓ "The sky is cloudy," said Jason, "So it's probably going to rain."

3. Which sentence has the correct capitalization?

   Ⓐ "Although we started out to the fair," said Lita, "We never got there."

   Ⓑ "Although we started out to the fair," Said Lita, "we never got there."

   Ⓒ "Although we started out to the fair," said Lita, "we never got there."

   Ⓓ "although we started out to the fair," said Lita, "we never got there."

4. Which sentence has the correct capitalization?

   Ⓐ On monday, we celebrate labor day.

   Ⓑ On Monday, we celebrate labor Day.

   Ⓒ On monday, we celebrate Labor Day.

   Ⓓ On Monday, we celebrate Labor Day.

5. Which sentence has the correct capitalization?

   Ⓐ February 14 is Valentine's Day.

   Ⓑ February 14 is Valentine's day.

   Ⓒ february 14 is Valentine's Day.

   Ⓓ February 14 is valentine's day.

    Language Fundamentals • EMC 2755 • © Evan-Moor Corp.

The names of people and pets should be capitalized.

Ishana   Fluffy

The title before a person's name should also be capitalized.

Professor Mehta

Names of specific places should be capitalized.

Santa Fe, New Mexico   Mesa Verde National Park   Snake River

Circle the word or words that should begin with a capital letter.

city	texas	mike
ben	river	state
girl	dr. cata	america
rhode island	stream	dog
country	gulf of mexico	ocean
new orleans	county	atlanta
oak drive	calvert city	colorado river

> The names of buildings, bridges, monuments, and schools should also be capitalized.
>
> **White House**   **Triborough Bridge**   **Gateway Arch**   **Texas A&M University**

Rewrite the sentences correctly.

1. There's more to see in San Francisco than just the golden gate bridge.

_____

_____

2. The transamerica pyramid is a world-famous skyscraper.

_____

_____

3. The exploratorium is a museum that makes science fun.

_____

_____

4. There is a great view from the top of coit tower, a memorial to firefighters.

_____

_____

5. Schools like san francisco state university make the area a great place to learn.

_____

_____

Capitalize the titles of books, songs, and poems. Unless they are the first or last words in the title, do not capitalize prepositions, such as *for* or *in;* articles, such as *a* or *the;* or coordinating conjunctions, such as *and.*

    Julie of the Wolves   "Star Spangled Banner"   "Old Ironsides"

Follow the same rules for capitalizing the titles of short stories, magazines, and newspapers.

    "The Wonderful Story of Henry Sugar"   "Ode to a Tomato"
    National Geographic Kids   Dallas Morning News

Rewrite the titles using the correct capitalization.

1. "the walrus and the carpenter"

   _____

2. miami herald

   _____

3. "how the camel got his hump"

   _____

4. my life with the chimpanzees

   _____

5. discovery girls magazine

   _____

6. a wrinkle in time

   _____

Fill in the bubble next to the word or words that should begin with capital letters.

1. Ⓐ girl
   Ⓑ mary
   Ⓒ daughter
   Ⓓ sister

2. Ⓐ stadium
   Ⓑ arena
   Ⓒ shea stadium
   Ⓓ gym

3. Ⓐ garfield
   Ⓑ cat
   Ⓒ kitten
   Ⓓ pet

4. Ⓐ math teacher
   Ⓑ soccer coach
   Ⓒ school nurse
   Ⓓ principal davis

5. Ⓐ monument
   Ⓑ washington monument
   Ⓒ building
   Ⓓ place

6. Ⓐ war
   Ⓑ struggle
   Ⓒ french-indian war
   Ⓓ fight

7. Ⓐ fortson company
   Ⓑ business
   Ⓒ corporation
   Ⓓ company

8. Ⓐ *james and the giant peach*
   Ⓑ book
   Ⓒ library
   Ⓓ volume

9. Ⓐ song
   Ⓑ "row, row, row your boat"
   Ⓒ music
   Ⓓ melody

10. Ⓐ story
    Ⓑ writing
    Ⓒ literature
    Ⓓ "the three little bears"

Language Fundamentals • EMC 2755 • © Evan-Moor Corp.

An abbreviation is a short way of writing a word or group of words. Many abbreviations end with a period. Some abbreviations, such as the ones for states and some measurements, do not end with a period.

	Abbreviation
January	**Jan.**
inch	**in.**
pages	**pp.**
Avenue	**Ave.**
Kentucky	**KY**
centimeter	**cm**
University of Nevada, Reno	**UNR**
Internal Revenue Service	**IRS**

Write the abbreviation for each of the following words or group of words.

1. sports utility vehicle _____

2. as soon as possible _____

3. your state _____

4. emergency room _____

5. University of California, Los Angeles _____

6. foot _____

7. pages _____

8. Street _____

9. National Broadcasting Company _____

10. unidentified flying object _____

Name _____

The days of the week can be abbreviated.

Sunday	**Sun.**
Monday	**Mon.**
Tuesday	**Tues.**
Wednesday	**Wed.**
Thursday	**Thurs.**
Friday	**Fri.**
Saturday	**Sat.**

Help Martha shorten her list of things to do. Write the abbreviations
for the underlined words.

1. On <u>Saturday</u>, go see new apartment with Mom.   _____

2. On <u>Sunday</u>, paint bathroom walls.   _____

3. On <u>Monday</u>, help unpack clothes and dishes.   _____

4. On <u>Tuesday</u>, look for a nearby park.   _____

5. On <u>Wednesday</u>, send out moving cards.   _____

6. On <u>Thursday</u>, set up a work area.   _____

7. On <u>Friday</u>, invite friends over.   _____

Write a sentence about your plans for one of the days of the week.
Use an abbreviation for the name of the day.

8. _____

_____

_____

Language Fundamentals • EMC 2755 • © Evan-Moor Corp.

> There are abbreviations for the months of the year. These abbreviations are usually written with the first three letters of the name of the month and a period at the end.

January	**Jan.**	July	**July**
February	**Feb.**	August	**Aug.**
March	**Mar.**	September	**Sept.**
April	**Apr.**	October	**Oct.**
May	**May**	November	**Nov.**
June	**June**	December	**Dec.**

May, *June*, and *July* are not usually abbreviated because their names are already so short. *September* has four letters for its abbreviation.

Write the answer to each of the following questions. Use abbreviations for the names of the months.

1. What is the first month of the year? _____

2. What is the last month of the year? _____

3. What is your favorite month of the year? _____

4. What is your least favorite month of the year? _____

5. Where you live, what are the hottest months of the summer?

_____

6. Where you live, what are the coldest months of the winter?

_____

7. In what month does the school year start where you live? _____

8. In what month were you born? _____

> The titles that come before or after people's names are usually abbreviated. Start the title with a capital letter and end it with a period.

Title	Abbreviation
married or unmarried man/mister	**Mr.**
married woman/mistress	**Mrs.**
married or unmarried woman	**Ms.**
doctor	**Dr.**
Junior	**Jr.**
Senior	**Sr.**

Read Eugene's letter to a pen pal in France. Circle six titles that could be written correctly as abbreviations. Write the abbreviations on the lines below.

Dear Henri,

You asked me to describe my family. My father is Mister Eugene S. Louis, Senior. He works in real estate, so we're never sure when he'll be home or when he'll have to run out. My mother is Mistress Karen Louis. She teaches at my elementary school. She doesn't teach my class, though. My teacher is Ms. Cora Simpson. She is a very tough grader, but we all like her because we learn so much from her.

My aunt is Doctor Lila Louis. She is a pediatrician. That means her patients are children. She is so busy that we don't get to see her very much.

My grandfather, Doctor Jacob Louis, is a retired veterinarian, which is what we call an animal doctor. He lives on a farm out in the country. I love to visit him because he has all kinds of animals, including horses we can ride!

Now I want to hear about your family!

Your pal,
Eugene S. Louis, Junior

1. _____   4. _____

2. _____   5. _____

3. _____   6. _____

Fill in the bubble next to the correct answer.

1. In which sentence is the abbreviation written correctly?
   Ⓐ Mr. Li teaches math.
   Ⓑ His assistant is Mrs Stevens.
   Ⓒ Doctor. P. K. Matthews wrote the book.
   Ⓓ Robert. Smith is the tutor.

2. In which sentence is the abbreviation written correctly?
   Ⓐ School starts in Sep.
   Ⓑ School starts in Sept.
   Ⓒ School ends in Jun.
   Ⓓ School ends in june.

3. In which sentence is the abbreviation written correctly?
   Ⓐ Mrs Smith teaches science.
   Ⓑ Her hero is Dctr Albert Einstein.
   Ⓒ Carl Fox, Jur is my lab partner.
   Ⓓ His dad is Dr. Fox.

4. In which sentence is the abbreviation written correctly?
   Ⓐ On Mon, I have piano.
   Ⓑ On Tues., I have karate.
   Ⓒ On Thu., I have Girl Scouts.
   Ⓓ On Fri, I have tennis.

5. In which sentence is the abbreviation written correctly?
   Ⓐ The answer is on page 6.
   Ⓑ I live on Central ave.
   Ⓒ Mom drove me to the ER when I broke my arm.
   Ⓓ My dad drives an S.U.V.

The names of roads, streets, and highways can be abbreviated. The abbreviations begin with a capital letter and are written with a period at the end.

21 Atherton **Pl.**	Place
201 American **Hwy.**	Highway
7507 Santa Rosa **Ave.**	Avenue
3333 Park **Dr.**	Drive
352 Solano **Blvd.**	Boulevard
3 Jackson **St.**	Street
45 Palace **Ct.**	Court
15 Dove **Ln.**	Lane

Circle the abbreviations in the schedule below. Write the word that each abbreviation stands for.

My Saturday Schedule

1. Meet Juan at 104 Sutton Pl. _____

2. Go to soccer game on North St. _____

3. Get lunch at deli on Franklin Blvd. _____

4. Go to Brooke's house on Bracken Hwy. _____

5. Sign up for tennis camp on Circle Ct. _____

6. Visit Uncle Leo on Gilbert Ln. _____

7. Dinner with Mom at Moe's on Farley Dr. _____

8. Do homework at Jose's on Cliff Ave. _____

Name _____

The names of states have two-letter abbreviations that are used in addresses. These abbreviations are written with two capital letters and no period.

Alabama AL	Alaska AK	Arizona AZ	Arkansas AR	California CA
Colorado CO	Connecticut CT	Delaware DE	Florida FL	Georgia GA
Hawaii HI	Idaho ID	Illinois IL	Indiana IN	Iowa IA
Kansas KS	Kentucky KY	Louisiana LA	Maine ME	Maryland MD
Massachusetts MA	Michigan MI	Minnesota MN	Mississippi MS	Missouri MO
Montana MT	Nebraska NE	Nevada NV	New Hampshire NH	New Jersey NJ
New Mexico NM	New York NY	North Carolina NC	North Dakota ND	Ohio OH
Oklahoma OK	Oregon OR	Pennsylvania PA	Rhode Island RI	South Carolina SC
South Dakota SD	Tennessee TN	Texas TX	Utah UT	Vermont VT
Virginia VA	Washington WA	West Virginia WV	Wisconsin WI	Wyoming WY

Write the answer to each of the following questions. Use state abbreviations.

1. In which state do you live? _____

2. Which state would you most like to visit? _____

3. Write the names of any states where relatives live. _____

_____

4. Write the name of the state in which you were born. _____

5. In which state was your teacher born? _____

Most measurements can be abbreviated. The abbreviation is the same for the singular and plural form of the measurement. For example, the abbreviation *ft.* can stand for both *foot* and *feet.*

inch	**in.**
foot	**ft.**
yard	**yd.**
mile	**mi.**

Abbreviations for measurements in the metric system are <u>not</u> written with periods.

meter	**m**
centimeter	**cm**
millimeter	**mm**
kilometer	**km**

Write the letter of the correct abbreviation next to each of the following words.

1. millimeter _____   a. yd.

2. inch   _____   b. mm

3. centimeter _____   c. cm

4. yard   _____   d. in.

Rewrite the following sentences using abbreviations for the measurement words.

7. There are 5,280 feet in a mile.

   _____

8. In a kilometer, there are 1,000 meters.

   _____

Language Fundamentals • EMC 2755 • © Evan-Moor Corp.

Words that measure weight can be abbreviated. If the abbreviation is for a metric measurement, it is <u>not</u> written with a period.

ounce	**oz.**
pound	**lb.**
kilogram	**kg**
liter	**L**

Words that measure time can also be abbreviated. These abbreviations are usually written with a period at the end.

second	**sec.**
minute	**min.**
year	**yr.**
before noon	**a.m.**
after noon	**p.m.**

Write the word that each underlined abbreviation stands for.

1. Marta bought $3\frac{1}{2}$ <u>lb.</u> of chicken at the grocery store.   _____

2. For her recipe, she needed 2 <u>kg</u> of potatoes.   _____

3. She bought 6 <u>oz.</u> of cheese while she was at the store.   _____

Write the correct abbreviation for each underlined word.

4. Kaitlin is coming to visit again in a <u>week</u>.   _____

5. We are counting the <u>minutes</u> until she is here.   _____

6. It took Dad 63 <u>seconds</u> to find his car keys.   _____

Answer the questions using abbreviations.

7. At what time did you get up this morning?   _____

8. At what time did you go to bed last night?   _____

Fill in the bubble next to the correct abbreviation or word(s).

1. feet
   - Ⓐ f.
   - Ⓑ ft.
   - Ⓒ FT
   - Ⓓ FE

2. ounces
   - Ⓐ oz.
   - Ⓑ os.
   - Ⓒ on.
   - Ⓓ ozs.

3. CT
   - Ⓐ California
   - Ⓑ Colorado
   - Ⓒ Connecticut
   - Ⓓ District of Columbia

4. before noon
   - Ⓐ a.m.
   - Ⓑ am
   - Ⓒ A.M.
   - Ⓓ AM

5. MI
   - Ⓐ Mississippi
   - Ⓑ Michigan
   - Ⓒ Missouri
   - Ⓓ Maine

6. kilometers
   - Ⓐ km.
   - Ⓑ km
   - Ⓒ kilos
   - Ⓓ kl

7. NE
   - Ⓐ Nevada
   - Ⓑ New York
   - Ⓒ New Mexico
   - Ⓓ Nebraska

8. pound
   - Ⓐ pd.
   - Ⓑ pnd.
   - Ⓒ lb.
   - Ⓓ lb

> Statements and most commands end with a period (.).
>
> It is very important to eat a good breakfast.
>
> Please bring me some cereal.
>
> Interrogative sentences end with a question mark (?).
>
> What did you have for breakfast?
>
> Exclamatory sentences and strong commands end with an exclamation point (!).
>
> This oatmeal is the best I have ever tasted!
>
> Run for your life!

Write the name of the punctuation mark needed for each sentence.

1. You may have eggs or cereal for breakfast _____

2. Do we have any bacon _____

3. No, but we do have sausage _____

4. That's my favorite _____

5. Please give me two fried eggs _____

6. Will you have eggs, Olivia _____

7. I hate eggs _____

8. Fix me a bowl of granola, please _____

9. Am I late for school _____

10. No, sit down and eat _____

> Use commas to separate a series of three or more words or phrases.
>
> Do you like **classical, jazz, country, or rock music?**
>
> The audience listened to **two country bands, three rock bands, and two folk bands**.

Add commas to separate three or more words or phrases in a series.

1. You may hear classical music at a concert on the radio or on your own CDs.

2. The Boston Symphony New York Philharmonic and National Symphony are famous orchestras.

3. Orchestras usually have stringed woodwind brass and percussion sections.

4. Violins cellos violas and harps are stringed instruments.

5. Woodwinds include the flute the oboe the clarinet and the bassoon.

6. You will find trombones trumpets and tubas in the brass section.

7. Snare drums cymbals xylophones and pianos are all part of the percussion section.

8. The banjo guitar and fiddle are used in country music.

9. A rock band may use guitars drums and keyboards.

10. In a jazz band, you might play piano saxophone trumpet drums or bass.

Write two sentences of your own about music. Use a series in each sentence.

11. _____

_____

12. _____

_____

> Remember to use commas to separate items in a series of three or more.
>
> We **went to the restaurant, ate dinner, and paid the check.**
>
> **I had clams, Mom had lobster, and Dad had squid**.

Circle *correct* or *incorrect* to show whether commas are used correctly in the following sentences.

1. On Saturday, we got up, went to the park, and went home.   correct   incorrect

2. We packed a lunch, got in the car, and went on a picnic.   correct   incorrect

3. Then we bought food cooked dinner, and then ate it.   correct   incorrect

4. Then I got in my pajamas, brushed, my teeth and went to bed.   correct   incorrect

5. My parents cleaned up, invited friends over, and had a party.   correct   incorrect

6. Everyone sang around the piano played games, or danced.   correct   incorrect

Rewrite each sentence, placing commas where they are needed.

7. Joshua went to the gym got into his uniform and began to stretch.

_____

_____

8. Julia got into her uniform walked to the field and got ready to play ball.

_____

_____

> Use a comma between the day and the year in a date.
>
> December 7, 1941
>
> March 15, 1580
>
> Use a comma after the year if more of the sentence follows.
>
> On January 10, 1960, there was a huge blizzard.

Proofread the following paragraph. Add commas where they belong.

I am keeping track of my family's birthdays for my family tree project. I was born on December 16 1997; my little brother was born on June 13 2002; and my baby sister was born on August 1 2004. On November 27 1965 my father was born, and on February 6 1966 my mother was born. My father's mother was born on December 3 1940 and my father's father was born on June 9 1942. My mother's mother was born on March 15 1945 and my mother's father was born on July 4 1945.

Write a sentence about an important date to you. Remember to use commas to set off the date.

1. _____

_____

Complete the sentence with the date and the year.

2. The best holiday I had was _____

_____

> Use a comma between the name of the city and the name of the state, country, or province.

Brooklyn, New York

Paris, France

Calgary, Alberta

If there are words after the state, country, or province name, use another comma to set it off from the rest of the sentence.

In Reno, Nevada, the weather is cooler than in Cairo, Egypt.

She lives in Toronto, Ontario, which is a wonderful city!

Write these sentences correctly by adding commas where they are needed.

1. In Ashland Oregon there is a fine theater.

   _____

2. In New York New York there are many beautiful theaters.

   _____

3. Chicago Illinois is another good town for seeing plays.

   _____

4. Edinburgh Scotland has a wonderful theater festival.

   _____

Write a sentence about a city you'd like to visit. Remember to use commas to separate the name of the city from its state, province, or country.

5. _____

   _____

> Use a comma in a compound sentence. Place the comma before the conjunction *(and, but, or)* that joins the two main parts of the sentence.

I am 10 years old**, and** I am in the fifth grade.

My brother likes tuna**, but** I like salami.

I think Dad will be home tonight**, or** he may not get here until tomorrow.

Circle the comma that separates the two sentences in each compound sentence.

1. My father, Alan Johnson, sells computer systems, and he travels a lot.

2. Dylan, Hannah, and I miss him, but we are always glad when he comes home.

3. He usually brings us souvenirs, or he may bring a toy, a book, or a computer game.

4. Mom likes to travel with my father, but she usually has too much work at her office, Bryant and Meyers, to be able to go.

5. Dad enjoys his work, but he wishes he didn't have to be gone so much, traveling from one city to the next.

Add a comma to correctly punctuate each compound sentence.

6. I go to Lincoln Elementary School and my brother Dylan goes to River Middle School.

7. I may attend River next year or I may go to Washington or Douglas.

8. Dylan teases me sometimes but I still want to go to his school.

9. He helps me with my homework and he protects my little sister Hannah and me.

10. Dylan is a great brother but he is also a good friend.

Fill in the bubble next to the sentence that uses the correct punctuation.

1. Ⓐ There have been many fads in America?

    Ⓑ In the 1920s, college students wore raccoon fur overcoats

    Ⓒ Do you think that women's bobbed hair looked good.

    Ⓓ People liked escapist movies in the 1930s.

2. Ⓐ Rhythm and blues, Broadway standards and rock and roll were popular in the 1950s.

    Ⓑ Poodle skirts letter sweaters, and ponytails were also popular.

    Ⓒ Children watched *The Howdy Doody Show* and *Captain Kangaroo.*

    Ⓓ The jitterbug the stroll and the Madison were the dances in style then.

3. Ⓐ In the, 1960s, rock and roll music changed.

    Ⓑ On February 9, 1964, the Beatles appeared on *The Ed Sullivan Show.*

    Ⓒ The Beatles were from Liverpool England, and they were incredibly popular.

    Ⓓ On August 10 1970 the Beatles broke up their band.

4. Ⓐ All across the United States CB radios were popular with drivers in the 1970s.

    Ⓑ In San Francisco, California, a man made millions selling pet rocks.

    Ⓒ From New York City New York the hustle became a huge dance fad.

    Ⓓ Born on the Isle of Man Great Britain the Bee Gees were a hit in the U.S.

5. Ⓐ Smurfs were popular in the 1980s and Cabbage Patch dolls were all the rage.

    Ⓑ Young women wore high heels with ankle socks and young men wore T-shirts with sports jackets.

    Ⓒ Some people loved New Wave bands but others preferred rap music.

    Ⓓ The Brat Pack was a group of famous young actors, but it was hard for them to stay popular.

> Use a comma to set off a person's name if he or she is being addressed directly.
>
> Concheta, would you please pass me the salt?
>
> What did you think of the roast, Eli?
>
> I can tell, Dad, that you spent a long time cooking it.

Correct these sentences by adding commas where they are needed.

1. Daniel what are you doing on Saturday?

2. I'm not sure Zach.

3. Daniel let's go to the movies.

4. Mom is that okay with you?

5. I can tell Daniel that you really want to go.

6. What do you want to see Zach?

7. Let's see that new comedy Daniel.

8. Julia do you want to go with us?

9. Thanks Daniel but I have other plans.

10. I guess we're the only ones going Zach.

Write two more sentences for this conversation, adding commas where they are needed.

11. _____

    _____

12. _____

    _____

> Use commas to set off introductory phrases of four or more words.
>
> **At the beginning of the month,** we will change our schedule.

With a short introductory phrase, no comma is needed.

> **After breakfast** we have to walk to school.

Add commas where they are needed.

1. At the beginning of the year Chen went to a new school.

2. At first he was very nervous.

3. As the weeks went by he made some friends.

4. Soon he felt right at home.

5. During the winter break Chen missed school.

6. By the middle of the year he started a new club.

7. Along with his friends he thought he could help others.

8. In order to do just that they made a Newcomers' Club.

9. When new students started they were invited to join.

10. In no time at all the new students felt right at home, too.

Write two sentences about new students. Use a long and a short introductory phrase.

11. _____

_____

12. _____

_____

> In a friendly letter, use a comma after the greeting
> and after the closing.
>
> Dear Uncle Anil,
>
> Sincerely yours,

Add commas where they belong. In the space provided, write *greeting* or *closing*.

Dear Grandma _____   Dear Mr. Sorento _____

Yours truly _____   Sincerely _____

Dearest Aimee _____   Dear Brother _____

Love _____   Much love _____

Dear Uncle Joel _____   With kind regards _____

Fondly _____   Dear Mrs. Dobosz _____

Read the letter from Mina to her cousin. Insert commas where they belong.

March 15, 2007

Dear Hansa

    I wish that you could be here with me. It's wonderful to travel in India. There are so many exciting things to see. It has also been great to meet my cousins and aunts and uncles. I'm taking pictures everywhere I go. You won't believe your eyes when you see them!

    I'll write more soon. I can't wait to see you.

Love

Mina

> When you write the exact words that someone says, use commas to set off the quotation from the rest of the sentence.
>
> Earl said, "I wish that we could go to a restaurant tonight."
>
> "You can help me cook a delicious meal instead," said Earl's sister.
>
> If the quotation already ends in a question mark or an exclamation point, you don't need the comma.
>
> "Do you want to make pizza or spaghetti?" Earl asked.
>
> "Neither!" his sister said laughingly.

Add commas where they are necessary.

1. Jared asked "Who is the greatest basketball player ever?"

2. Mrs. Young said that Jerry West was the best.

3. "I think Shaquille O'Neal is better" Pedro said.

4. "Michael Jordan rules!" Betty exclaimed.

5. "I don't know" Maria said.

6. "Ann Meyers is the best" Lydia said.

7. Hector said "No, it's Wilt Chamberlain."

8. Mr. Perez thought that Bill Russell was incredible.

9. "I don't know any of the players" Will admitted.

10. "Rebecca Lobo changed the game" Neka said.

Fill in the bubble next to the sentence that uses the correct punctuation.

1. Ⓐ Dad can we go to Joe's Pizzeria for dinner?

   Ⓑ I don't know Noah.

   Ⓒ Mom what do you think?

   Ⓓ Sure, Noah, since it's got such good food.

2. Ⓐ At this wonderful restaurant they serve all kinds of pizza.

   Ⓑ After a long, wait we ordered our pizza.

   Ⓒ By the time we got our salads, we were ready to eat.

   Ⓓ Because we weren't regulars we didn't know the staff.

3. Ⓐ "I'd like a meatball hero," Dad said.

   Ⓑ "I want pizza" Mom said.

   Ⓒ "I'll have lasagna" Noah said.

   Ⓓ "I recommend the minestrone" said the waiter.

4. Ⓐ The chef asked "Did you like your meal?"

   Ⓑ Dad said, "I loved it!"

   Ⓒ Mom said "The food was delicious."

   Ⓓ The waiter said "Here's our dessert menu."

5. Which greeting for a friendly letter is written correctly?

   Ⓐ Dear Ray

   Ⓑ Dear, Haley

   Ⓒ Dear Jacob:

   Ⓓ Dear Ava,

> When writing the exact words that someone says, use quotation
> marks before and after the quoted words and punctuation.
>
> "This was my best birthday ever!" said Olivia.
>
> Payat said, "I like pool parties."

For each sentence, write *yes* or *no* to tell whether it needs quotation marks.

1. Mira said that her homework was hard.   _____

2. I had no trouble, said Andrew.   _____

3. Leah said, It took me forever to finish!   _____

4. The teacher said that she was proud of their work.   _____

Rewrite each sentence correctly. Remember to use quotation marks.

5. Do you have any hobbies? asked Connor.

   _____

6. I like playing board games, said Natalie.

   _____

7. Connor said, I'm too competitive to enjoy them.

   _____

8. I thought you liked them, Natalie responded.

   _____

Use quotation marks to set off a quotation from other words in a sentence. If a quotation is interrupted by words indicating who is speaking, use quotation marks to set off each part of the speaker's words.

"It's a close game," said Jose, "and I can't say who'll win."

Add quotation marks to the sentences where they are needed.

1. I like watching movies on TV, said Anna, but I don't like going to the movies.

2. Going to the movies is fun, Mrs. Ramos said, when you have someone to go with.

3. I don't like people talking, Anna said, because it makes it hard for me to hear.

4. I like seeing movies at big theaters, said Nate, where the screens are huge.

5. I know what you mean, said Anna, but I'd rather wait for the DVDs.

6. I don't watch many movies, said Tyler, because Mom thinks they're a waste of time.

7. I know what she means, said Mrs. Ramos, because I've seen a lot of junk out there.

8. Tyler, said Anna, does she let you play video games?

9. No, said Tyler, she thinks that they're a waste of time, too.

10. My mother lets me play only 30 minutes a day, said Luke, if I finish my homework.

11. Maybe my mother would agree to that, Tyler said thoughtfully.

12. It's worth a try, Mrs. Ramos said, if you're sure it won't affect your grades.

> Use quotation marks around the titles of short stories, poems, and songs.
>
> My mom loves the story "Bernice Bobs Her Hair" by F. Scott Fitzgerald.
>
> "How Not to Have to Dry the Dishes" is my favorite Shel Silverstein story.
>
> "We Shall Overcome" is a powerful song from the civil rights movement.

Rewrite these sentences using the correct punctuation for each title.

1. One of my favorite stories is The Circuit by Francisco Jiménez.

   _____

   _____

2. My favorite song is Who Let the Dogs Out?

   _____

3. I like the poem If I Had a Brontosaurus by Shel Silverstein.

   _____

   _____

4. Have you ever read the story The Captain's Story by Mark Twain?

   _____

   _____

5. The Gardener is a great poem by Robert Louis Stevenson.

   _____

   _____

> <u>Underline</u> the titles of books, movies, television shows, newspapers, and magazines.
>
> | | |
> |---:|:---|
> | **Book** | <u>The Giver</u> by Lois Lowry |
> | **Movie** | <u>Ice Age</u> |
> | **Television Show** | <u>History Detectives</u> |
> | **Newspaper** | <u>Sacramento Bee</u> |
> | **Magazine** | <u>Time for Kids</u> |
>
> If you are using a computer, you can use *italics* instead of underlining.
>
> *The Giver* 　 *Ice Age* 　 *History Detectives*

Correct the following paragraph. Remember to underline the titles of movies, books, newspapers, magazines, and television shows.

 I loved the movie Shrek. I thought I would like it because I used to love William Steig's picture books, like Sylvester and the Magic Pebble and Doctor DeSoto. I especially loved his fairy-tale book Shrek. I was surprised by how different the movie was from the book, but I think they're both great. Movie critics from Time and Entertainment Weekly agreed!

Answer each question. Remember to underline the titles of movies, books, and television shows.

1. What movie have you watched again and again?

   _____

2. What is your favorite book?

   _____

3. What television show would you recommend to friends?

   _____

Fill in the bubble next to the correct answer.

1. Which sentence is punctuated correctly?

   Ⓐ Mika said "I want to be on the soccer team."

   Ⓑ Her mother said, "I don't think that's such a good idea."

   Ⓒ Mika asked "But why?"

   Ⓓ "You've never played" said her mother.

2. Which sentence is punctuated correctly?

   Ⓐ Nicholas said that "he likes to read sports magazines."

   Ⓑ Abigail said, "I like to watch sports on television."

   Ⓒ Julia said that, "she likes playing sports."

   Ⓓ Will said, I just like sports.

3. Which sentence is punctuated correctly?

   Ⓐ "Did you know, said Hailey "that I want to be an actress when I grow up?"

   Ⓑ "The trouble with that plan" said Hailey's mother "is that so few are successful."

   Ⓒ "I don't care," said Hailey, "because I have real talent."

   Ⓓ "Of course you do" said Hailey's mother, "because you're my daughter."

4. Which poem title is written correctly?

   Ⓐ The Magic Eraser

   Ⓑ The "Magic" Eraser

   Ⓒ The Magic Eraser

   Ⓓ "The Magic Eraser"

5. Which book title is written correctly?

   Ⓐ Where the Sidewalk Ends

   Ⓑ "Where the Sidewalk Ends"

   Ⓒ Where the Sidewalk Ends

   Ⓓ Where the Sidewalk Ends

> A contraction is a shortened form of two words. A contraction uses an apostrophe in place of the missing letter or letters.
>
> have + not = **haven't**
>
> they + would = **they'd**
>
> I + will = **I'll**

Match each set of words with its contraction. Write the letter on the line.

1. could not _____   a. they're

2. does not _____   b. we've

3. he will _____   c. he'll

4. we have _____   d. haven't

5. they are _____   e. doesn't

6. have not _____   f. couldn't

In the sentences below, look for the contractions that need apostrophes. Write the words correctly.

7. Youd be surprised by how long we have been on this bus.   _____

8. If I didnt know better, I would say that we are lost.   _____

9. We wouldnt be lost if we had paid more attention.   _____

10. Isnt Tanya's house near the grocery store?   _____

> Possessive nouns show ownership.

Singular = Add 's	Plural Ending in s = Add '	Plural Not Ending in s = Add 's
Tino's temperature	the Johnsons' pool	the children's story hour
the dog's tail	the animals' habitats	the women's group

Rewrite the following sentences correctly.

1. The Campbells pictures were ready for pickup.

   _____

2. Coreys photograph of the sunset was beautiful.

   _____

3. The pictures of the mens barbecue were hilarious.

   _____

4. The Garcias photographs were ready at the same time.

   _____

   _____

5. Talitas and Juans photographs of their classmates were good.

   _____

   _____

6. The colors of the childrens clothing were vivid.

   _____

> When writing the time, use a colon between the numbers
> that show the hour and the minutes.
>
> The bus arrived at 3:24.
>
> It got us there by 6:00.
>
> At 8:30, I finished my homework.

Correct the sentences below. Write the time on the line next to the sentence.

1. We went to the park at 100 p.m. _____

2. By 145, we were hot in the sun. _____

3. Luckily, at 205 Lee came with snacks and drinks. _____

4. Still, by 230 I was ready to go home. _____

5. We decided to meet later at 400. _____

6. I waited until 425, but nobody came. _____

7. At 500 p.m., I went home for dinner. _____

8. Lee picked me up for school at 820 the next morning. _____

9. She said that they started their homework at 330 p.m. _____

10. They didn't finish until 600 p.m. _____

11. They forgot to call until 900 p.m. _____

12. Lee knew I went to bed at 830. _____

> When writing a business letter, use a colon after the greeting.
>
> To Whom It May Concern:
>
> Dear Senator Carey:
>
> Dear Sir or Madam:

Read the greetings below. Circle whether the greetings are for a business or friendly letter.

1. Dear Sis,   business   friendly

2. Dear Doctor Petersen: business   friendly

3. Dear General Ramirez: business   friendly

4. Dear Aunt Lila,   business   friendly

5. Dear Sir: business   friendly

Write your own business letter to someone. Pitch your idea for a new invention. You don't need to include your address, the inside address, or the date.

Dear _____

_____

_____

_____

_____

_____

Sincerely,

_____

Fill in the bubble next to the correct answer.

1. Which contraction is written correctly?

   Ⓐ couldn't

   Ⓑ havent

   Ⓒ weve

   Ⓓ wouldnt

2. Which singular possessive is written correctly?

   Ⓐ Claras' present

   Ⓑ Sadies toy

   Ⓒ Ethan's lunch

   Ⓓ Connors snack

3. Which plural possessive is written correctly?

   Ⓐ girl's hobbies

   Ⓑ the boys' collections

   Ⓒ the dogs kennel

   Ⓓ the birds feeder

4. Which time is written correctly?

   Ⓐ 945

   Ⓑ 9:45

   Ⓒ nine:45

   Ⓓ 9:forty-five

5. Which greeting is written correctly for a business letter?

   Ⓐ Dear Sarah,

   Ⓑ Dear Madam

   Ⓒ To Whom It May Concern,

   Ⓓ Dear Mr. Gomez:

> Be careful not to confuse subject and object pronouns.

- Subject pronouns should be used as the subject of a sentence or clause.

I   you   he   she   it   we   they

Incorrect   **Him** and **me** play in the orchestra

Correct   **He** and **I** play in the orchestra.

- Object pronouns take the place of a word or group of words that are the object of a verb or a preposition.

me   you   him   her   it   us   them

Incorrect   Ms. Winters gave lessons to **he** and **she**.

Correct   Ms. Winters gave lessons to **him** and **her**.

Complete each sentence correctly.

1. The students auditioned for _____.

2. Ms. Winters asked to hear _____.

3. She gave _____ and me some sheet music to read.

4. Connor and _____ played a duet.

5. _____ sounded good together.

Correct the pronoun errors in this paragraph.

Evan and me play guitar together. We practice every Saturday. My

mother taught he and I to play. Sometimes her watches us practice and gives

us advice. It helps Evan and I. My little sister and me sit down with the guitar

sometimes. Tomorrow she's going to play for Mom and I.

> Negatives are words that mean "no." When there are two negatives in the same sentence, it's called a double negative. Avoid double negatives.
>
> no   not   never   none   nothing   nobody   nowhere   hardly   barely
>
> **Incorrect**   I **didn't** eat **no** lunch today.
> **Correct**   I **didn't** eat any lunch today.

Rewrite each sentence to eliminate the double negative.

1. I didn't hear no bell at lunchtime today.

_____

2. When I looked up from my book, there wasn't nobody left in the classroom.

_____

_____

3. I didn't never miss lunch before.

_____

4. I didn't lose no time racing out of the room.

_____

5. I was afraid there wouldn't be no lunch left when I got to the cafeteria.

_____

_____

6. Lunch ends at 12:45, and they don't let no one in the cafeteria after that.

_____

_____

People often confuse these word pairs: *good* and *well*; *bad* and *badly*.

- The word *good* is an adjective. It describes a noun or pronoun.
  The word *well* is usually an adverb. It describes a verb or sometimes an adjective.

- The word *bad* is an adjective. It describes a noun or pronoun. Do not use *bad* as an adverb.
  The word *badly* is an adverb. It describes a verb or adjective.

Incorrect	Correct
Manuel performed **good** on his test today.	Manuel performed **well** on his test today.
I did **bad** on the test.	I did **badly** on the test. I got a **bad** score.

Complete each sentence correctly.

1. Did you have a _____ time at the movies last night?

2. I had studied _____ in the afternoon, so my mom let me go.

3. Cara and I thought the movie was really _____ and boring.

4. The lead actress played the part _____.

Write a sentence using the word in parentheses ( ).

5. (good) _____

_____

6. (well) _____

_____

7. (bad) _____

_____

8. (badly) _____

_____

Fill in the bubble next to the correct answer.

1. Which sentence is written correctly?

   Ⓐ Sandra likes to walk to school with Tami and I.

   Ⓑ What did they give Ashley and she?

   Ⓒ They gave Ashanti and me a round of applause.

   Ⓓ Her and I sang our favorite Beatles song.

2. Which sentence is written correctly?

   Ⓐ Tony and I play soccer after school.

   Ⓑ Tony and me are good players.

   Ⓒ The other players kick the ball to him or I.

   Ⓓ The other team doesn't want to play against he or I.

3. Which sentence is written correctly?

   Ⓐ Ekram didn't see no bicycles on the path.

   Ⓑ There wasn't anyone in sight.

   Ⓒ Nobody was doing nothing in the park that early.

   Ⓓ Ekram hadn't never seen the park so empty.

4. Which sentence is written correctly?

   Ⓐ We danced good at our recital.

   Ⓑ Ms. Weiss said I danced well in my solo.

   Ⓒ It was a well performance for everyone.

   Ⓓ Even my little brother did good.

5. Which sentence is written correctly?

   Ⓐ My brother Roberto cooks good.

   Ⓑ The dinner he made last night was really well.

   Ⓒ Roberto learned our grandmother's lessons good.

   Ⓓ She taught him to be a good cook.

> The words *can* and *may* are often confused. They mean different things. Be sure to use the word whose meaning fits what you're trying to say.
>
> - *can* means "able to"
>
>   Emily **can** run two miles.
>
> - *may* means "allowed to"
>
>   "You **may** spend the night at Aidan's house," said Dad.

Write *can* or *may* to complete each sentence correctly.

1. Emily and Yuko _____ both run very fast.

2. "_____ I run with you?" asked David.

3. "How fast _____ you run?" asked Yuko.

4. "I _____ run pretty fast," David replied.

5. "You _____ run with us this afternoon," Emily said.

6. "That way, we _____ see if we are good running buddies," said Yuko.

7. David showed that he _____ run as fast as Emily and Yuko.

8. They told him that he _____ run with them anytime.

Write two sentences using the words in parentheses ( ).

9. (can) _____

_____

10. (may) _____

_____

The words *lie* and *lay* are often confused.

- Use *lie* to mean "to rest or recline."
- Use *lay* to mean "to put or place."

	lie	lay
Present	**I lie** down when I'm tired.	**I lay** my books on the table.
Future	**I will lie** down tomorrow.	**I will lay** them on the table tomorrow.

Write *lie* or *lay* on the line to complete each sentence.

1. My father likes to _____ down for a nap after Sunday dinner.

2. He will _____ the paper down on the floor and stretch out on the couch.

3. Our cat likes to _____ next to him.

4. She will _____ her toy mouse next to Dad's head.

Write four sentences using the form of *lie* or *lay*.

5. lie—present tense: _____

_____

6. lay—present tense: _____

_____

7. lie—future tense: _____

_____

8. lay—future tense: _____

_____

The words *lie* and *lay* are often confused.

- Use *lie* to mean "to rest or recline."
- Use *lay* to mean "to put or place."

	lie	lay
Present	I **lie** down when I'm tired.	I **lay** my books on the table.
Past	Yesterday, I **lay** down for a while.	I know I **laid** them there yesterday.

Write the correct past tense form of *lie* or *lay* to complete each sentence.

1. Before I _____ down, I organized my desk.

2. My friend _____ CDs on my desk, so I put them back on the shelf.

3. Papers were scattered, so I gathered them and _____ them in a pile.

4. I _____ my schoolbooks next to the papers.

5. While I was organizing, my cat _____ on top of my computer.

6. I picked her up and _____ her on the bed.

7. She _____ her paw on my pillow.

8. After a few more minutes, I _____ down with her for a nice nap.

Write two sentences of your own, using the past tense of *lie* and *lay*.

9. _____

_____

10. _____

_____

Homophones, words that sound alike, are often confused.

- *To, too,* and *two* all sound the same, but the different spellings have different meanings.

    Too many people were in line to get on the boat.

    They gave the tickets **to** the man at the gate.

    The **two** of them climbed on board.

- *There, their,* and *they're* are also words that are often confused.

    There are life preservers on board.

    They're listening to the announcement.

    Those are **their** seats.

Write the correct word on the line to complete each sentence.

1. The Lopez family didn't want to go _____ far on a boat.

2. They asked their friends the Washingtons _____ recommend a trip.

3. "The _____ of us took a boat around Manhattan," said Mrs. Washington.

4. "_____ were so many things to see," said Mr. Washington.

5. The Lopez family made a reservation and packed _____ bags.

6. _____ taking a train into the city on Saturday.

7. The train went to Grand Central Station, and they caught a cab from _____.

8. "We can get out here," said Mrs. Lopez _____ the cab driver.

9. "It's not _____ far to walk to the boat," said Mrs. Lopez.

10. The Washingtons said _____ going to come back next summer.

Fill in the bubble next to the correct answer.

1. Which sentence is written correctly?
   Ⓐ Thuy asked, "Can I stay up tonight?"
   Ⓑ "Please, can María stay with us tonight, Mom?" asked Ella.
   Ⓒ My mom said I can stay for dinner.
   Ⓓ My mom said I may stay for dinner.

2. Which sentence is written correctly?
   Ⓐ Jin Hoon told his dog to lay down.
   Ⓑ Would you please lay those placemats on the table?
   Ⓐ Benita wanted to lay down for a nap.
   Ⓐ Isaac will lie the cloth on the table.

3. Which sentence is written correctly?
   Ⓐ Denitra went to the store to get a newspaper.
   Ⓑ There were only too papers left.
   Ⓒ Denitra thought, "That's two bad."
   Ⓓ "I wanted something too read," she said.

4. Which sentence is written correctly?
   Ⓐ Their not sitting over there.
   Ⓑ There not sitting over their.
   Ⓒ They're not sitting over their.
   Ⓓ They're not sitting over there.

5. Which sentence is written correctly?
   Ⓐ It's too bad you two didn't get to meet.
   Ⓑ It's two bad you to didn't get to meet.
   Ⓒ It's to bad you two didn't get to meet.
   Ⓓ It's too bad you to didn't get two meet.

> A base word, also called a word root, is the main part of a word before word parts are added at the beginning or the end.
>
> pre**view**
> un**thank**ful
> dis**appear**ance
> dis**charge**d

Circle the base word in each underlined word.

1. Lily is never <u>careless</u> when it comes to math.

2. She likes to <u>preview</u> the next chapter in her math book before it's <u>assigned</u>.

3. She is always <u>excited</u> to learn new skills.

4. Shayla is <u>unafraid</u> when it comes to taking tests.

5. There is no <u>nervousness</u> when she sits down to write her answers.

6. She is <u>careful</u> as she answers the equations.

7. Miguel loves science, and he is <u>hopeful</u> about his future.

8. He wants to be a vet because he has a real <u>fondness</u> for animals.

9. He even likes <u>dangerous</u> snakes and spiders.

10. Sean, however, is a <u>powerful</u> athlete.

11. He is <u>multitalented</u> and plays many sports.

12. He thinks it would be <u>wonderful</u> to be a <u>professional</u> athlete.

A prefix is a word part that comes before a base word. Adding a prefix to a word changes the word's meaning.

- The prefix *pre–* means "before, ahead."

    pre + assign = preassign means "to assign ahead of time"

    Are you going to **preassign** seats for this trip?

- The prefix *re–* means "again."

    re + assign = reassign means "to assign again"

    They told me they were going to **reassign** my seat.

Add the correct prefix to the base word to match the meaning.

1. look at before   _____view

2. wind again   _____wind

3. attach again   _____attach

4. heat beforehand   _____heat

Add a prefix to the word in parentheses ( ) and write the new word on the line to complete each sentence.

5. Let's _____ the plan we came up with yesterday.
                (visit)

6. I want to _____ for the tickets.
            (pay)

7. Then we won't have to _____ our steps.
               (trace)

8. I want to get there in time for the _____ show.
                    (game)

A prefix is a word part that comes before a base word. Adding a prefix to a word changes the word's meaning.

The prefixes *un-* and *dis-* mean "not" or "the opposite of."

un + asked = unasked means "not asked"

That was the question that remained **unasked.**

dis + agreement = disagreement means "the opposite of agreement"

We had a **disagreement** over when to leave for the game.

Circle a word in the puzzle to match each definition. The words can be read across, down, or diagonally. Write each word next to its meaning.

1. the opposite of *trust* _____   4. the opposite of *regard* _____

2. not safe _____   5. not certain _____

3. the opposite of *comfort* _____   6. not answered _____

A	U	N	C	E	R	T	A	I	N	T
U	D	I	S	C	O	M	F	O	R	T
Q	N	L	D	M	T	O	V	W	Y	R
U	E	A	N	U	L	T	A	R	T	E
L	Y	N	N	N	V	E	M	N	P	T
C	D	D	I	S	T	R	U	S	T	U
J	F	G	K	A	W	M	M	L	B	Q
U	I	N	L	F	O	E	A	N	R	L
D	I	S	R	E	G	A	R	D	A	Z
S	N	O	L	E	L	N	C	E	D	I
Y	W	R	R	R	N	A	I	L	D	E

A prefix is a word part that comes before a base word. Adding a prefix to a word changes the word's meaning.

- The prefix *in–* means "not" or "the opposite of."

   in + appropriate = inappropriate or "not appropriate"

   It was **inappropriate** for people to talk while she was singing.

- The prefix *under–* means "below" or "less than required."

   under + age = underage or "less than the required age"

   They were **underage** to get into the movie.

Draw a line to match each word to its meaning.

1. not advisable   •   • underwater

2. less than nourished   •   • infrequent

3. below water   •   • undervalued

4. not frequent   •   • inadvisable

5. not complete   •   • undernourished

6. valued below its worth •   • incomplete

Write a sentence for each word.

7. (underwater) _____

_____

8. (incomplete) _____

_____

A suffix is a word part that comes after a base word.
Adding a suffix to a word changes the word's meaning.

- The suffix *–less* means "without."

    use + **less** = useless means "without use"

    She thought the directions for the model were **useless.**

- The suffix *–ness* means "the state of being."

    kind + **ness** = kindness means "the state of being kind"

    She showed her friends great **kindness.**

Write the answer to each clue in the puzzle.

Across
1. without harm
3. state of being kind
5. without thought
6. without color

Down
1. joy
2. without seams
4. state of being silly

A suffix is a word part that comes after a base word.
Adding a suffix to a word changes the word's meaning.

The suffixes *–er* and *–or* mean "someone who."
The suffix *–er* is the more commonly used.

> teach + **er** = teacher or "someone who teaches"
>
> > The **teacher** taught the class how to speak Spanish.
>
> act + **or** = actor or "someone who acts"
>
> > The **actor** did a wonderful job playing the part.

Add a suffix to each word in parentheses ( ) and write the new word
to complete the sentence. Hint: Two answers end in *or*.

1. The _____ talked about ways to help the community.
   (speak)

2. She was as interesting to listen to as a good _____.
   (act)

3. Raul is a good _____, so he learned a lot.
   (listen)

4. This _____ uses nothing but compost to make her plants grow.
   (garden)

5. That _____ helps out by bringing vegetables to the homeless shelter.
   (farm)

6. The _____ campaigns on behalf of immigrants.
   (senate)

Add *er* to each word and use it in a sentence.

7. (work) _____

   _____

8. (write) _____

   _____

A suffix is a word part that comes after a base word.
Adding a suffix to a word changes the word's meaning.

- The suffix –*able* means "capable of."
    wash + **able** = washable or "capable of being washed"
        He was glad the shirt was **washable** when he spilled his drink on it.

- For most words ending in *e*, drop the *e* when you add a suffix
  that begins with a vowel.
        recycle – **e** + **able** = recyclable or "capable of being recycled"
        Evan collects the **recyclable** trash.

Add the suffix –*able* to the word in parentheses ( ) to complete each sentence.

1. I'm not _____ with the amount of trash in our house.
     (comfort)

2. Much of what we discard is actually _____.
                                              (reuse)

3. Most cans are _____.
                     (recycle)

4. Soda cans are _____ for a deposit.
                     (return)

5. Even _____ bottles can be recycled.
          (break)

Write three sentences about recycling using the words in parentheses ( ).

6. (recyclable) _____

   _____

7. (reusable) _____

   _____

8. (perishable) _____

   _____

Words that share the same base words or root words are usually related in meaning.

use	mark	sight
misuse	remarkable	sightsee
useful	marked	sighted
using	marks	sightless
usable	unmarked	sighting

Choose the correct word with the base word *use* to complete each sentence.

1. Karen is _____ the computer for her project.

2. The _____ of power tools can be dangerous.

Choose the correct word with the base word *mark* to complete each sentence.

3. Her skills on the balance beam are _____.

4. The _____ street was hard to find.

Choose the correct word with the base word *sight* to complete each sentence.

5. The family will _____ while they are in Paris.

6. The ship's crew _____ land!

Write two sentences using other words from the rule box.

7. _____

_____

8. _____

_____

Fill in the bubble next to the correct answer.

1. Which one is the base word in *disappear?*

   Ⓐ pear

   Ⓑ appear

   Ⓒ dis

   Ⓓ ear

2. Which one is the correct meaning of the word *preview?*

   Ⓐ look after

   Ⓑ look through

   Ⓒ look out

   Ⓓ look at ahead of time

3. Which sentence uses a form of the base word *sight* correctly?

   Ⓐ The latest sighting of Bigfoot was faked.

   Ⓑ A man without sightsee said he met the creature.

   Ⓒ If I sighting Bigfoot, I wouldn't tell anyone.

   Ⓓ People would think I was sightful!

4. Which sentence uses a form of the word *nervous* correctly?

   Ⓐ "The recital is next week," Lucy said nervousor.

   Ⓑ Lucy is nervousless about her next recital.

   Ⓒ Lucy's nervousness disappeared as soon as she heard the applause.

   Ⓓ The applause sounded nervously.

5. Which sentence uses a form of the word *comfort* correctly?

   Ⓐ Alice thought that the couch was very uncomfort.

   Ⓑ Alice thought the couch was very comfortness.

   Ⓒ Alice thought the couch was very uncomfortless.

   Ⓓ Alice thought the couch was very uncomfortable.

Language Fundamentals • EMC 2755 • © Evan-Moor Corp.

Synonyms are words that have almost the same meaning.
You can use synonyms to vary your writing, avoid repetition,
or make your use of language more precise.

run—race, lope, speed, dash, tear, gallop

talk—babble, gossip, gush, say, chat, discuss

nice—kind, helpful, attentive, giving, friendly

big—huge, tremendous, gigantic, large, towering

A thesaurus is a reference book that lists synonyms.

Complete the paragraph by writing synonyms for the words in parentheses ( ).

My Uncle Clyde is considered the head of the Dettman family. He is

a really _____ man. Everyone _____ him,
　　　　　　　(nice)　　　　　　　　　　　　　　　(likes)

even animals. When my family gets together, all the adults

_____ until the noise level gets so high, Uncle Clyde has
　　(talk)

to whistle to get them to _____. Uncle Clyde is a
　　　　　　　　　　　　　　　　(stop)

_____ man with a really loud whistle. Once everyone
　　(big)

stops _____, Uncle Clyde will say, "Dinner's ready,"
　　　　　(talking)

and we all _____ to the table to eat.
　　　　　　(run)

Write a sentence about someone you know for each synonym.

1. (hilarious) _____

_____

2. (silly) _____

_____

> There are usually slight differences in meaning among synonyms. Think about the meaning you want to help you choose the right synonym.
>
> When she saw the comedy, she **laughed** out loud.
>
> When her brother said something silly at the table, she **giggled.**
>
> Dad used **large** stones to edge the planting bed.
>
> It took four men to move the **enormous** boulders.

Circle the synonym that best fits the meaning of the sentence. Write the word you circled in the blank to complete the sentence.

1. Maddy _____ longingly at the new baseball glove.
   (gazed, glanced)

2. This weekend was her chance to show what an _____ player she is.
   (okay, excellent)

3. Maddy had practiced her _____ every day after school.
   (pitching, tossing)

4. She was getting better and better at _____ the ball, too.
   (getting, catching)

5. Maddy was _____ about her playing.
   (certain, confident)

6. She knew that the _____ mitt was just what she needed for the game.
   (new, unused)

7. Maddy would _____ her mother tonight if she could buy it.
   (demand, ask)

8. Maddy's mother was very _____ of Maddy's playing.
   (supportive, helping)

> Antonyms are words that have opposite meanings.
>
> **slowly**—quickly, rapidly, hurriedly, speedily, swiftly
>
> **whisper**—scream, yell, holler, shout, screech
>
> **kind**—nasty, mean, awful, cruel, miserly
>
> **sad**—happy, thrilled, delighted, beaming, joyous

Write an antonym for each word.

1. gloomy   _____

2. energetic   _____

3. cowardly   _____

4. wisely   _____

5. difficult   _____

6. insulted   _____

7. polite   _____

8. feast   _____

Write a sentence for each antonym. Tell about movies or TV shows you've watched recently. Be sure to underline titles.

9. (exciting) _____

_____

10. (boring) _____

_____

> Antonyms are words that have opposite meanings. You can use antonyms to compare and contrast things.
>
> Roberto is very **sociable,** but his little brother Eduardo is very **shy.**
>
> I think the new library is **beautiful,** but the old one was **ugly!**

Use antonyms from the word box to complete the comparisons.

(always   neither   alike   hot   hates)

1. My friend Benny loves baseball, but he _____ football.

2. I never watch baseball, but I _____ watch football.

3. I like to be outdoors when it's cold, and Benny likes to be outdoors

   when it's _____.

4. Benny and I can be opposite in our tastes, but in other ways we're _____.

5. Both of us love basketball, and _____ of us likes skating.

Write three sentences using antonyms comparing your favorite sport with your least favorite sport.

6. _____

   _____

7. _____

   _____

8. _____

   _____

Language Fundamentals • EMC 2755 • © Evan-Moor Corp.

> Homophones are words that sound alike but have different spellings and meanings.
>
> My sister and I are **so** different.
>
> She can make a pair of pants, and I can't even **sew** on a button!
>
> There is **no** obstacle to our success with this.
>
> I **know** we will come up with a great science project.

Circle the correct homophone to match the meaning.

1. also	too	two
2. put down on paper	right	write
3. belonging to them	they're	their
4. in that place	there	they're
5. in this place	here	hear
6. 3 minus 2	won	one

Write a sentence for each of these homophones. Make sure that you use the correct meaning for the word's spelling in your sentence.

7. (through)_____

_____

8. (threw) _____

_____

Homophones are words that sound alike but have different spellings and meanings. Homophones are often confused with each other. Make sure your spelling matches the meaning that you intend.

Aleta **heard** the **herd** of horses thunder across the canyon.

      Herd means "large group of animals, such as cows."

      Heard means "listened to."

Did you hear the **tale** about how the monkey got its **tail?**

      Tail means "appendage on an animal, such as a horse."

      Tale means "story."

Write the answers to the clues in the puzzle.

no	herd	new	red	threw
know	heard	knew	read	through

Across

  2. past tense of *know*

  3. past tense of *throw*

  4. bright color

  5. none

  7. not used before

  8. listened to

Down

  1. past tense of *read*

  2. understand

  3. finished

  6. large group of animals

Name _____

Fill in the bubble next to the correct answer.

1. Which word is a synonym for *happiness?*
   Ⓐ joy
   Ⓑ sadness
   Ⓒ happy
   Ⓓ joyful

2. Which word is an antonym for *sharp?*
   Ⓐ knife
   Ⓑ sharpness
   Ⓒ pointy
   Ⓓ dull

3. What does the word *they're* mean?
   Ⓐ that place
   Ⓑ belonging to them
   Ⓒ they are
   Ⓓ they will

4. Which words are synonyms?
   Ⓐ *hear* and *here*
   Ⓑ *kind* and *nice*
   Ⓒ *sick* and *well*
   Ⓓ *wrong* and *right*

5. Which words are homophones?
   Ⓐ *happy* and *sad*
   Ⓑ *know* and *no*
   Ⓒ *glad* and *joyful*
   Ⓓ *no* and *never*

Compound words are words that are made up of two smaller words.

camp + ground = **campground**

motor + boat = **motorboat**

bed + room = **bedroom**

sun + rise = **sunrise**

black + board = **blackboard**

back + pack = **backpack**

Choose two words from the word box to make a compound word.
Write the compound words. How many can you find?

book	ground	back	black	see
base	case	ball	boat	motor
sight	sun	board	bed	set
room	lady	pack	camp	bug

1. _____

2. _____

3. _____

4. _____

5. _____

6. _____

7. _____

8. _____

9. _____

10. _____

11. _____

12. _____

13. _____

14. _____

15. _____

16. _____

> Many related words in English come from Greek and Latin roots.
>
> - The root *vis* comes from the Latin word for *see*.
>
>   **vis**ion   **vis**it   in**vis**ible   **vis**ta
>
> - The root *phys* comes from the Greek word for *body*.
>
>   **phys**ician   **phys**ics   **phys**iology   **phys**ical
>
> - The root *struct* comes from the Greek word for *build*.
>
>   **struct**ure   in**struct**   con**struct**   de**struct**ion

Use the clues to complete the puzzle with the Greek and Latin roots *vis, phys*, and *struct*.

Across

3. of or relating to the body

5. someone who visits

6. something that is built

8. to destroy

9. to teach or give direction to someone

Down

1. a person who treats illnesses and injuries; a doctor

2. able to be seen

3. the study of how living things function

4. not able to be seen

7. to build something large like a bridge, building, or road

Many words in English come from other languages, such as Arabic, Spanish, or Hindi.

The word *giraffe* comes from the Arabic word *zaraafah*.

The word *canyon* comes from the Spanish word *cañón*.

The word *bandana* comes from the Hindi word *bāndhni*.

Use your understanding of word meanings to match each word with its language of origin. Write the letter of the origin next to the English word.

1. absurd _____

2. goulash _____

3. knapsack _____

4. ukulele _____

5. moccasin _____

6. bazaar _____

7. cookie _____

8. liberty _____

a. from the Hungarian *gulyás*

b. from Hawaiian for a type of instrument

c. from Persian meaning "market"

d. from the French word *liberté* meaning "freedom"

e. from an Algonquin word for *shoe*

f. from the Dutch *knapzak*

g. from the French *absurde*

h. from the Dutch word *koekje* meaning "little cake"

Read each word and its origin. Write a sentence using the word in English.

9. *hurricane,* from the Spanish word *huracán* _____

_____

10. *parka,* from the Russian word for *jacket* _____

_____

Language Fundamentals • EMC 2755 • © Evan-Moor Corp.

Name _____

Fill in the bubble next to the correct answer.

1. Which word is a compound word?

Ⓐ camping

Ⓑ campground

Ⓒ grounded

Ⓓ camper

2. Which word does <u>not</u> come from the Greek word for *build?*

Ⓐ instrument

Ⓑ instruct

Ⓒ structure

Ⓓ deconstruction

3. Which word comes from the Latin root *vis,* meaning "see"?

Ⓐ divide

Ⓑ valley

Ⓒ very

Ⓓ visible

4. Which word comes from the Spanish word *cañón,* meaning "deep valley"?

Ⓐ can't

Ⓑ cannon

Ⓒ carrot

Ⓓ canyon

5. Which word comes from the Italian word *mascera,* meaning "something you wear to cover your face"?

Ⓐ me

Ⓑ match

Ⓒ mask

Ⓓ marble

> You can add word endings, such as *–s*, *–ed*, *–ing*, *–er*, and *–est*, to base words to make new words.
>
> Manuel stop**s** train**ing** today.
>
> Yesterday he stopp**ed** runn**ing** after school.
>
> He is pac**ing** himself because tomorrow is the 10K race.

Add *–s*, *–ed*, *–ing*, *–er*, or *–est* to each word to complete the sentence.

1. Sonya wait_____ for the bus every morning with her friends Ashanti and Kevin.

2. They don't mind wait_____, as long as they can do it together.

3. The bus stop_____ at the corner of Olive and Elm.

4. It take_____ the bus fifteen minutes to get them to school.

5. It takes long_____ to get there when the weather is bad.

6. The long_____ it ever took to get to school was one hour!

7. It had started snow_____ that morning, and the roads hadn't been cleared.

8. The snowplows clear_____ the roads later, so the ride home was quicker.

Write a sentence for each form of the word *rain*.

9. (rains) _____

_____

10. (raining) _____

_____

Name

Word endings, such as –s, –ed, –ing, –er, and –est, are added to base words depending on how the word is being used in the sentence.

The endings –s, –ed, and –ing can be added to verbs.

Jerome play**s** the saxophone.

He play**ed** at the dance on Friday night.

Play**ing** the saxophone is something he loves do**ing.**

The endings –er and –est can be added to adjectives and adverbs to compare.

The crowd was bigg**er** Friday than it was at the last dance.

It was the bigg**est** crowd ever for a school dance.

Add –s, –ed, –ing, –er, or –est to each word in parentheses ( ) and write it on the line.

1. Jerome _____ on the saxophone every day for an hour.
   (practice)

2. His father is a jazz musician, and Jerome _____ to be one, too.
   (want)

3. Jerome's music teacher _____ Jerome to play in the jazz ensemble.
   (ask)

4. Jerome is always _____ on his solo parts.
   (work)

5. He is practicing _____ this week than last.
   (hard)

6. This is the _____ solo he has ever played.
   (tough)

7. Jerome's father will be _____ his son play Friday.
   (watch)

8. He _____ his son is great!
   (think)

> Often you can tell a word's meaning by looking at the other words and groups of words around it.
>
> The solution was **obvious.** Everyone saw it.
>
> *Obvious* means "everyone can see it."

Read each sentence. Then write what the underlined word means.

1. Frankie had never been so <u>distracted</u>. She couldn't keep her mind on her work.

   The word *distracted* means _____.

2. The <u>routine</u> she had repeated over and over was slipping away.

   The word *routine* means _____.

3. She had practiced her scales <u>diligently</u>, never forgetting to do them.

   The word *diligently* means _____.

4. With <u>trepidation,</u> Frankie sat down to play, fearful that people wouldn't like her playing.

   The word *trepidation* means _____.

5. The audience applauded Frankie <u>enthusiastically</u> after she played, cheering her on.

   The word *enthusiastically* means _____.

6. The concert increased Frankie's <u>determination</u> to continue her playing. Nothing was going to stop her.

   The word *determination* means _____.

> Often you can tell a word's meaning by looking at the other words and groups of words around it.
>
> The panther's body was **sleek** and muscular. There wasn't an ounce of fat on him.
>
> The word *sleek* means "lean" or "trim."

Read the paragraph. Then answer the questions.

There was a <u>scavenger hunt</u> at school. Everyone was <u>anticipating</u> the fun to come. Last year, they had had a great time searching high and low for the things on the list. They couldn't wait! Everyone <u>congregated</u> in the gym as the rules were explained and the lists were passed out. Then the group <u>dispersed</u>, and the search began. After hours of <u>poring</u> over the clues, trying to figure out what they meant, and then scrambling to find the things on the list, everyone began to head back to the school. Andy Lopez's team <u>triumphed</u> because they found everything on the list first. They won a free lunch at Sundae's.

1. *scavenger hunt* means _____

2. *anticipating* means _____

3. *congregrated* means _____

4. *dispersed* means _____

5. *poring* means _____

6. *triumphed* means _____

Fill in the bubble next to the correct answer.

1. Which sentence is written correctly?

   Ⓐ Samantha walking two miles every day.

   Ⓑ Samantha walks two miles every day.

   Ⓒ Samantha walker two miles every day.

   Ⓓ Samantha walkest two miles every day.

2. Which sentence is written correctly?

   Ⓐ She was hoped to stick with her exercise routine.

   Ⓑ She was hoping to stick with her exercise routine.

   Ⓒ She hopeful to stick with her exercise routine.

   Ⓓ She hope to stick with her exercise routine.

3. Which sentence is written correctly?

   Ⓐ That was the farther she had ever walked.

   Ⓑ That was the far she had ever walked.

   Ⓒ That was the farthed she had ever walked.

   Ⓓ That was the farthest she had ever walked.

4. What does the word *insightful* mean in this sentence?
   She made some insightful comments that helped people understand the topic.

   Ⓐ helping to explain

   Ⓑ seeing

   Ⓒ interfering

   Ⓓ understanding

5. What does the word *threatened* mean in this sentence?
   The kitten felt threatened by the big barking dog.

   Ⓐ excited

   Ⓑ treated

   Ⓒ frightened

   Ⓓ angry

 Language Fundamentals • EMC 2755 • © Evan-Moor Corp.

Proofreading Marks

Use these marks to show corrections.

Mark	Meaning	Example
ℱ	Take this out (delete).	I love ℱo to read.
⊙	Add a period.	It was late⊙
≡	Make this a capital letter.	First prize went to maria.
/	Make this a lowercase letter.	We saw a Black Cat.
——	Fix the spelling.	This is our ~~hause~~ house.
⋏	Add a comma.	Goodnight⋏ Mom.
⌄	Add an apostrophe.	That⌄s Lil⌄s bike.
⌄⌄ ⌄⌄	Add quotation marks.	⌄⌄Come in, he said.⌄⌄
!̣ ?̣ ⋀ ⋀	Add an exclamation point or a question mark.	Help!⋀Can you help me?⋀
⊼	Add a hyphen.	I've read three⊼fourths of the book.
⌒	Close the space.	Foot⌒ball is fun.
⋀	Add a word or letter.	The⋀pen is mine. (red)
——	Underline the words.	We read <u>Old Yeller</u>.
⦂̣	Add a colon.	Alex arrived at 4⦂00.

Name _____

Proofread this paragraph. Use proofreading marks to correct
the 10 errors. Hint: One two-word proper noun is counted as one error.

      Kenya Stubbs and her parents had a big family reunion over the Fourth

of july weekend. More than 70 peoples showed up. Kenyas family has a huge

farmhouse in upstate new york, so that's where the reunion was held. Some

people had to stay in hotel's, but 37 people stayed at the farm! That included

6 babys, 11 childs under twelve year old, and 20 teen and adults. There were

plenty of good cooks, so there was plenty of food to eat. Everyone had a great

time. Kenya's Uncle DuBois said it was one of the best partys he had ever

been to.

Write the errors correctly on the lines below.

1. _____

2. _____

3. _____

4. _____

5. _____

6. _____

7. _____

8. _____

9. _____

10. _____

Language Fundamentals • EMC 2755 • © Evan-Moor Corp.

Name _____

Proofread this paragraph. Use proofreading marks to correct the 10 errors.

Earl and his five brothers live in indiana on a farm. Everyone in Earls family loves animale. Earl's brother carl wants to be a veterinarian someday. Carl spends most of his time with the horse's, grooming them and training them. Carl also keeps track of the medical supplys that need to be kept on hand in case any of the animals get sick. Earl's brother tommy is the oldest, so he has the most responsibility. Tommys' main chore is to tend to the cows, making sure they have been milked every morning. Earl is the youngest, and he and his brother Ken look after the sheeps. Next month, they are all going to show their animals at the pulaski County Fair.

Write the errors correctly on the lines below.

1. _____   6. _____

2. _____   7. _____

3. _____   8. _____

4. _____   9. _____

5. _____   10. _____

Proofread these paragraphs. Find the 10 errors, cross them out, and write the words correctly above them.

In social studies, we are studying America History. My mother is a california, and my father is a New yorker, so I decided to do a comparison/contrast essay about those two states.

The annual average temperature in California is warmerer than New York's annual average. Overall, California has few cold days than New York does. California is also largest than New York. California's higher point is Mt. Whitney, which is 14,494 feet above sea level. New York's most high point is Mt. Marcy, which is 5,344 feet above sea level.

Most presidents were born in New York than in California. Martin Van Buren, Millard Fillmore, Theodore Roosevelt, and Franklin Delano Roosevelt were all born in New York. Richard Nixon is the one President who was a native California.

Both California and New York are exciting states to study. I'd be happy to live in either one.

Proofread this paragraph. Use proofreading marks to correct the 10 errors.

My family lives in one of the interestingest parts of Boston. Our

neighborhood is called Brighton, and people move here from all over the

world. One of the bestest things about Brighton is all the wonderful

restaurants. This restaurants are known all over Boston. We have Italy

restaurants, chinese restaurants, and indian restaurants. There are many

Vietnam restaurants, too. One of these restaurants has the better spring rolls

I've ever tasted! Some days, we have the worse time deciding where to go.

Next week, we're going to try a new pakistani place. I can't wait!

Write the errors correctly on the lines below.

1. _____

2. _____

3. _____

4. _____

5. _____

6. _____

7. _____

8. _____

9. _____

10. _____

Name _____

Proofread these paragraphs. Find the 10 errors, cross them out, and write the words correctly above them.

When Bree started taking violin lessons last year, it seemed like the harder thing she had ever tried. She would practice and practice, but every day it sounded worser than the day before. She tried playing quietly, but that didn't seem to help. Then she tried playing louder, but that only made her dog, Midnight, howl.

"I'm never going to learn how to play this thing," she said dejectedly as she threw her bow down. Midnight stopped howling, but Bree didn't feel any better. Suddenly, hope appeared on the horizon. Bree's father came into the room carrying a largest pitcher of punch and a tray of the bigger cookies Bree had ever seen!

"Anyone ready for a little refreshment?" Bree's dad asked as he set the loads tray down on a table. It was getting darkest outside as the winter sun set.

"I'll never get any more good than I am now, Dad," she complained. "I'm the worse violinist ever!"

"You're going to get better at this," her dad said soothingly. "The more often you practice, the more your technique will improve. In the meantime, have a bigger cookie and give yourself and the dog a break."

With that, Bree, her dad, and Midnight sat down for their well-earned snack.

Language Fundamentals • EMC 2755 • © Evan-Moor Corp.

Proofread these paragraphs. Find the 10 errors, cross them out, and write the words correctly above them.

My big sister, Steffi, took my little sister, my brother, and I for a bike ride on Sunday. Her, Lani, Theo, and me went to Oakhurst Park, where there are lots of good bike trails.

Steffi and me led the way once we were on the trails, since we do the most biking. Theo wanted to go off on his own, but we promised Mom us would stay together.

We had a great ride! The trees didn't block the sun, so we could feel their warmth the whole time we were out.

Finally, at about 5:30 Steffi said to us, "It's time to head home, or they will be late for supper."

When we got home, Theo and me helped Lani wipe down her bike and put it away.

Dad called Steffi, Theo, Lani, and I in for dinner. As we sat down to eat, he said, "It's nice for your mother and I to know we can leave you in Steffi's capable hands. Thanks, Steffi, for being such a good big sister."

"Thanks, Steffi," we all repeated as we dug into our food. "You're the best!"

Proofread these paragraphs. Find the 10 errors, cross them out, and write the words correctly above them.

Whenever my family goes to the beach, you have a great time. The hard part of the trip comes when it's time for we to gather our belongings, load the car, and head home.

"Is this my or yours?" my brother asks as he holds up a shoe.

"It's not mines," I reply, "so they must be yours."

My father always loses his' towel. He turns to my mom and I and says, "Has anyone seen my towel?"

Then my mom and me go searching for it. It's usually half-buried in the sand somewhere.

"Here it is," one of us will say while pulling the towel out from the sand. "I believe this is your."

Every family has traditions, and I guess this is one of ours'.

Language Fundamentals • EMC 2755 • © Evan-Moor Corp.

Proofread these paragraphs. Find the 10 errors, cross them out, and write the words correctly above them.

My friends and me belong to a hiking club. We go hiking once a month in the hills near where us live. We have a guide who takes them on these hikes. Her name is Andrea, and she knows a lot about the animals, birds, and flowers we find on our hikes.

We have to wear special clothes when we hike. Ginnie and me have the same kind of hiking boots. The shoes are very comfortable, but their very sturdy, too. Lourdes's boots are also very sturdy and comfortable, plus it's really cool looking. They have green stripes on the sides.

Andrea tells us about the birds they see on our hikes. She knows just about every bird there is! One time, we saw a bald eagle sitting high up in a tree. When we looked through binoculars, we could see it's nest. We see quail all the time. They are so cute with they little crests that look like a big teardrop!

When we're old enough, Lourdes and me want to become guides like Andrea. It must be great to spend all that time outdoors!

Proofread these paragraphs. Find the 10 errors, cross them out, and write the words correctly above them.

Last weekend, our school putted on its first ever Dog Wash and Bake Sale to raise money for our school music program. We studied different types of school fundraisers, and it come down to two: a dog wash and a bake sale. We couldn't decide which one, so instead we went ahead with plans for both.

The fifth-grade class were in charge of organizing the baked goods, and the sixth-graders were in charge of the dog wash. The other classes drawed pictures for posters and decorated the playground.

On Saturday morning, people brang their dogs and line up in the dog wash area. We had huge tubs and hoses, as well as plenty of dog shampoo. It got very wet in the dog wash area, and a couple of kids slided on the soapsuds and fell. They got back up and kept washing dogs, so we knew they were okay.

Everyone, including some of the dogs, eat lots of cookies and cupcakes. We selled all the baked goods and made $475. The dog wash raised another $263. That meant we raised $738 to help the school buy sheet music for our music program.

Proofread these paragraphs. Use proofreading marks to correct
the 10 errors.

Tanya has a big test tomorrow, and she is studying for it tonight. She
studied all last weekend and every night this week, but it's an important test,
so she want to make sure she's ready. She be reviewing every chapter in her
social studies book, and her brothers is taking turns quizzing her on the
material covered. Tanya answers the questions, and sometimes she write
down special things she need to remember.

Tanya's mother will calls her when dinner is ready. Tanya's mother
believe that you can't learn anything if you don't eats properly. Tanya's
family knows that Tanya will do well on the test. She always do.

Write the errors correctly on the lines below.

1. _____

2. _____

3. _____

4. _____

5. _____

6. _____

7. _____

8. _____

9. _____

10. _____

Proofread these paragraphs. Use proofreading marks to correct
the 10 errors.

Our neighborhood have a community garden. Because we lives in the

city, most people don't has a garden in their backyard, so someone donate

a plot of land, and everyone work to keep it clean and productive.

Last year my family growed string beans, tomatoes, squash, and lettuce.

This year my friend Phailin's family is grown peppers, a special kind of basil,

and mustard greens. Phailin's grandmother said she'd going to make me

a special dish. She asked me if I like to try new food. I tell her that once I

even tryed octopus. She laughed and promised me no octopus, just some

good Thai home cooking.

Write the errors correctly on the lines below.

1. _____   6. _____

2. _____   7. _____

3. _____   8. _____

4. _____   9. _____

5. _____   10. _____

Proofread these paragraphs. Find the 10 errors, cross them out, and write the words correctly above them.

Shane's birthday was coming up, and his father ask him what he wanted to do.

"I want to go bowling," Shane replyed, as he finished loading his dishes into the dishwasher.

"Bowling!" his fathered said in complete surprise. "Where did you get that idea?"

"From Makayla's Grandma Lucy," Shane answered. "She has bin bowling since she was a teenager, and she teached Makayla to bowl. I went with them once, and it's pretty cool."

"Okay," Shane's father said doubtfully. "It's your birthday."

Shane sended out invitations to ten friends. Some of them laughed when they heared what they were going to do, but they all said yes.

Makayla's Grandma Lucy was there, and she give everyone pointers on how to stand and how to move their arms slowly so that they has the most control over the ball.

Once Shane's friends got into it, they have a great time. As a matter of fact, two of Shane's friends decided to have their next birthday parties at the bowling alley.

"Well, Shane," his father said with a smile, "it looks as if you'd started a trend. I might even take up bowling myself!"

Proofread these paragraphs. Find the 10 errors, cross them out, and write the words correctly above them.

Rachel felt ready for her soccer game. She had played bad in her last game, but that's because she had hurt her ankle. As soon as she twisted it, it hurt terrible, and it continued to throb painfully through the rest of the game.

Rachel sat out the next three games reluctantly, but she knew her ankle would throb worst if she didn't listen to Coach's advice. She watched the team play worse in each game. Rachel was their best kicker, and she could run quicklier than anyone except Nina, who was as fast as the wind.

Last week, Coach had finally said that Rachel was ready to get back into the game. Today, as soon as the game started Rachel knew she was going to play best than she ever had before. Soccer was something she loved more than anything, and she had missed it bad.

As the game progressed, Rachel's kicks went right where she meant them to go. Her team showed what they could do, playing more good and more good as the end of the game drew nearer. In the final minutes of the game, someone sudden kicked the ball to Rachel. As she slammed it past the other team's goalie, she heard voices roar loud from the stands. They'd won! That's when Rachel knew that she wanted to play soccer forever! There was nothing like it.

Language Fundamentals • EMC 2755 • © Evan-Moor Corp.

Proofread this paragraph.
Correct the incomplete sentences by adding words to make them complete. Then rewrite the paragraph on the lines.

Like to camp? So my family. We every summer for two weeks. Our

favorite place to camp Lake of the Ozarks. Many great campgrounds there.

Camped at one last year that had a playground for kids, with swings and a

seesaw. My little brothers and sisters. My sister Anika and I love to swim, so

it near the lake. This summer for three weeks. Get to bring a friend this time.

_____

_____

_____

_____

_____

_____

_____

_____

_____

Find each run-on sentence in these paragraphs and correct it.
You can create two sentences or make the run-on sentence into
a compound or complex sentence using conjunctions.

The famous Pullman porters were African-American men who worked on sleeping-car trains during the 19th and 20th centuries, they carried luggage, made up beds, and served food and drinks. African-American men weren't allowed to work at many steady, good-paying jobs, being a Pullman porter was a desirable job.

People used to travel long distances by train, the old Pullman cars had sleeping berths so people could sleep on their long journeys. The Pullman porters saw to the passengers' needs the quality of their service was well-known among frequent travelers. Up until the 1920s though, the porters worked many hours for very little money, they had been trying to organize to change their working conditions for years. In 1925, A. Philip Randolph joined with a large number of porters, they founded the Brotherhood of Sleeping Car Porters, the first African-American-controlled union in U.S. history. The strength of the union was behind them Pullman porters' working conditions and pay improved. In 1978, the Brotherhood of Sleeping Car Porters ceased to be an independent organization it merged with the Brotherhood of Railway and Airline Clerks.

Read this paragraph and rewrite it to make it read more smoothly. Combine sentences to avoid choppiness and unnecessary repetition. Use compound sentences, complex sentences, and other sentence-combining techniques.

My grandparents are baseball fans. They love to watch baseball games all during baseball season. There's only one problem. The problem is that Nana is a Red Sox fan. Grandpa is a Yankee fan. There has been a rivalry for years. The rivalry is between Red Sox fans and Yankee fans. The Red Sox are the Boston baseball team. The Yankees are a New York baseball team. The Red Sox fans have never forgotten the great baseball player. His name was Babe Ruth. Babe Ruth left the Boston Red Sox. Babe Ruth went to play for the Yankees. This happened way back in 1920. The Red Sox fans still talk about it.

_____

_____

_____

_____

_____

_____

_____

_____

_____

Read these paragraphs and then rewrite them to make them read more smoothly. Combine sentences to avoid choppiness and unnecessary repetition. Use compound sentences, complex sentences, and other sentence-combining techniques.

One of Lupe's family's favorite things to do is invite friends over. The family invites them over for a taco feast.

Everyone in the family helps. They help get ready for the party. Lupe's older brother chops onions. He chops chiles. He chops tomatoes. He puts them in bowls. The bowls are special bowls. They are used only when company comes.

Lupe's mother makes guacamole. Guacamole is a dip. The dip is wonderful. It is made from avocados. Lupe's Abuela taught Lupe's mother how to make this dip. This dip is very popular with everyone. Abuela also taught Lupe how to make tortillas. Abuela's are better.

_____

_____

_____

_____

_____

_____

_____

_____

_____

_____

Proofread this paragraph. Use proofreading marks to correct
the 10 errors. Hint: Two two-word proper nouns and one four-word
proper noun count as one error each.

My Uncle Jason lives in new jersey. he works in New York City. I like to
visit him there on school vacations. my parents let me fly by myself from
chicago because Uncle jason meets me at the airport in newark. sometimes,
Uncle Jason lets me go to work with him at his law office. then we go to
lunch together at the museum of modern art. Later we go to central park
and watch people sail miniature boats on this really cool pond.

Rewrite the paragraph on the lines below. Remember to use capital letters where
they belong.

_____

_____

_____

_____

_____

_____

_____

_____

Proofread this paragraph. Use proofreading marks to correct
the 10 errors. Hint: Two two-word holiday names and one three-word
holiday name count as one error each.

What's your favorite holiday? I love the fourth of july. I'm a big fan of

fireworks, patriotic songs, and cookouts. Other people prefer the winter

holidays, such as hanukkah, kwanzaa, or christmas. There's something about

a december holiday that breaks up the long stretch of dreary weather. My

mom likes any holiday that involves a monday off from work. We always

do something special on presidents' day, labor day, and Memorial Day.

Sometimes, Mom can get friday off, too, so we can leave as soon as school

lets out and head to the beach or the woods to go camping. Last september,

we went to the beach for five days. It was great!

Rewrite the paragraph on the lines below. Remember to use capital letters where
they belong.

_____

_____

_____

_____

_____

_____

_____

_____

_____

Name _____

Write the titles correctly.

1. Folk Tales

   "beauty and the beast" _____

   "why opossum has a bare tail" _____

   "anansi and turtle" _____

2. Magazines

   ranger rick _____

   time for kids _____

3. Books

   maniac magee _____

   bridge to terabithia _____

4. Songs

   "swing low, sweet chariot" _____

   "my favorite things" _____

5. Poem

   "eletelephony" _____

Answer the following questions.

6. What is your favorite book?

   _____

7. What is your favorite song?

   _____

Proofread this paragraph. Use proofreading marks to correct
the 10 errors.

Do you like roller-coaster rides. I used to be scared of them, but now I
ride on one every time I go to an amusement park My brother, Jeb, likes to
ride on them, too. Last summer, we went to Coney Island with my parents,
Jeb and I rode on the Cyclone, which some people think is the best roller
coaster ever? The ride was so cool We screamed like maniacs the whole way
down Do you know what Jeb said as soon as we got off the ride? "Let's go
again," he said. So we did My mom thinks we're nuts to want to ride on
roller coasters all the time, My dad is pretty cool about it He used to like to
go on roller coasters himself, but now he says he's too old and too smart to
do it again

Proofread this paragraph. Use proofreading marks to correct
the 10 errors.

What's your favorite season. Is it fall, when the leaves turn colors, and
the air gets that nice crisp feeling to it! Or is winter your favorite. Winter
brings snow to the mountains and the smell of burning wood as people use
their fireplaces to make their houses all nice and cozy, Spring is the favorite
season for many people That sound of the first returning robin is just
amazing The buds appear on the trees, and the flowers begin to poke through
the ground! Before you know it, it's summer The days get longer and
warmer, and the smell of barbecue fills the summer evening air, That has to
make summer the best season of all

Proofread these paragraphs. Use proofreading marks to correct
the 10 errors.

> "What time do you have? Ella asked her friend Luis. My watch broke,
> so I'm wearing Susans, but I dont think it's working either."
>
> Its 2:45," Luis said. "Why? Do you have to be somewhere this
> afternoon?"
>
> "I'm supposed to be home by 315," Ella responded. My mom's taking
> me shopping for a new bike.
>
> "Get a move on Ella," Luis said. "What's more important than shopping
> for a new bike?"

Write the corrected paragraphs on the lines below. Remember to include
the correct punctuation.

_____

_____

_____

_____

_____

_____

_____

_____

_____

Language Fundamentals • EMC 2755 • © Evan-Moor Corp.

Proofread these paragraphs. Use proofreading marks to correct
the 10 errors.

Liam's great-grandmother, Gigi, was born on April 16 1914. When Gigi
was a little girl automobiles were a new invention. People traveled on
streetcars and trains or they walked long distances to get to where they
wanted to go.

Most families didnt have cars but Gigi's family had one. They would go
for long Sunday rides and theyd have a picnic somewhere along the way.
They would always bring sandwiches fruit punch and cookies that Gigi's
mother had made. After they had eaten they would pile back into the car
and head home for a nice long nap!

Write the corrected first paragraph on the lines below. Remember to include
the correct punctuation.

_____

_____

_____

_____

_____

_____

_____

_____

Proofread these paragraphs. Use proofreading marks to correct the 10 errors.

Terrys family was going river rafting on Saturday and they said he could bring one friend along.

"Terry why don't you invite that boy who moved in across the street last month? his mother asked.

"Mom I hardy know him! He could turn out to be a total freak," Terry objected. Terry wasnt' crazy about the idea of being the first one to try out the new kid.

Just remember, Terry, that being new feels pretty rotten until someone makes you feel like you belong," his mother pointed out.

"Yeah, youre right," Terry said as he picked up the phone.

"That would be great, said Jorge when Terry asked him to go river rafting.

And thats exactly what the trip turned out to be—great! Jorge was funny and fun, and best of all, he loved to paddle!

Proofread these paragraphs. Use proofreading marks to correct the 10 errors.

Zachs school newspaper took a survey of students and teachers to find out peoples' favorite books, poems, stories movies, songs, and television shows.

The fifth-grade students favorite book was Harry Potter and the Goblet of Fire. The third-grade student's favorite book was Charlotte's Web.

The favorite movie for first-graders was Shrek. The favorite story for fourth-graders was On Board the Titanic.

The big surprise was the teachers choice for best song. The majority of the teachers chose On Top of Spaghetti as their favorite song!

Proofread this friendly letter. Use proofreading marks to correct the 10 errors.

June 3 2006

Dear Tío Roberto

    Thank you so much for the birthday present. Ive wanted my own tent for ages and the one you bought me is perfect!

    Two weeks from now Dr and Mrs Marquez are coming with their son Jaime to stay with us for ten days. Dad said that Jaime and I can camp out in the backyard. Since the tent sleeps two Jaime and I will be able to stay in it.

    Thanks again for the gift Tío Roberto. You're the best!

                  Love

                  José

Proofread this business letter. Use proofreading marks to correct the 10 errors.

November 1 2007

Who Are You Costume Company

17 Lowell Av.

New Rochelle Ny 10952

To Whom It May Concern

On September 18 2007 I purchased a pirate costume made by your company to wear to a Halloween party.

The party began at 700. By 8:30, the costume began to fall apart. I had to leave the party early before the costume was completely destroyed.

I am returning the costume to you and I would appreciate a full refund. My receipt is enclosed.

Sincerely

Jeremy Nyack

Proofread these paragraphs. Find the 10 errors, cross them out, and write the words correctly above them.

My friends and I like to play baseball, but we don't have no baseball fields in our neighborhood. Jenette's backyard is huge though, and it works really good as a baseball diamond.

First, we measure out the distances between the bases, and then we lie the bases down where they belong. There isn't nobody who can lie out bases like Jenette. We may count on those bases to be exactly where they're supposed to be.

Julia is our star batter. There isn't no one who can hit a ball as far as she can. She bats so good that hardly anyone wants to be in the outfield when she hits the ball. Once during practice, she hit it to Chen and I. Instead of trying to catch the ball, we both ran away from it. We didn't want no part of that fast fly ball. Good thing we're on her team!

Language Fundamentals • EMC 2755 • © Evan-Moor Corp.

Proofread these paragraphs. Find the 10 errors, cross them out, and write the words correctly above them.

"Mom, can I go to Mary Catherine's house to play video games?" Tanja asked her mother. "Her parents invited me for dinner, to. There making jambalaya tonight."

"Have you finished your homework?" Mom asked.

"I plan too do the last of it when I get home," Tanja said. "Their isn't that much left to do."

"Okay, sweetie," Mom replied, "as long as you're sure you can finish up by bedtime. Say hi to Mary Catherine's parents for me. Their nice people. We should have them over for dinner sometime. Before you go, Tanja, would you please wake your father? He went to lay down for a nap before supper."

"I'd be only two happy to wake him," Tanja said with a grin.

"On second thought, you don't have too. You go on ahead and have fun with Mary Catherine," Mom said as Tanja left. "I'm glad you to are such great friends!"

Answer Key

Page 11

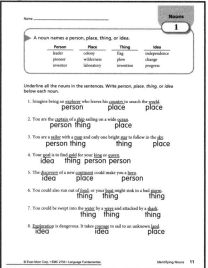

Page 12

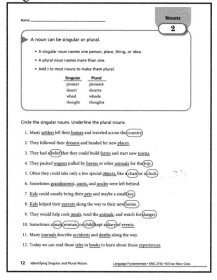

Page 13

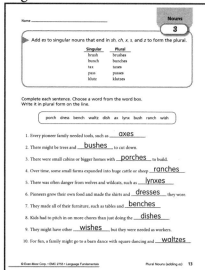

Page 14

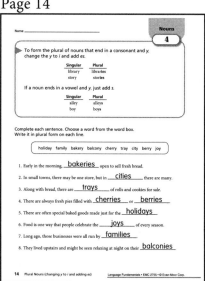

Page 15

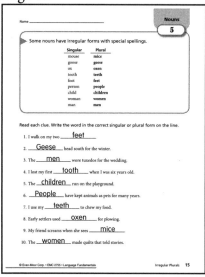

Page 16

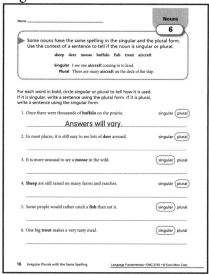

Page 17

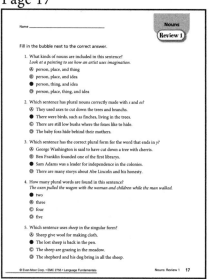

Page 18

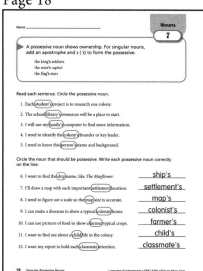

Page 19

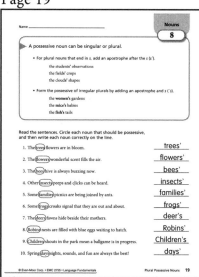

Language Fundamentals • EMC 2755 • © Evan-Moor Corp.

Page 20

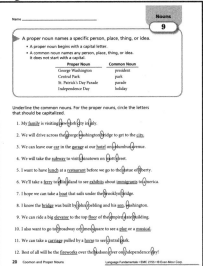

Page 21

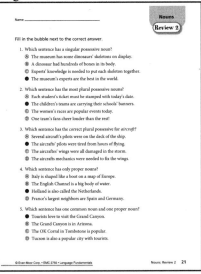

Page 22

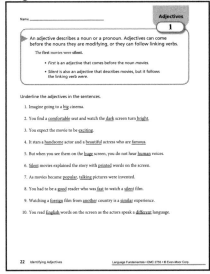

Page 23

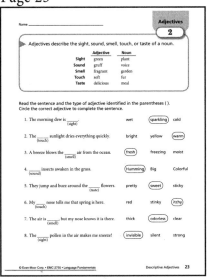

Page 24

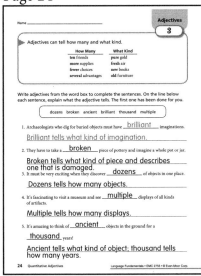

Page 25

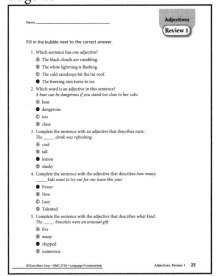

Page 26

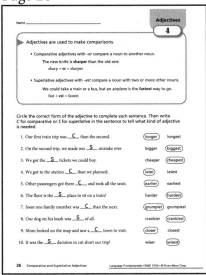

Page 27

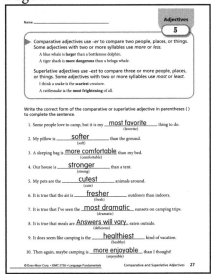

Page 28

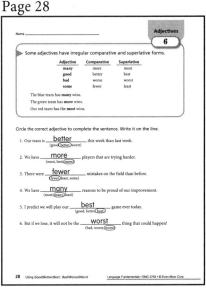

Page 29

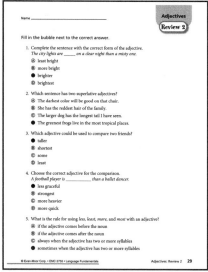

Page 30

Page 31

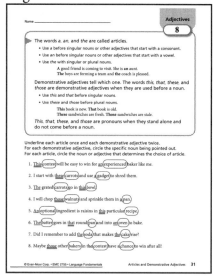

Page 32

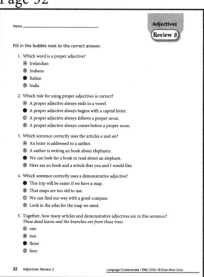

Page 33

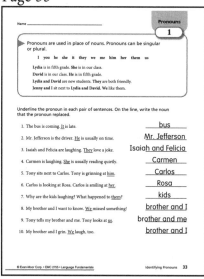

Page 34

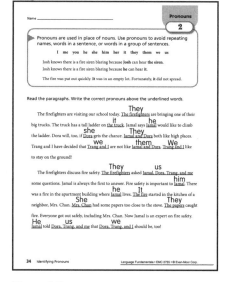

Page 35

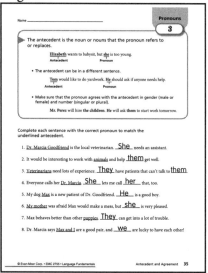

Page 36

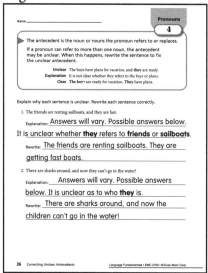

Page 37

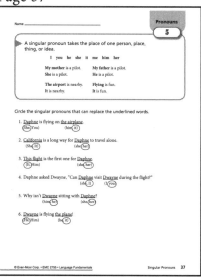

Page 38

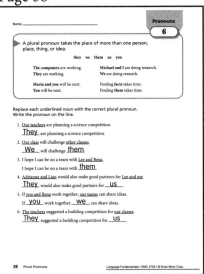

Pronouns 6

A plural pronoun takes the place of more than one person, place, thing, or idea.

they   we   them   us   you

The **computers** are working.   **Michael and I** are doing research.
They are working.   **We** are doing research.

Maria and you will be next.   Finding **facts** takes time.
You will be next.   Finding **them** takes time.

Replace each underlined noun with the correct plural pronoun. Write the pronoun on the line.

1. Our teachers are planning a science competition.
   They are planning a science competition.
2. Our class will challenge other classes.
   We will challenge **them**.
3. I hope I can be on a team with Lee and Bena.
   I hope I can be on a team with **them**.
4. Adrianne and Lian would also make good partners for Lee and me.
   They would also make good partners for **us**.
5. If you and Bena work together, our teams can share ideas.
   If **you** work together, **we** can share ideas.
6. The teachers suggested a building competition for our classes.
   They suggested a building competition for **us**.

38 Plural Pronouns   Language Fundamentals • EMC 2755 • © Evan-Moor Corp.

Page 39

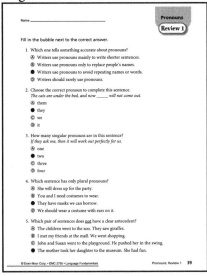

Pronouns Review 1

Fill in the bubble next to the correct answer.

1. Which one tells something accurate about pronouns?
   Ⓐ Writers use pronouns mainly to write shorter sentences.
   Ⓑ Writers use pronouns only to replace people's names.
   ● Writers use pronouns to avoid repeating names or words.
   Ⓓ Writers should rarely use pronouns.

2. Choose the correct pronoun to complete this sentence.
   The cats are under the bed, and now _____ will not come out.
   Ⓐ them
   ● they
   Ⓒ we
   Ⓓ it

3. How many singular pronouns are in this sentence?
   If they ask me, then it will work out perfectly for us.
   Ⓐ one
   ● two
   Ⓒ three
   Ⓓ four

4. Which sentence has only plural pronouns?
   Ⓐ She will dress up for the party.
   Ⓑ You and I need costumes to wear.
   ● They have masks we can borrow.
   Ⓓ We should wear a costume with ears on it.

5. Which pair of sentences does not have a clear antecedent?
   Ⓐ The children went to the zoo. They saw giraffes.
   Ⓑ I met my friends at the mall. We went shopping.
   ● John and Susan went to the playground. He pushed her in the swing.
   Ⓓ The mother took her daughter to the museum. She had fun.

© Evan-Moor Corp. • EMC 2755 • Language Fundamentals   Pronouns: Review 1   39

Page 40

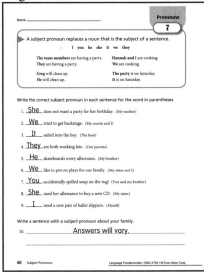

Pronouns 7

A subject pronoun replaces a noun that is the subject of a sentence.

I   you   he   she   it   we   they

The **team members** are having a party.   **Hannah and I** are cooking.
They are having a party.   **We** are cooking.

Greg will clean up.   The **party** is on Saturday.
He will clean up.   **It** is on Saturday.

Write the correct subject pronoun in each sentence for the word in parentheses.

1. **She** does not want a party for her birthday. (My mother)
2. **We** tried to get backstage. (My cousin and I)
3. **It** sailed into the bay. (The boat)
4. **They** are both working late. (Our parents)
5. **He** skateboards every afternoon. (My brother)
6. **We** like to put on plays for our family. (My sister and I)
7. **You** accidentally spilled soup on the rug! (You and my brother)
8. **She** used her allowance to buy a new CD. (My sister)
9. **I** need a new pair of ballet slippers. (Myself)

Write a sentence with a subject pronoun about your family.

10. **Answers will vary.**

40 Subject Pronouns   Language Fundamentals • EMC 2755 • © Evan-Moor Corp.

Page 41

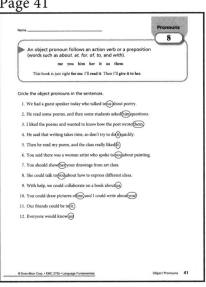

Pronouns 8

An object pronoun follows an action verb or a preposition (words such as *about, at, for, of, to,* and *with*).

me   you   him   her   it   us   them

This book is just right **for me**. I'll **read it**. Then I'll **give it to her.**

Circle the object pronouns in the sentences.

1. We had a guest speaker today who talked to (us) about poetry.
2. He read some poems, and then some students asked (him) questions.
3. I liked the poems and wanted to know how the poet wrote (them).
4. He said that writing takes time, so don't try to do (it) quickly.
5. Then he read my poem, and the class really liked (it).
6. You said there was a woman artist who spoke to (you) about painting.
7. You should show (her) your drawings from art class.
8. She could talk to (you) about how to express different ideas.
9. With help, we could collaborate on a book about (us).
10. You could draw pictures of (me) and I could write about (you).
11. Our friends could be in (it).
12. Everyone would know (us).

© Evan-Moor Corp. • EMC 2755 • Language Fundamentals   Object Pronouns   41

Page 42

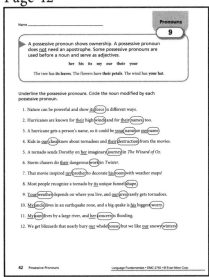

Pronouns 9

A possessive pronoun shows ownership. A possessive pronoun does not need an apostrophe. Some possessive pronouns are used before a noun and serve as adjectives.

her   his   its   my   our   their   your

The tree has **its leaves.** The flowers have **their petals.** The wind has **your hat.**

Underline the possessive pronouns. Circle the noun modified by each possessive pronoun.

1. Nature can be powerful and show its (force) in different ways.
2. Hurricanes are known for their high (winds) and for their (names) too.
3. A hurricane gets a person's name, so it could be your (name) or my (name).
4. Kids in our (class) knew about tornadoes and their (destruction) from the movies.
5. A tornado sends Dorothy on her imaginary (journey) in *The Wizard of Oz.*
6. Storm chasers do their dangerous (work) in *Twister.*
7. That movie inspired my (brother) to decorate his (room) with weather maps!
8. Most people recognize a tornado by its unique funnel (shape).
9. Your (weather) depends on where you live, and your (area) rarely gets tornadoes.
10. My (uncle) lives in an earthquake zone, and a big quake is his biggest (worry).
11. My (aunt) lives by a large river, and her (concern) is flooding.
12. We get blizzards that nearly bury our whole (house) but we like our snowy (winters).

42 Possessive Pronouns   Language Fundamentals • EMC 2755 • © Evan-Moor Corp.

Page 43

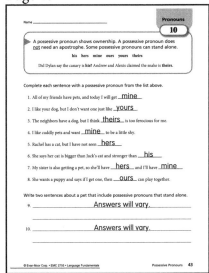

Pronouns 10

A possessive pronoun shows ownership. A possessive pronoun does not need an apostrophe. Some possessive pronouns can stand alone.

his   hers   mine   ours   yours   theirs

Did Dylan say the canary is **his?** Andrew and Alexis claimed the snake is **theirs.**

Complete each sentence with a possessive pronoun from the list above.

1. All of my friends have pets, and today I will get **mine**.
2. I like your dog, but I don't want one just like **yours**.
3. The neighbors have a dog, but I think **theirs** is too ferocious for me.
4. I like cuddly pets and want **mine** to be a little shy.
5. Rachel has a cat, but I have not seen **hers**.
6. She says her cat is bigger than Jack's cat and stronger than **his**.
7. My sister is also getting a pet, so she'll have **hers** and I'll have **mine**.
8. She wants a puppy and says if I get one, then **ours** can play together.

Write two sentences about a pet that include possessive pronouns that stand alone.

9. **Answers will vary.**

10. **Answers will vary.**

© Evan-Moor Corp. • EMC 2755 • Language Fundamentals   Possessive Pronouns   43

Page 44

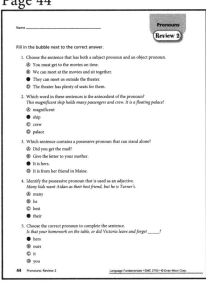

Pronouns Review 2

Fill in the bubble next to the correct answer.

1. Choose the sentence that has both a subject pronoun and an object pronoun.
   Ⓐ You must get to the movies on time.
   ● We can meet at the movies and sit together.
   Ⓒ They can meet us outside the theater.
   Ⓓ The theater has plenty of seats for them.

2. Which word in these sentences is the antecedent of the pronoun?
   This magnificent ship holds many passengers and crew. It is a floating palace!
   Ⓐ magnificent
   ● ship
   Ⓒ crew
   Ⓓ palace

3. Which sentence contains a possessive pronoun that can stand alone?
   Ⓐ Did you get the mail?
   Ⓑ Give the letter to your mother.
   ● It is hers.
   Ⓓ It is from her friend in Maine.

4. Identify the possessive pronoun that is used as an adjective.
   Many kids want Aidan as their best friend, but he is Turner's.
   Ⓐ many
   Ⓑ he
   Ⓒ best
   ● their

5. Choose the correct pronoun to complete the sentence.
   Is that your homework on the table, or did Victoria leave and forget _____?
   ● hers
   Ⓑ ours
   Ⓒ it
   Ⓓ you

44 Pronouns: Review 2   Language Fundamentals • EMC 2755 • © Evan-Moor Corp.

Page 45

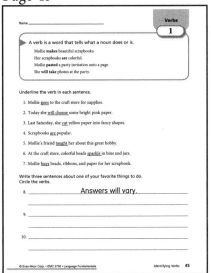

Verbs 1

A verb is a word that tells what a noun does or is.

Mollie **makes** beautiful scrapbooks.
Her scrapbooks **are** colorful.
Mollie **pasted** a party invitation onto a page.
She will **take** photos at the party.

Underline the verb in each sentence.

1. Mollie goes to the craft store for supplies.
2. Today she will choose some bright pink paper.
3. Last Saturday, she cut yellow paper into fancy shapes.
4. Scrapbooks are popular.
5. Mollie's friend taught her about this great hobby.
6. At the craft store, colorful beads sparkle in bins and jars.
7. Mollie buys beads, ribbons, and paper for her scrapbook.

Write three sentences about one of your favorite things to do. Circle the verbs.

8. **Answers will vary.**

9.

10.

© Evan-Moor Corp. • EMC 2755 • Language Fundamentals   Identifying Verbs   45

Page 46

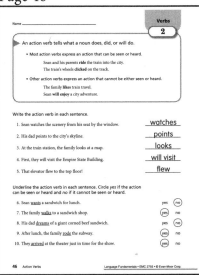

Verbs 2

An action verb tells what a noun does, did, or will do.

• Most action verbs express an action that can be seen or heard.
   Sean and his parents **ride** the train into the city.
   The train's wheels **clicked** on the track.
• Other action verbs express an action that cannot be either seen or heard.
   The family **likes** train travel.
   Sean will **enjoy** a city adventure.

Write the action verb in each sentence.

1. Sean watches the scenery from his seat by the window.   **watches**
2. His dad points to the city's skyline.   **points**
3. At the train station, the family looks at a map.   **looks**
4. First, they will visit the Empire State Building.   **will visit**
5. That elevator flew to the top floor!   **flew**

Underline the action verb in each sentence. Circle *yes* if the action can be seen or heard and *no* if it cannot be seen or heard.

6. Sean wants a sandwich for lunch.   yes (no)
7. The family walks to a sandwich shop.   (yes) no
8. His dad dreams of a giant corned beef sandwich.   yes (no)
9. After lunch, the family rode the subway.   (yes) no
10. They arrived at the theater just in time for the show.   (yes) no

46 Action Verbs   Language Fundamentals • EMC 2755 • © Evan-Moor Corp.

Page 47

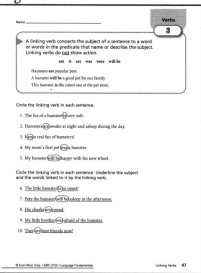

Name _____

Verbs 3

A linking verb connects the subject of a sentence to a word or words in the predicate that name or describe the subject. Linking verbs do not show action.

am is are was were will be

Hamsters **are** popular pets.
A hamster **will be** a good pet for our family.
This hamster **is** the cutest one at the pet store.

Circle the linking verb in each sentence.

1. The fur of a hamster (is) very soft.
2. Hamsters (are) awake at night and asleep during the day.
3. I (am) a big fan of hamsters!
4. My mom's first pet (was) a hamster.
5. My hamster (will be) happy with his new wheel.

Circle the linking verb in each sentence and underline the subject and the words linked to it by the linking verb.

6. The little hamster (is) so sweet!
7. Pete the hamster (will be) asleep in the afternoon.
8. His cheeks (are) round.
9. My little brother (was) afraid of the hamster.
10. They (are) best friends now!

Page 48

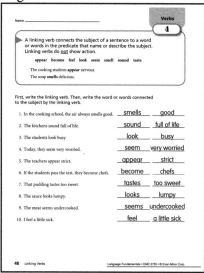

Verbs 4

A linking verb connects the subject of a sentence to a word or words in the predicate that name or describe the subject. Linking verbs do not show action.

appear become feel look seem smell sound taste

The cooking students **appear** nervous.
The soup **smells** delicious.

First, write the linking verb. Then, write the word or words connected to the subject by the linking verb.

1. In the cooking school, the air always smells good. — smells — good
2. The kitchens sound full of life. — sound — full of life
3. The students look busy. — look — busy
4. Today, they seem very worried. — seem — very worried
5. The teachers appear strict. — appear — strict
6. If the students pass the test, they become chefs. — become — chefs
7. That pudding tastes too sweet. — tastes — too sweet
8. The sauce looks lumpy. — looks — lumpy
9. The meat seems undercooked. — seems — undercooked
10. I feel a little sick. — feel — a little sick

Page 49

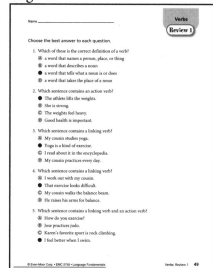

Verbs Review 1

Choose the best answer to each question.

1. Which of these is the correct definition of a verb?
   Ⓐ a word that names a person, place, or thing
   Ⓑ a word that describes a noun
   ● a word that tells what a noun is or does
   Ⓓ a word that takes the place of a noun

2. Which sentence contains an action verb?
   ● The athlete lifts the weights.
   Ⓑ She is strong.
   Ⓒ The weights feel heavy.
   Ⓓ Good health is important.

3. Which sentence contains a linking verb?
   Ⓐ My cousin studies yoga.
   ● Yoga is a kind of exercise.
   Ⓒ I read about it in the encyclopedia.
   Ⓓ My cousin practices every day.

4. Which sentence contains a linking verb?
   Ⓐ I work out with my cousin.
   ● That exercise looks difficult.
   Ⓒ My cousin walks the balance beam.
   Ⓓ He raises his arms for balance.

5. Which sentence contains a linking verb and an action verb?
   Ⓐ How do you exercise?
   Ⓑ Jose practices judo.
   Ⓒ Karen's favorite sport is rock climbing.
   ● I feel better when I swim.

Page 50

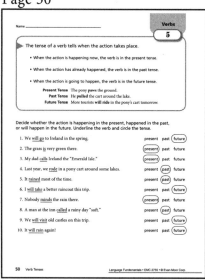

Verbs 5

The tense of a verb tells when the action takes place.

- When the action is happening, the verb is in the present tense.
- When the action has already happened, the verb is in the past tense.
- When the action is going to happen, the verb is in the future tense.

Present Tense The pony **paws** the ground.
Past Tense He **pulled** the cart around the lake.
Future Tense More tourists **will ride** in the pony's cart tomorrow.

Decide whether the action is happening in the present, happened in the past, or will happen in the future. Underline the verb and circle the tense.

1. We will go to Ireland in the spring. — present past (future)
2. The grass is very green there. — (present) past future
3. My dad calls Ireland the "Emerald Isle." — (present) past future
4. Last year, we rode in a pony cart around some lakes. — present (past) future
5. It rained most of the time. — present (past) future
6. I will take a better raincoat this trip. — present past (future)
7. Nobody minds the rain there. — (present) past future
8. A man at the inn called a rainy day "soft." — present (past) future
9. We will visit old castles on this trip. — present past (future)
10. It will rain again! — present past (future)

Page 51

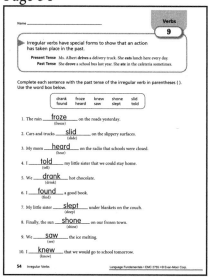

Verbs 6

A present tense verb tells that the action:

Is Happening Now The quarterback **makes** a touchdown.
Happens Regularly My dad **watches** our favorite team every week.

Underline the present tense verbs. Then write whether the action is happening now or happens regularly.

1. Every Sunday, my dad and I relax in front of the television. — regularly
2. We sit on the couch and wear our team hats. — regularly
3. Today our team plays an important game. — now
4. They are playing their biggest rival. — now
5. I am eating popcorn for a snack. — now
6. During every game, I call the plays like a professional announcer. — regularly
7. The quarterback fumbles that ball! — now
8. The coach looks pretty upset! — now
9. The coach throws his hat whenever he is mad. — regularly
10. For the second time today, the kicker makes the extra point. — now
11. That wraps it up! — now
12. We love football. — regularly

Write two sentences in the present tense about sports.

13. Now: _____ Answers will vary.

14. Regularly: _____

Page 52

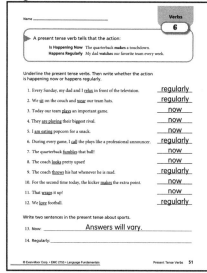

Verbs 7

A past tense verb tells that an action took place in the past and is over.

The class **elected** a new president yesterday.
Susan **won** the election.
Most of our class **voted** for her.

Underline the sentence in each pair that has a past tense verb. Circle the past tense verb.

1. The class has an election every year. Yesterday we (put) our ballots in the box.
2. I (lost) the election. Susan is our new class president.
3. My friends feel sorry for me. I (worked) hard in the campaign.
4. I am happy for Susan. She (ran) a fair campaign.
5. Our class (made) a good choice. I will support President Susan.

Rewrite each sentence in the past tense. Answers will vary. Possible answers below.

6. I design a poster for my presidential campaign.
   I designed a poster for my presidential campaign.

7. My sister helps me color in the letters.
   My sister helped me color in the letters.

8. I write some good speeches.
   I wrote some good speeches.

Page 53

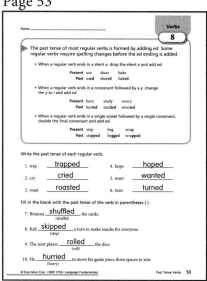

Verbs 8

The past tense of most regular verbs is formed by adding ed. Some regular verbs require spelling changes before the ed ending is added.

- When a regular verb ends in a silent e, drop the silent e and add ed.
  Present use share bake
  Past used shared baked

- When a regular verb ends in a consonant followed by a y, change the y to i and add ed.
  Present bury study worry
  Past buried studied worried

- When a regular verb ends in a single vowel followed by a single consonant, double the final consonant and add ed.
  Present stop beg wrap
  Past stopped begged wrapped

Write the past tense of each regular verb.

1. trap — trapped
2. cry — cried
3. roast — roasted
4. hope — hoped
5. want — wanted
6. turn — turned

Fill in the blank with the past tense of the verb in parentheses ( ).

7. Brianna **shuffled** the cards. (shuffle)
8. Keli **skipped** a turn to make snacks for everyone. (skip)
9. The next player **rolled** the dice. (roll)
10. He **hurried** to move his game piece three spaces to win. (hurry)

Page 54

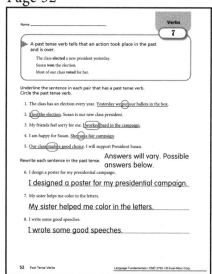

Verbs 9

Irregular verbs have special forms to show that an action has taken place in the past.

Present Tense Ms. Albert **drives** a delivery truck. She **eats** lunch here every day.
Past Tense She **drove** a school bus last year. She **ate** in the cafeteria sometimes.

Complete each sentence with the past tense of the irregular verb in parentheses ( ). Use the word box below.

drank froze knew shone slid
found heard saw slept told

1. The rain **froze** on the roads yesterday. (freeze)
2. Cars and trucks **slid** on the slippery surfaces. (slide)
3. My mom **heard** on the radio that schools were closed. (hear)
4. I **told** my little sister that we could stay home. (tell)
5. We **drank** hot chocolate. (drink)
6. I **found** a good book. (find)
7. My little sister **slept** under blankets on the couch. (sleep)
8. Finally, the sun **shone** on our frozen town. (shine)
9. We **saw** the ice melting. (see)
10. I **knew** that we would go to school tomorrow. (know)

Page 55

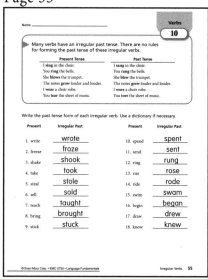

Verbs 10

Many verbs have an irregular past tense. There are no rules for forming the past tense of these irregular verbs.

Present Tense	Past Tense
I **sing** in the choir.	I **sang** in the choir.
You **ring** the bells.	You **rang** the bells.
She **blows** the trumpet.	She **blew** the trumpet.
The notes **grow** louder and louder.	The notes **grew** louder and louder.
I **wear** a choir robe.	I **wore** a choir robe.
You **tear** the sheet of music.	You **tore** the sheet of music.

Write the past tense form of each irregular verb. Use a dictionary if necessary.

Present	Irregular Past	Present	Irregular Past
1. write	wrote	10. spend	spent
2. freeze	froze	11. send	sent
3. shake	shook	12. ring	rung
4. take	took	13. rise	rose
5. steal	stole	14. ride	rode
6. sell	sold	15. swim	swam
7. teach	taught	16. begin	began
8. bring	brought	17. draw	drew
9. stick	stuck	18. know	knew

Page 56

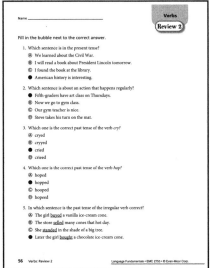

Page 57

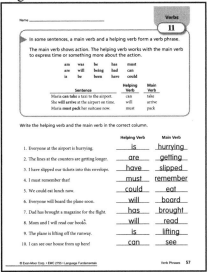

Page 58

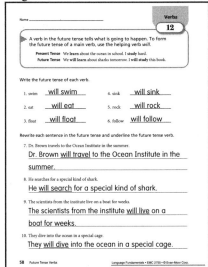

Page 59

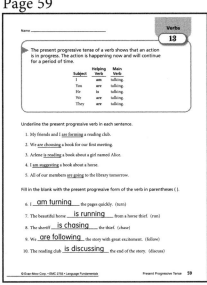

Page 60

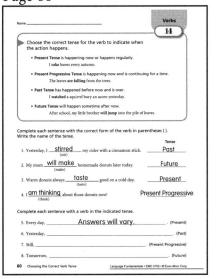

Page 61

Page 62

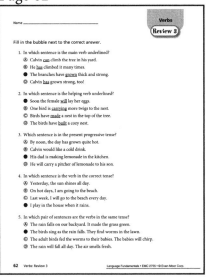

Page 63

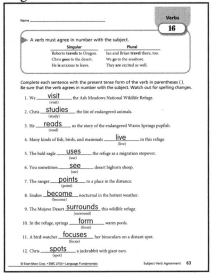

Page 64

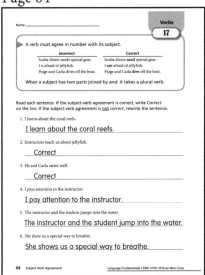

Page 65

Name ____________________

Verbs — **Review 4**

Fill in the bubble next to the correct answer.

1. In which sentence do the subject and verb agree in number?
   - Ⓐ Nina sprain her ankle.
   - ● She limps along the sidewalk.
   - Ⓒ The doctor give her a pair of crutches.
   - Ⓓ Manny carry her books.
2. Which one is the correct rule for making a regular present tense verb agree with a singular subject?
   - Ⓐ Change the *y* to *i* and add *ed*.
   - Ⓑ Use the plural form of the verb.
   - Ⓒ Make no change to the verb.
   - ● Add *s* or *es* to the verb.
3. In which sentence do the subject and the verb agree in number?
   - Ⓐ You dances well.
   - Ⓑ I dances well, too.
   - Ⓒ He dance well.
   - ● She dances well, too.
4. In which sentence do the subject and the verb agree in number?
   - Ⓐ Nina and Manny meets after school.
   - ● They meet at the bus stop.
   - Ⓒ Manny help Nina.
   - Ⓓ He help her with her crutches.
5. In which sentence do the subject and the verb agree in number?
   - ● Manny and Nina go to the library on Saturday.
   - Ⓑ Eddie and Fran goes to the library, too.
   - Ⓒ They meets their friends there.
   - Ⓓ I sees them together at a table.

© Evan-Moor Corp. • EMC 2755 • Language Fundamentals — Verbs: Review 4 — 65

Page 66

Name ____________________

Adverbs — **1**

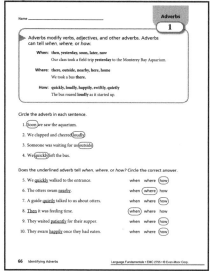

Adverbs modify verbs, adjectives, and other adverbs. Adverbs can tell *when, where,* or *how.*

When: **then, yesterday, soon, later, now**
Our class took a field trip **yesterday** to the Monterey Bay Aquarium.

Where: **there, outside, nearby, here, home**
We took a bus **there.**

How: **quickly, loudly, happily, swiftly, quietly**
The bus roared **loudly** as it started up.

Circle the adverb in each sentence.

1. (Soon) we saw the aquarium.
2. We clapped and cheered (loudly).
3. Someone was waiting for us (outside).
4. We (quickly) left the bus.

Does the underlined adverb tell *when, where,* or *how?* Circle the correct answer.

5. We quickly walked to the entrance. — when where (how)
6. The otters swam nearby. — when (where) how
7. A guide quietly talked to us about otters. — when where (how)
8. Then it was feeding time. — (when) where how
9. They waited patiently for their supper. — when where (how)
10. They swam happily once they had eaten. — when where (how)

66 Identifying Adverbs — Language Fundamentals • EMC 2755 • © Evan-Moor Corp.

Page 67

Name ____________________

Adverbs — **2**

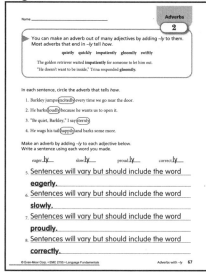

You can make an adverb out of many adjectives by adding *–ly* to them. Most adverbs that end in *–ly* tell *how.*

quietly quickly impatiently gloomily swiftly

The golden retriever waited **impatiently** for someone to let him out.
"He doesn't want to be inside," Trina responded **gloomily.**

In each sentence, circle the adverb that tells *how.*

1. Barkley jumps (excitedly) every time we go near the door.
2. He barks (loudly) because he wants us to open it.
3. "Be quiet, Barkley," I say (sternly).
4. He wags his tail (happily) and barks some more.

Make an adverb by adding *–ly* to each adjective below. Write a sentence using each word you made.

eager ly   slow ly   proud ly   correct ly

5. Sentences will vary but should include the word eagerly.
6. Sentences will vary but should include the word slowly.
7. Sentences will vary but should include the word proudly.
8. Sentences will vary but should include the word correctly.

© Evan-Moor Corp. • EMC 2755 • Language Fundamentals — Adverbs with –ly — 67

Page 68

Name ____________________

Adverbs — **3**

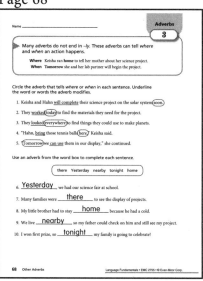

Many adverbs do not end in *–ly*. These adverbs can tell *where* and *when* an action happens.

Where Keisha ran **home** to tell her mother about her science project.
When **Tomorrow** she and her lab partner will begin the project.

Circle the adverb that tells *where* or *when* in each sentence. Underline the word or words the adverb modifies.

1. Keisha and Hahn will complete their science project on the solar system (soon).
2. They worked (today) to find the materials they need for the project.
3. They looked (everywhere) to find things they could use to make planets.
4. "Hahn, bring those tennis balls (here)," Keisha said.
5. "(Tomorrow) we can use them in our display," she continued.

Use an adverb from the word box to complete each sentence.

there Yesterday nearby tonight home

6. Yesterday we had our science fair at school.
7. Many families were there to see the display of projects.
8. My little brother had to stay home because he had a cold.
9. We live nearby, so my father could check on him and still see my project.
10. I won first prize, so tonight my family is going to celebrate!

68 Other Adverbs — Language Fundamentals • EMC 2755 • © Evan-Moor Corp.

Page 69

Name ____________________

Adverbs — **4**

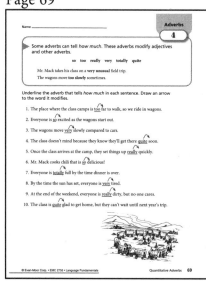

Some adverbs can tell *how much.* These adverbs modify adjectives and other adverbs.

so too really very totally quite

Mr. Mack takes his class on a **very unusual** field trip.
The wagons move **too slowly** sometimes.

Underline the adverb that tells *how much* in each sentence. Draw an arrow to the word it modifies.

1. The place where the class camps is too far to walk, so we ride in wagons.
2. Everyone is so excited as the wagons start out.
3. The wagons move very slowly compared to cars.
4. The class doesn't mind because they know they'll get there quite soon.
5. Once the class arrives at the camp, they set things up really quickly.
6. Mr. Mack cooks chili that is so delicious!
7. Everyone is totally full by the time dinner is over.
8. By the time the sun has set, everyone is very tired.
9. At the end of the weekend, everyone is really dirty, but no one cares.
10. The class is quite glad to get home, but they can't wait until next year's trip.

© Evan-Moor Corp. • EMC 2755 • Language Fundamentals — Quantitative Adverbs — 69

Page 70

Name ____________________

Adverbs — **5**

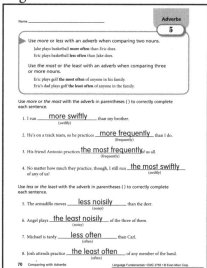

Use *more* or *less* with an adverb when comparing two nouns.
Jake plays basketball **more often** than Eric does.
Eric plays basketball **less often** than Jake does.

Use *the most* or *the least* with an adverb when comparing three or more nouns.
Eric plays golf **the most often** of anyone in his family.
Eric's dad plays golf **the least often** of anyone in the family.

Use *more* or *the most* with the adverb in parentheses ( ) to correctly complete each sentence.

1. I run more swiftly (swiftly) than my brother.
2. He's on a track team, so he practices more frequently (frequently) than I do.
3. His friend Antonio practices the most frequently (frequently) of us all.
4. No matter how much they practice, though, I still run the most swiftly (swiftly) of any of us!

Use *less* or *the least* with the adverb in parentheses ( ) to correctly complete each sentence.

5. The armadillo moves less noisily (noisy) than the deer.
6. Angel plays the least noisily (noisy) of the three of them.
7. Michael is tardy less often (often) than Carl.
8. Josh attends practice the least often (often) of any member of the band.

70 Comparing with Adverbs — Language Fundamentals • EMC 2755 • © Evan-Moor Corp.

Page 71

Name ____________________

Adverbs — **6**

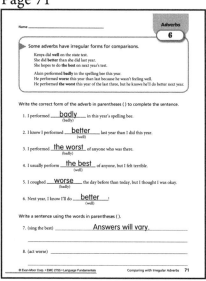

Some adverbs have irregular forms for comparisons.

Kenya did **well** on the state test.
She did **better** than she did last year.
She hopes to do **the best** on next year's test.

Alain performed **badly** in the spelling bee this year.
He performed **worse** this year than last because he wasn't feeling well.
He performed **the worst** this year of the last three, but he knows he'll do better next year.

Write the correct form of the adverb in parentheses ( ) to complete the sentence.

1. I performed badly (badly) in this year's spelling bee.
2. I know I performed better (well) last year than I did this year.
3. I performed the worst (badly) of anyone who was there.
4. I usually perform the best (well) of anyone, but I felt terrible.
5. I coughed worse (badly) the day before than today, but I thought I was okay.
6. Next year, I know I'll do better (well)!

Write a sentence using the words in parentheses ( ).

7. (sing the best) Answers will vary.
8. (act worse) ____________________

© Evan-Moor Corp. • EMC 2755 • Language Fundamentals — Comparing with Irregular Adverbs — 71

Page 72

Name ____________________

Adverbs — **7**

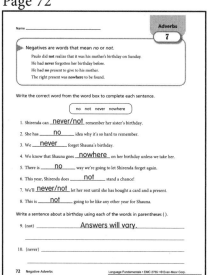

Negatives are words that mean *no* or *not.*

Paulo did **not** realize that it was his mother's birthday on Sunday.
He had **never** forgotten her birthday before.
He had **no** present to give to his mother.
The right present was **nowhere** to be found.

Write the correct word from the word box to complete each sentence.

no not never nowhere

1. Shirenda can never/not remember her sister's birthday.
2. She has no idea why it's so hard to remember.
3. We never forget Shauna's birthday.
4. We know that Shauna goes nowhere on her birthday unless we take her.
5. There is no way we're going to let Shirenda forget again.
6. This year, Shirenda does not stand a chance!
7. We'll never/not let her rest until she has bought a card and a present.
8. This is not going to be like any other year for Shauna.

Write a sentence about a birthday using each of the words in parentheses ( ).

9. (not) Answers will vary.
10. (never) ____________________

72 Negative Adverbs — Language Fundamentals • EMC 2755 • © Evan-Moor Corp.

Page 73

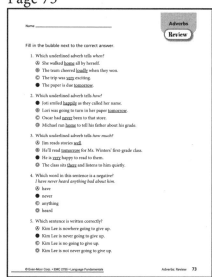

Name ____________________

Adverbs — **Review**

Fill in the bubble next to the correct answer.

1. Which underlined adverb tells *when?*
   - Ⓐ She walked home all by herself.
   - Ⓑ The team cheered loudly when they won.
   - Ⓒ The trip was very exciting.
   - ● The paper is due tomorrow.
2. Which underlined adverb tells *how?*
   - ● Joti smiled happily as they called her name.
   - Ⓑ Lori was going to turn in her paper tomorrow.
   - Ⓒ Oscar had never been to that store.
   - Ⓓ Michael ran home to tell his father about his grade.
3. Which underlined adverb tells *how much?*
   - Ⓐ Jim reads stories well.
   - Ⓑ He'll read tomorrow for Ms. Winters' first-grade class.
   - ● He is very happy to read to them.
   - Ⓓ The class sits there and listens to him quietly.
4. Which word in this sentence is a negative?
   I have never heard anything bad about him.
   - Ⓐ have
   - ● never
   - Ⓒ anything
   - Ⓓ heard
5. Which sentence is written correctly?
   - Ⓐ Kim Lee is nowhere going to give up.
   - ● Kim Lee is never going to give up.
   - Ⓒ Kim Lee is no going to give up.
   - Ⓓ Kim Lee is not never going to give up.

© Evan-Moor Corp. • EMC 2755 • Language Fundamentals — Adverbs: Review — 73

Page 74

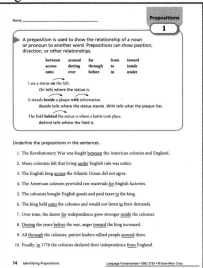

Prepositions 1

A preposition is used to show the relationship of a noun or pronoun to another word. Prepositions can show position, direction, or other relationships.

between	around	for	from	toward
across	during	through	to	inside
onto	over	before	in	under

I see a statue **on** the hill.
On tells where the statue is.

It stands **beside** a plaque **with** information.
Beside tells where the statue stands. *With* tells what the plaque has.

The field **behind** the statue is where a battle took place.
Behind tells where the field is.

Underline the prepositions in the sentences.

1. The Revolutionary War was fought <u>between</u> the American colonies and England.
2. Many colonists felt that living <u>under</u> English rule was unfair.
3. The English king <u>across</u> the Atlantic Ocean did not agree.
4. The American colonies provided raw materials <u>for</u> English factories.
5. The colonists bought English goods and paid taxes <u>to</u> the king.
6. The king held <u>onto</u> the colonies and would not listen <u>to</u> their demands.
7. Over time, the desire <u>for</u> independence grew stronger <u>inside</u> the colonies.
8. <u>During</u> the years <u>before</u> the war, anger <u>toward</u> the king increased.
9. All <u>through</u> the colonies, patriot leaders rallied people <u>around</u> them.
10. Finally, <u>in</u> 1776 the colonies declared their independence <u>from</u> England.

74 Identifying Prepositions

Page 75

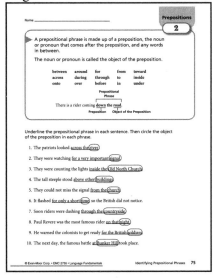

Prepositions 2

A prepositional phrase is made up of a preposition, the noun or pronoun that comes after the preposition, and any words in between.

The noun or pronoun is called the object of the preposition.

between	around	for	from	toward
across	during	through	to	inside
onto	over	before	in	under

Prepositional Phrase
There is a rider coming **down the road**.
Preposition   Object of the Preposition

Underline the prepositional phrase in each sentence. Then circle the object of the preposition in each phrase.

1. The patriots looked <u>across the (river)</u>.
2. They were watching <u>for a very important (signal)</u>.
3. They were counting the lights <u>inside the (Old North Church)</u>.
4. The tall steeple stood <u>above other (buildings)</u>.
5. They could not miss the signal <u>from the (church)</u>.
6. It flashed <u>for only a short (time)</u> so the British did not notice.
7. Soon riders were dashing <u>through the (countryside)</u>.
8. Paul Revere was the most famous rider <u>on that (night)</u>.
9. He warned the colonists to get ready <u>for the British (soldiers)</u>.
10. The next day, the famous battle <u>at (Bunker Hill)</u> took place.

Identifying Prepositional Phrases 75

Page 76

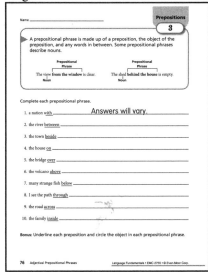

Prepositions 3

A prepositional phrase is made up of a preposition, the object of the preposition, and any words in between. Some prepositional phrases describe nouns.

Prepositional Phrase
The view **from the window** is clear.
Noun

Prepositional Phrase
The shed **behind the house** is empty.
Noun

Complete each prepositional phrase.

1. a nation with _____ Answers will vary.
2. the river between _____
3. the town beside _____
4. the house on _____
5. the bridge over _____
6. the volcano above _____
7. many strange fish below _____
8. I see the path through _____
9. the road across _____
10. the family inside _____

Bonus: Underline each preposition and circle the object in each prepositional phrase.

76 Adjectival Prepositional Phrases

Page 77

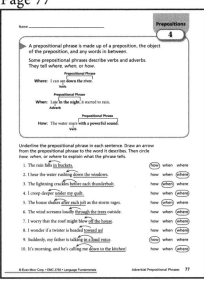

Prepositions 4

A prepositional phrase is made up of a preposition, the object of the preposition, and any words in between.

Some prepositional phrases describe verbs and adverbs. They tell *where, when,* or *how.*

Prepositional Phrase
Where: I can see **down the river.**
Verb

Prepositional Phrase
When: Late **in the night,** it started to rain.
Adverb

Prepositional Phrase
How: The water roars **with a powerful sound.**
Verb

Underline the prepositional phrase in each sentence. Draw an arrow from the prepositional phrase to the word it describes. Then circle how, when, or where to explain what the phrase tells.

1. The rain falls <u>in buckets.</u> how when (where)
2. I hear the water rushing <u>down the windows.</u> (how) when where
3. The lightning crackles <u>before each thunderbolt.</u> how (when) where
4. I creep deeper <u>under my quilt.</u> how when (where)
5. The house shakes <u>after each jolt</u> as the storm rages. how (when) where
6. The wind screams loudly <u>through the trees</u> outside. how when (where)
7. I worry that the roof might blow <u>off the house.</u> how when (where)
8. I wonder if a twister is headed <u>toward us!</u> how when (where)
9. Suddenly, my father is talking <u>in a loud voice.</u> (how) when where
10. It's morning, and he's calling me <u>down to the kitchen!</u> how when (where)

Adverbial Prepositional Phrases 77

Page 78

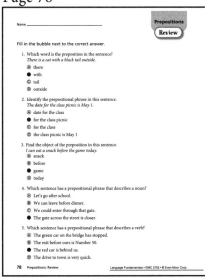

Prepositions Review

Fill in the bubble next to the correct answer.

1. Which word is the preposition in the sentence?
   There is a cat with a black tail outside.
   (A) there
   ● with
   (C) tail
   (D) outside

2. Identify the prepositional phrase in this sentence.
   The date for the class picnic is May 1.
   (A) date for the class
   ● for the class picnic
   (C) for the class
   (D) the class picnic is May 1

3. Find the object of the preposition in this sentence.
   I can eat a snack before the game today.
   (A) snack
   (B) before
   ● game
   (D) today

4. Which sentence has a prepositional phrase that describes a noun?
   (A) Let's go after school.
   (B) We can leave before dinner.
   ● We could enter through that gate.
   (D) The gate across the street is closer.

5. Which sentence has a prepositional phrase that describes a verb?
   (A) The green car on the bridge has stopped.
   (B) The exit before ours is Number 50.
   ● The red car is behind us.
   (D) The drive to town is very quick.

78 Prepositions: Review

Page 79

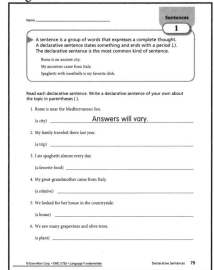

Sentences 1

A sentence is a group of words that expresses a complete thought. A declarative sentence states something and ends with a period (.). The declarative sentence is the most common kind of sentence.

Rome is an ancient city.
My ancestors came from Italy.
Spaghetti with meatballs is my favorite dish.

Read each declarative sentence. Write a declarative sentence of your own about the topic in parentheses ( ).

1. Rome is near the Mediterranean Sea.
   (a city) _____ Answers will vary.

2. My family traveled there last year.
   (a trip) _____

3. I ate spaghetti almost every day.
   (a favorite food) _____

4. My great-grandmother came from Italy.
   (a relative) _____

5. We looked for her house in the countryside.
   (a house) _____

6. We saw many grapevines and olive trees.
   (a plant) _____

Declarative Sentences 79

Page 80

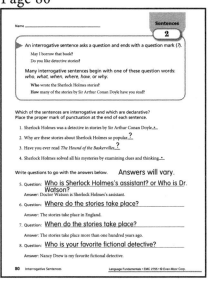

Sentences 2

An interrogative sentence asks a question and ends with a question mark (?).

May I borrow that book?
Do you like detective stories?

Many interrogative sentences begin with one of these question words: *who, what, when, where, how,* or *why.*

Who wrote the Sherlock Holmes stories?
How many of the stories by Sir Arthur Conan Doyle have you read?

Which of the sentences are interrogative and which are declarative? Place the proper mark of punctuation at the end of each sentence.

1. Sherlock Holmes was a detective in stories by Sir Arthur Conan Doyle <u>.</u>
2. Why are these stories about Sherlock Holmes so popular <u>?</u>
3. Have you ever read *The Hound of the Baskervilles* <u>?</u>
4. Sherlock Holmes solved all his mysteries by examining clues and thinking <u>.</u>

Write questions to go with the answers below. Answers will vary.

5. Question: Who is Sherlock Holmes's assistant? or Who is Dr. Watson?
   Answer: Doctor Watson is Sherlock Holmes's assistant.

6. Question: Where do the stories take place?
   Answer: The stories take place in England.

7. Question: When do the stories take place?
   Answer: The stories take place more than one hundred years ago.

8. Question: Who is your favorite fictional detective?
   Answer: Nancy Drew is my favorite fictional detective.

80 Interrogative Sentences

Page 81

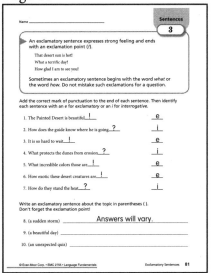

Sentences 3

An exclamatory sentence expresses strong feeling and ends with an exclamation point (!).

That desert is hot!
What a terrific day!
How glad I am to see you!

Sometimes an exclamatory sentence begins with the word *what* or the word *how.* Do not mistake such exclamations for a question.

Add the correct mark of punctuation to the end of each sentence. Then identify each sentence with an e for *exclamatory* or an i for *interrogative.*

1. The Painted Desert is beautiful <u>!</u>   <u>e</u>
2. How does the guide know where he is going <u>?</u>   <u>i</u>
3. It is so hard to wait <u>!</u>   <u>e</u>
4. What protects the dunes from erosion <u>?</u>   <u>i</u>
5. What incredible colors those are <u>!</u>   <u>e</u>
6. How exotic these desert creatures are <u>!</u>   <u>e</u>
7. How do they stand the heat <u>?</u>   <u>i</u>

Write an exclamatory sentence about the topic in parentheses ( ). Don't forget the exclamation point!

8. (a sudden storm) _____ Answers will vary.
9. (a beautiful day) _____
10. (an unexpected quiz) _____

Exclamatory Sentences 81

Page 82

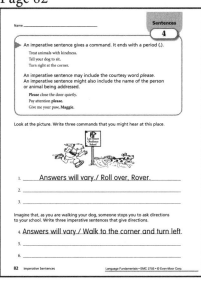

Sentences 4

An imperative sentence gives a command. It ends with a period (.).

Treat animals with kindness.
Tell your dog to sit.
Turn right at the corner.

An imperative sentence may include the courtesy word *please.* An imperative sentence might also include the name of the person or animal being addressed.

Please close the door quietly.
Pay attention **please.**
Give me your paw, **Maggie.**

Look at the picture. Write three commands that you might hear at this place.

1. _____ Answers will vary./ Roll over, Rover.
2. _____
3. _____

Imagine that, as you are walking your dog, someone stops you to ask directions to your school. Write three imperative sentences that give directions.

4. _____ Answers will vary./ Walk to the corner and turn left.
5. _____
6. _____

82 Imperative Sentences

Page 83

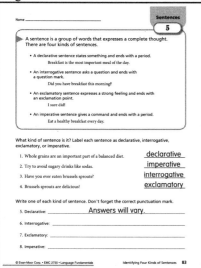

Sentences 5

A sentence is a group of words that expresses a complete thought. There are four kinds of sentences.

• A declarative sentence states something and ends with a period.
  Breakfast is the most important meal of the day.
• An interrogative sentence asks a question and ends with a question mark.
  Did you have breakfast this morning?
• An exclamatory sentence expresses a strong feeling and ends with an exclamation point.
  I sure did!
• An imperative sentence gives a command and ends with a period.
  Eat a healthy breakfast every day.

What kind of sentence is it? Label each sentence as declarative, interrogative, exclamatory, or imperative.

1. Whole grains are an important part of a balanced diet. __declarative__
2. Try to avoid sugary drinks like sodas. __imperative__
3. Have you ever eaten brussels sprouts? __interrogative__
4. Brussels sprouts are delicious! __exclamatory__

Write one of each kind of sentence. Don't forget the correct punctuation mark.

5. Declarative: __Answers will vary.__
6. Interrogative: _____
7. Exclamatory: _____
8. Imperative: _____

© Evan-Moor Corp. • EMC 2755 • Language Fundamentals   Identifying Four Kinds of Sentences   83

Page 84

Sentences 6

A sentence must express a complete thought. A group of words that does not express a complete thought is called a sentence fragment.

Sentence Fragment New Zealand
Complete Sentence New Zealand is green and beautiful.
Sentence Fragment On the map.
Complete Sentence I found New Zealand on the map.

Write sentence if the group of words expresses a complete thought and fragment if the group of words does not express a complete thought.

1. Shaped by volcanoes. __fragment__
2. Volcanoes formed New Zealand. __sentence__
3. The ash and lava created interesting landforms. __sentence__
4. With active volcanoes. __fragment__
5. New Zealanders live with active volcanoes. __sentence__
6. Live on ranches in New Zealand. __fragment__
7. Millions of sheep live on ranches in New Zealand. __sentence__
8. Rugby, a kind of football. __fragment__
9. New Zealanders love to play rugby, a kind of football. __sentence__

Write a sentence of your own about a place you would like to visit.

10. __Answers will vary.__

84   Complete Sentences v. Sentence Fragments   Language Fundamentals • EMC 2755 • © Evan-Moor Corp.

Page 85

Sentences 7

A complete sentence must have a subject and a predicate. A sentence fragment is missing a subject or a predicate or both.

Sentence Fragment Our marching band. (missing predicate)
Complete Sentence Our marching band practices on Tuesday.
Sentence Fragment Polished their instruments. (missing subject)
Complete Sentence The horn players polished their instruments.
Sentence Fragment Onto the football field. (missing subject and predicate)
Complete Sentence The band marched onto the football field.

Write sentence or fragment after each group of words.

1. The Jefferson School parade started early. __sentence__
2. Later, the drill squad. __fragment__
3. The band's lively tunes. __fragment__
4. The tuba played the low notes. __sentence__
5. Practiced hard every week. __fragment__
6. The drum major wears a tall hat. __sentence__
7. The honor guard carries the flags. __sentence__
8. On the day of the game. __fragment__
9. Everyone is excited. __sentence__

Choose one of the fragments above and turn it into a complete sentence.

10. __Answers will vary.__

© Evan-Moor Corp. • EMC 2755 • Language Fundamentals   Complete Sentences v. Sentence Fragments   85

Page 86

Sentences Review 1

Fill in the bubble next to the correct answer.

1. Which group of words expresses a complete thought?
   Ⓐ Skate in the competition.
   Ⓑ The best students in Ms. Boe's class.
   ● Lindsey laces her skates.
   Ⓓ Impresses the judges.

2. Which sentence is declarative?
   Ⓐ Dancing on roller skates is hard!
   ● The skaters move together around the rink.
   Ⓒ Did you make your own costume?
   Ⓓ Arrive on time for rehearsal.

3. Which sentence is interrogative?
   Ⓐ Many talented skaters are competing.
   Ⓑ Tony looks confident.
   ● Are those new skates?
   Ⓓ These judges are tough!

4. Which sentence is imperative?
   Ⓐ I can't skate to that music!
   Ⓑ Is it too fast?
   ● Listen closely.
   Ⓓ You should take the turn slowly.

5. Which sentence is exclamatory?
   ● What a great dance routine!
   Ⓑ Will they skate as a team?
   Ⓒ Isaac and Angelina always practice together.
   Ⓓ Watch them as they circle the rink.

86   Sentences: Review 1   Language Fundamentals • EMC 2755 • © Evan-Moor Corp.

Page 87

Sentences 8

Every sentence has two parts, a subject and a predicate.

• The subject tells who or what the sentence is about.
• The predicate tells what the subject is or does.

Subject | Predicate
Our old computer | crashed last week.
This new keyboard | feels strange to me.

Draw one line under the subject and two lines under the predicate in each sentence.

1. I opened a new file for my document.
2. My friend helped me.
3. We are working together on this project.
4. He downloads photographs.
5. I type the report.

Make the best match of subjects to predicates. Draw a line to connect each pair.

Subject | Predicate
6. Information — are posted every day.
7. My friend — is easy to find with a computer.
8. Online dictionaries — do not always work right.
9. Weather reports — tells me about great Web sites.
10. Computers — help us with our spelling.

© Evan-Moor Corp. • EMC 2755 • Language Fundamentals   Subjects and Predicates   87

Page 88

Sentences 9

A complete sentence has two parts, a subject and a predicate.

• The subject names the person, place, or thing that the sentence is about.
• The predicate tells what the subject is or does.

Subject | Predicate
The city | is a lively place.
Drivers | honk their horns.
He | ran a red light.

Write the subject and predicate of each sentence.

1. Shoppers rush into the department store.
   __Shoppers__ (Subject)   __rush into the department store__ (Predicate)
2. This jacket is on sale!
   __This jacket__ (Subject)   __is on sale__ (Predicate)
3. We will eat lunch in a restaurant.
   __We__ (Subject)   __will eat lunch in a restaurant__ (Predicate)
4. This juicy hamburger with pickles tastes good.
   __This juicy hamburger with pickles__ (Subject)   __tastes good__ (Predicate)

Write one sentence about something you do on a Saturday. Divide it into subject and predicate.

5. __Answers will vary.__
   _____ (Subject)   _____ (Predicate)

88   Subjects and Predicates   Language Fundamentals • EMC 2755 • © Evan-Moor Corp.

Page 89

Sentences 10

In an imperative sentence, you is always the subject, even though it is not stated. We understand that the subject is you, so we say that the subject is "you, understood."

(You) Raise the curtain.
(You) Focus the spotlight on the star of the show.
(You) Take a bow.

Write the subject of each sentence. When the sentence is an imperative sentence, write you, understood.

1. The stage is set. __The stage__
2. Programs have been printed. __Programs__
3. Hand a program to each person. __you, understood__
4. Listen to the director. __you, understood__
5. The audience takes their seats. __The audience__
6. Be quiet. __you, understood__

Write four imperative sentences. Write the understood subject in the parentheses ( ).

7. (__You__) __Answers will vary.__
8. (__You__) _____
9. (__You__) _____
10. (__You__) _____

© Evan-Moor Corp. • EMC 2755 • Language Fundamentals   You as the Understood Subject   89

Page 90

Sentences 11

The complete subject of a sentence includes all the words that tell about the subject. The simple subject is the main noun or pronoun in the complete subject.

Complete Subject | Simple Subject
The people in my neighborhood are very friendly. | people
The kids on this street get along well. | kids
Laurie Perkins plays with everyone. | Laurie Perkins

Choose a noun from the word box that is the best simple subject for each sentence.

poles   game   evening   backyard   kids

1. My favorite outdoor __game__ is volleyball.
2. That family's large __backyard__ gives us a perfect place to play.
3. Two metal __poles__ hold an old volleyball net.
4. The oldest __kids__ become team captains.
5. A warm summer __evening__ is the perfect time for a game.

Underline each complete subject. Circle the noun that is the simple subject.

6. Our next-door neighbor lent some tools to my parents.
7. The neighborhood children like to play kickball.
8. Our parents invited us to play in the backyard.
9. The youngest kids play in the sandbox.
10. My friend's parents are planning a neighborhood barbecue.

90   Simple and Complete Subjects   Language Fundamentals • EMC 2755 • © Evan-Moor Corp.

Page 91

Sentences 12

The simple subject is the most important word in the complete subject.

• Sometimes the simple subject is the same as the complete subject.
  Readers value their public library.
  Complete Subject Readers
  Simple Subject Readers
• Sometimes the simple subject is made up of two or more words that name a person or a place.
  The Gordon Library in our town has very helpful librarians.
  Complete Subject The Gordon Library in our town
  Simple Subject Gordon Library

Underline the complete subject and circle the simple subject in each sentence.

1. The students in my class visit our school library almost every day.
2. The school librarian answers our questions.
3. My classmate is writing a report on an author.
4. Laura Ingalls Wilder wrote a series of popular books.
5. She wrote stories about her life on the prairie.
6. The helpful librarian found a biography of the author.
7. A nineteenth-century author is the subject of my report.
8. Robert Louis Stevenson's books are very exciting.
9. My time in the library is spent with his book Treasure Island.
10. I can't put that book down!

© Evan-Moor Corp. • EMC 2755 • Language Fundamentals   Simple and Complete Subjects   91

Page 92

Name ____________________

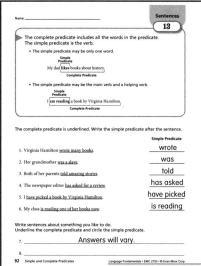

Sentences **13**

The complete predicate includes all the words in the predicate. The simple predicate is the verb.

- The simple predicate may be only one word.

Simple Predicate

My dad **likes** books about history.

Complete Predicate

- The simple predicate may be the main verb and a helping verb.

Simple Predicate

I **am reading** a book by Virginia Hamilton.

Complete Predicate

The complete predicate is underlined. Write the simple predicate after the sentence.

	Simple Predicate
1. Virginia Hamilton wrote many books.	wrote
2. Her grandmother was a slave.	was
3. Both of her parents told amazing stories.	told
4. The newspaper editor has asked for a review.	has asked
5. I have picked a book by Virginia Hamilton.	have picked
6. My class is reading one of her books now.	is reading

Write sentences about something you like to do. Underline the complete predicate and circle the simple predicate.

7. Answers will vary.

8. ____________________

92 Simple and Complete Predicates — Language Fundamentals • EMC 2755 • © Evan-Moor Corp.

Page 93

Name ____________________

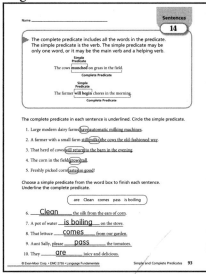

Sentences **14**

The complete predicate includes all the words in the predicate. The simple predicate is the verb. The simple predicate may be only one word, or it may be the main verb and a helping verb.

Simple Predicate

The cows **munched** on grass in the field.

Complete Predicate

Simple Predicate

The farmer **will begin** chores in the morning.

Complete Predicate

The complete predicate in each sentence is underlined. Circle the simple predicate.

1. Large modern dairy farms (have) automatic milking machines.
2. A farmer with a small farm still (milks) the cows the old-fashioned way.
3. That herd of cows (will return) to the barn in the evening.
4. The corn in the field (grows) tall.
5. Freshly picked corn (tastes) so good!

Choose a simple predicate from the word box to finish each sentence. Underline the complete predicate.

are Clean comes pass is boiling

6. Clean the silk from the ears of corn.
7. A pot of water is boiling on the stove.
8. That lettuce comes from our garden.
9. Aunt Sally, please pass the tomatoes.
10. They are juicy and delicious.

© Evan-Moor Corp. • EMC 2755 • Language Fundamentals — Simple and Complete Predicates 93

Page 94

Name ____________________

Sentences **Review 2**

Fill in the bubble next to the correct answer.

1. In which sentence is the complete subject underlined?
   - Ⓐ The table tennis players took their places at the table.
   - Ⓑ The table tennis players took their places at the table.
   - Ⓒ The table tennis players took their places at the table.
   - ● The table tennis players took their places at the table.
2. In which sentence is the simple subject underlined?
   - Ⓐ The taller player won the last match.
   - Ⓑ The taller player won the last match.
   - ● The taller player won the last match.
   - Ⓓ The taller player won the last match.
3. In which sentence is the complete predicate underlined?
   - Ⓐ One player will serve the ball.
   - Ⓑ One player will serve the ball.
   - ● One player will serve the ball.
   - Ⓓ One player will serve the ball.
4. In which sentence is the simple predicate underlined?
   - Ⓐ Mitch is handling his paddle well.
   - ● Mitch is handling his paddle well.
   - Ⓒ Mitch is handling his paddle well.
   - Ⓓ Mitch is handling his paddle well.
5. Which of these is the subject of every imperative sentence?
   - Ⓐ the first word
   - ● you, understood
   - Ⓒ the first noun
   - Ⓓ There is no subject.

94 Sentences: Review 2 — Language Fundamentals • EMC 2755 • © Evan-Moor Corp.

Page 95

Name ____________________

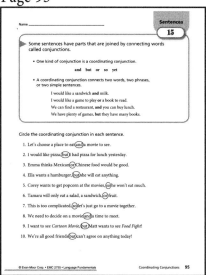

Sentences **15**

Some sentences have parts that are joined by connecting words called conjunctions.

- One kind of conjunction is a coordinating conjunction.

and but or so yet

- A coordinating conjunction connects two words, two phrases, or two simple sentences.

I would like a sandwich **and** milk.
I would like a game to play **or** a book to read.
We can find a restaurant, **and** you can buy lunch.
We have plenty of games, **but** they have many books.

Circle the coordinating conjunction in each sentence.

1. Let's choose a place to eat (and) a movie to see.
2. I would like pizza, (but) I had pizza for lunch yesterday.
3. Emma thinks Mexican (or) Chinese food would be good.
4. Ella wants a hamburger, (but) she will eat anything.
5. Corey wants to get popcorn at the movies, (so) he won't eat much.
6. Tamara will only eat a salad, a sandwich, (or) fruit.
7. This is too complicated, (so) let's just go to a movie together.
8. We need to decide on a movie (and) a time to meet.
9. I want to see *Cartoon Movie*, (but) Matt wants to see *Food Fight!*
10. We're all good friends (but) can't agree on anything today!

© Evan-Moor Corp. • EMC 2755 • Language Fundamentals — Coordinating Conjunctions 95

Page 96

Name ____________________

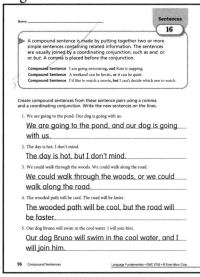

Sentences **16**

A compound sentence is made by putting together two or more simple sentences containing related information. The sentences are usually joined by a coordinating conjunction, such as *and, or,* or *but.* A comma is placed before the conjunction.

Compound Sentence I am going swimming, **and** Kate is napping.
Compound Sentence A weekend can be hectic, **or** it can be quiet.
Compound Sentence I'd like to watch a movie, **but** I can't decide which one to watch.

Create compound sentences from these sentence pairs using a comma and a coordinating conjunction. Write the new sentences on the lines.

1. We are going to the pond. Our dog is going with us.
   We are going to the pond, and our dog is going with us.
2. The day is hot. I don't mind.
   The day is hot, but I don't mind.
3. We could walk through the woods. We could walk along the road.
   We could walk through the woods, or we could walk along the road.
4. The wooded path will be cool. The road will be faster.
   The wooded path will be cool, but the road will be faster.
5. Our dog Bruno will swim in the cool water. I will join him.
   Our dog Bruno will swim in the cool water, and I will join him.

96 Compound Sentences — Language Fundamentals • EMC 2755 • © Evan-Moor Corp.

Page 97

Name ____________________

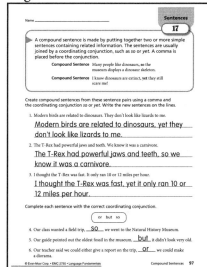

Sentences **17**

A compound sentence is made by putting together two or more simple sentences containing related information. The sentences are usually joined by a coordinating conjunction, such as *so* or *yet.* A comma is placed before the conjunction.

Compound Sentence Many people like dinosaurs, **so** the museum displays a dinosaur skeleton.
Compound Sentence I know dinosaurs are extinct, **yet** they still scare me!

Create compound sentences from these sentence pairs using a comma and the coordinating conjunction *so* or *yet.* Write the new sentences on the lines.

1. Modern birds are related to dinosaurs. They don't look like lizards to me.
   Modern birds are related to dinosaurs, yet they don't look like lizards to me.
2. The T-Rex had powerful jaws and teeth. We know it was a carnivore.
   The T-Rex had powerful jaws and teeth, so we know it was a carnivore.
3. I thought the T-Rex was fast. It only ran 10 or 12 miles per hour.
   I thought the T-Rex was fast, yet it only ran 10 or 12 miles per hour.

Complete each sentence with the correct coordinating conjunction.

or but so

4. Our class wanted a field trip, so we went to the Natural History Museum.
5. Our guide pointed out the oldest fossil in the museum, but it didn't look very old.
6. Our teacher said we could either give a report on the trip, or we could make a diorama.

© Evan-Moor Corp. • EMC 2755 • Language Fundamentals — Compound Sentences 97

Page 98

Name ____________________

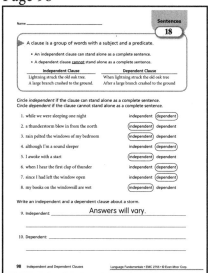

Sentences **18**

A clause is a group of words with a subject and a predicate.

- An independent clause can stand alone as a complete sentence.
- A dependent clause cannot stand alone as a complete sentence.

Independent Clause	Dependent Clause
Lightning struck the old oak tree.	When lightning struck the old oak tree
A large branch crashed to the ground.	After a large branch crashed to the ground

Circle *independent* if the clause can stand alone as a complete sentence. Circle *dependent* if the clause cannot stand alone as a complete sentence.

1. while we were sleeping one night — independent (dependent)
2. a thunderstorm blew in from the north — (independent) dependent
3. rain pelted the windows of my bedroom — (independent) dependent
4. although I'm a sound sleeper — independent (dependent)
5. I awoke with a start — (independent) dependent
6. when I hear the first clap of thunder — independent (dependent)
7. since I had left the window open — independent (dependent)
8. my books on the windowsill are wet — (independent) dependent

Write an independent and a dependent clause about a storm.

9. Independent: Answers will vary.

10. Dependent: ____________________

98 Independent and Dependent Clauses — Language Fundamentals • EMC 2755 • © Evan-Moor Corp.

Page 99

Name ____________________

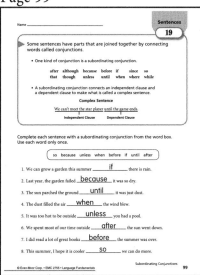

Sentences **19**

Some sentences have parts that are joined together by connecting words called conjunctions.

- One kind of conjunction is a subordinating conjunction.

after although because before if since so that though unless until when where while

- A subordinating conjunction connects an independent clause and a dependent clause to make what is called a complex sentence.

Complex Sentence

We can't meet the star player until the game ends.
Independent Clause — Dependent Clause

Complete each sentence with a subordinating conjunction from the word box. Use each word only once.

so because unless when before if until after

1. We can grow a garden this summer if there is rain.
2. Last year, the garden failed because it was so dry.
3. The sun parched the ground until it was just dust.
4. The dust filled the air when the wind blew.
5. It was too hot to be outside unless you had a pool.
6. We spent most of our time outside after the sun went down.
7. I did read a lot of great books before the summer was over.
8. This summer, I hope it is cooler so we can do more.

© Evan-Moor Corp. • EMC 2755 • Language Fundamentals — Subordinating Conjunctions 99

Page 100

Name ____________________

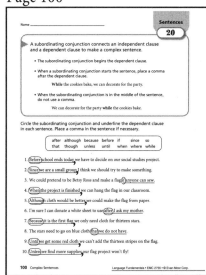

Sentences **20**

A subordinating conjunction connects an independent clause and a dependent clause to make a complex sentence.

- The subordinating conjunction begins the dependent clause.
- When a subordinating conjunction starts the sentence, place a comma after the dependent clause.

While the cookies bake, we can decorate for the party.

- When the subordinating conjunction is in the middle of the sentence, do not use a comma.

We can decorate for the party **while** the cookies bake.

Circle the subordinating conjunction and underline the dependent clause in each sentence. Place a comma in the sentence if necessary.

after although because before if since so that though unless until when where while

1. (Before) school ends today, we have to decide on our social studies project.
2. (Since) we are a small group, I think we should try to make something.
3. We could pretend to be Betsy Ross and make a flag (if) anyone can sew.
4. (When) the project is finished, we can hang the flag in our classroom.
5. (Although) cloth would be better, we could make the flag from paper.
6. I'm sure I can donate a white sheet to use (after) I ask my mother.
7. (Because) it is the first flag, we only need cloth for thirteen stars.
8. The stars need to go on blue cloth (that) we do not have.
9. (Until) we get some red cloth, we can't add the thirteen stripes on the flag.
10. (Unless) we find more supplies, our flag project won't fly!

100 Complex Sentences — Language Fundamentals • EMC 2755 • © Evan-Moor Corp.

Page 101

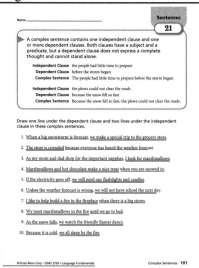

Page 102

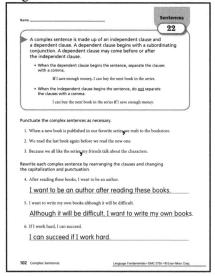

Page 103

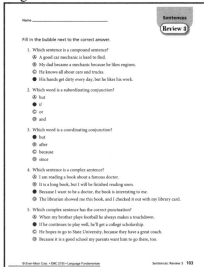

Page 104

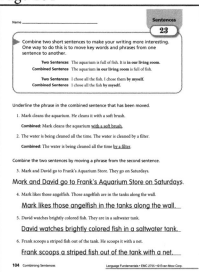

Page 105

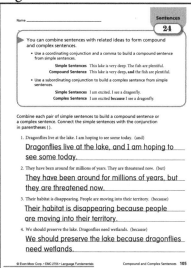

Page 106

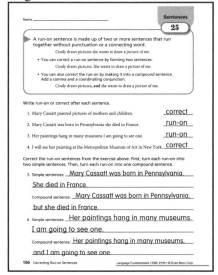

Page 107

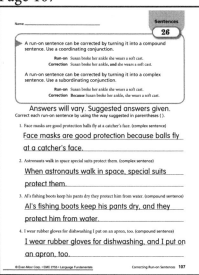

Page 108

Page 109

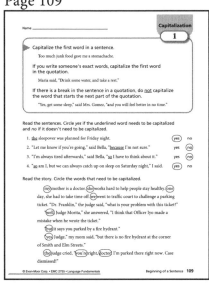

Page 110

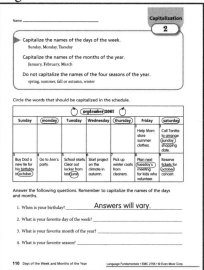

Capitalization 2

Capitalize the names of the days of the week.
Sunday, Monday, Tuesday

Capitalize the names of the months of the year.
January, February, March

Do not capitalize the names of the four seasons of the year.
spring, summer, fall or autumn, winter

Circle the words that should be capitalized in the schedule.

(september) 2007

Sunday	(monday)	Tuesday	Wednesday	(thursday)	Friday	(saturday)
					Help Mom store summer clothes.	Call Tanitia to arrange (sunday) shopping date.
Buy Dad a new tie for his (birthday) in (october).	Go to Ann's party.	School starts. Clear out locker from last (june).	Start project on the climate in autumn.	Pick up winter coats from cleaners.	Plan next (tuesday's) meeting for kids who volunteer.	Reserve tickets for (october) concert.

Answer the following questions. Remember to capitalize the names of the days and months.

1. When is your birthday? **Answers will vary.**

2. What is your favorite day of the week? _____

3. What is your favorite month of the year? _____

4. What is your favorite season? _____

110 Days of the Week and Months of the Year   Language Fundamentals • EMC 2755 • © Evan-Moor Corp.

Page 111

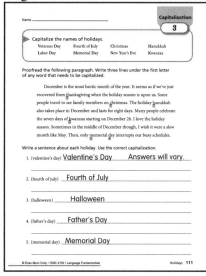

Capitalization 3

Capitalize the names of holidays.

Veterans Day	Fourth of July	Christmas	Hanukkah
Labor Day	Memorial Day	New Year's Eve	Kwanzaa

Proofread the following paragraph. Write three lines under the first letter of any word that needs to be capitalized.

December is the most hectic month of the year. It seems as if we've just recovered from thanksgiving when the holiday season is upon us. Some people travel to see family members on christmas. The holiday hanukkah also takes place in December and lasts for eight days. Many people celebrate the seven days of kwanzaa starting on December 26. I love the holiday season. Sometimes in the middle of December though, I wish it were a slow month like May. Then, only memorial day interrupts our busy schedules.

Write a sentence about each holiday. Use the correct capitalization.

1. (valentine's day) **Valentine's Day** _____ Answers will vary.

2. (fourth of july) **Fourth of July** _____

3. (halloween) **Halloween** _____

4. (father's day) **Father's Day** _____

5. (memorial day) **Memorial Day** _____

© Evan-Moor Corp. • EMC 2755 • Language Fundamentals   Holidays 111

Page 112

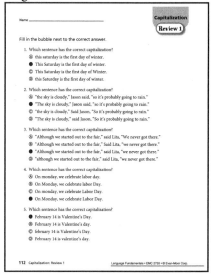

Capitalization Review 1

Fill in the bubble next to the correct answer.

1. Which sentence has the correct capitalization?
   - Ⓐ this saturday is the first day of winter.
   - ● This Saturday is the first day of winter.
   - Ⓒ This Saturday is the first day of Winter.
   - Ⓓ this Saturday is the first day of winter.

2. Which sentence has the correct capitalization?
   - Ⓐ "the sky is cloudy," Jason said, "so it's probably going to rain."
   - ● "The sky is cloudy," Jason said, "so it's probably going to rain."
   - Ⓒ "The sky is cloudy," Said Jason, "So it's probably going to rain."
   - Ⓓ "The sky is cloudy," said Jason, "So it's probably going to rain."

3. Which sentence has the correct capitalization?
   - Ⓐ "Although we started out to the fair," said Lita, "We never got there."
   - Ⓑ "Although we started out to the fair," Said Lita, "we never got there."
   - ● "Although we started out to the fair," said Lita, "we never got there."
   - Ⓓ "although we started out to the fair," said Lita, "we never got there."

4. Which sentence has the correct capitalization?
   - Ⓐ On monday, we celebrate labor day.
   - Ⓑ On Monday, we celebrate labor Day.
   - Ⓒ On monday, we celebrate Labor Day.
   - ● On Monday, we celebrate Labor Day.

5. Which sentence has the correct capitalization?
   - ● February 14 is Valentine's Day.
   - Ⓑ February 14 is Valentine's day.
   - Ⓒ february 14 is Valentine's Day.
   - Ⓓ February 14 is valentine's day.

112 Capitalization: Review 1   Language Fundamentals • EMC 2755 • © Evan-Moor Corp.

Page 113

Capitalization 4

The names of people and pets should be capitalized.
Ishana   Fluffy

The title before a person's name should also be capitalized.
Professor Mehta

Names of specific places should be capitalized.
Santa Fe, New Mexico   Mesa Verde National Park   Snake River

Circle the word or words that should begin with a capital letter.

city	(texas)	(mike)
(ben)	river	state
girl	(dr. cata)	(america)
(rhode island)	stream	dog
country	(gulf of mexico)	ocean
(new orleans)	county	(atlanta)
oak drive	(calvert city)	(colorado river)

© Evan-Moor Corp. • EMC 2755 • Language Fundamentals   Proper Nouns 113

Page 114

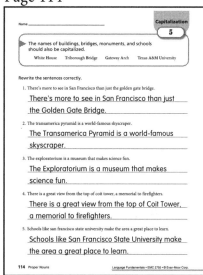

Capitalization 5

The names of buildings, bridges, monuments, and schools should also be capitalized.
White House   Triborough Bridge   Gateway Arch   Texas A&M University

Rewrite the sentences correctly.

1. There's more to see in San Francisco than just the golden gate bridge.
   There's more to see in San Francisco than just the Golden Gate Bridge.

2. The transamerica pyramid is a world-famous skyscraper.
   The Transamerica Pyramid is a world-famous skyscraper.

3. The exploratorium is a museum that makes science fun.
   The Exploratorium is a museum that makes science fun.

4. There is a great view from the top of coit tower, a memorial to firefighters.
   There is a great view from the top of Coit Tower, a memorial to firefighters.

5. Schools like san francisco state university make the area a great place to learn.
   Schools like San Francisco State University make the area a great place to learn.

114 Proper Nouns   Language Fundamentals • EMC 2755 • © Evan-Moor Corp.

Page 115

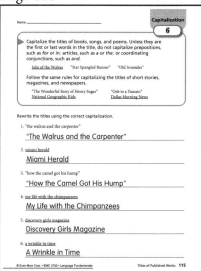

Capitalization 6

Capitalize the titles of books, songs, and poems. Unless they are the first or last words in the title, do not capitalize prepositions, such as *for* or *in*; articles, such as *a* or *the*; or coordinating conjunctions, such as *and*.

Julie of the Wolves   "Star Spangled Banner"   "Old Ironsides"

Follow the same rules for capitalizing the titles of short stories, magazines, and newspapers.

"The Wonderful Story of Henry Sugar"   "Ode to a Tomato"
National Geographic Kids   Dallas Morning News

Rewrite the titles using the correct capitalization.

1. "the walrus and the carpenter"
   "The Walrus and the Carpenter"

2. miami herald
   Miami Herald

3. "how the camel got his hump"
   "How the Camel Got His Hump"

4. my life with the chimpanzees
   My Life with the Chimpanzees

5. discovery girls magazine
   Discovery Girls Magazine

6. a wrinkle in time
   A Wrinkle in Time

© Evan-Moor Corp. • EMC 2755 • Language Fundamentals   Titles of Published Works 115

Page 116

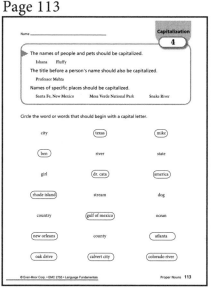

Capitalization Review 2

Fill in the bubble next to the word or words that should begin with capital letters.

1. Ⓐ girl
   ● mary
   Ⓒ daughter
   Ⓓ sister

2. Ⓐ stadium
   Ⓑ arena
   ● shea stadium
   Ⓓ gym

3. ● garfield
   Ⓑ cat
   Ⓒ kitten
   Ⓓ pet

4. Ⓐ math teacher
   Ⓑ soccer coach
   Ⓒ school nurse
   ● principal davis

5. Ⓐ monument
   ● washington monument
   Ⓒ building
   Ⓓ place

6. Ⓐ war
   ● struggle
   Ⓑ french-indian war
   Ⓓ fight

7. ● fortson company
   Ⓑ business
   Ⓒ corporation
   Ⓓ company

8. ● james and the giant peach
   Ⓑ book
   Ⓒ library
   Ⓓ volume

9. ● song
   Ⓑ "row, row, row your boat"
   Ⓒ music
   Ⓓ melody

10. Ⓐ story
    Ⓑ writing
    Ⓒ literature
    ● "the three little bears"

116 Capitalization: Review 2   Language Fundamentals • EMC 2755 • © Evan-Moor Corp.

Page 117

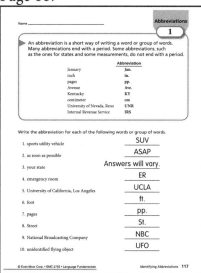

Abbreviations 1

An abbreviation is a short way of writing a word or group of words. Many abbreviations end with a period. Some abbreviations, such as the ones for states and some measurements, do not end with a period.

	Abbreviation
January	Jan.
inch	in.
pages	pp.
Avenue	Ave.
Kentucky	KY
centimeter	cm
University of Nevada, Reno	UNR
Internal Revenue Service	IRS

Write the abbreviation for each of the following words or group of words.

1. sports utility vehicle   **SUV**
2. as soon as possible   **ASAP**
3. your state   **Answers will vary.**
4. emergency room   **ER**
5. University of California, Los Angeles   **UCLA**
6. foot   **ft.**
7. pages   **pp.**
8. Street   **St.**
9. National Broadcasting Company   **NBC**
10. unidentified flying object   **UFO**

© Evan-Moor Corp. • EMC 2755 • Language Fundamentals   Identifying Abbreviations 117

Page 118

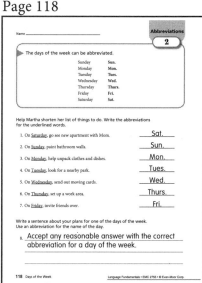

Abbreviations 2

The days of the week can be abbreviated.

Sunday	Sun.
Monday	Mon.
Tuesday	Tues.
Wednesday	Wed.
Thursday	Thurs.
Friday	Fri.
Saturday	Sat.

Help Martha shorten her list of things to do. Write the abbreviations for the underlined words.

1. On Saturday, go see new apartment with Mom.   **Sat.**
2. On Sunday, paint bathroom walls.   **Sun.**
3. On Monday, help unpack clothes and dishes.   **Mon.**
4. On Tuesday, look for a nearby park.   **Tues.**
5. On Wednesday, send out moving cards.   **Wed.**
6. On Thursday, set up a work area.   **Thurs.**
7. On Friday, invite friends over.   **Fri.**

Write a sentence about your plans for one of the days of the week. Use an abbreviation for the name of the day.

8. **Accept any reasonable answer with the correct abbreviation for a day of the week.**

118 Days of the Week   Language Fundamentals • EMC 2755 • © Evan-Moor Corp.

Page 119

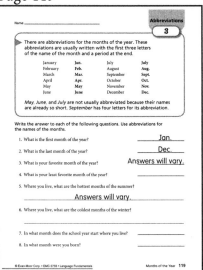

Abbreviations 3

There are abbreviations for the months of the year. These abbreviations are usually written with the first three letters of the name of the month and a period at the end.

January	**Jan.**	July	**July**
February	**Feb.**	August	**Aug.**
March	**Mar.**	September	**Sept.**
April	**Apr.**	October	**Oct.**
May	**May**	November	**Nov.**
June	**June**	December	**Dec.**

May, June, and *July* are not usually abbreviated because their names are already so short. *September* has four letters for its abbreviation.

Write the answer to each of the following questions. Use abbreviations for the names of the months.

1. What is the first month of the year? **Jan.**
2. What is the last month of the year? **Dec.**
3. What is your favorite month of the year? **Answers will vary.**
4. What is your least favorite month of the year?
5. Where you live, what are the hottest months of the summer? **Answers will vary.**
6. Where you live, what are the coldest months of the winter?
7. In what month does the school year start where you live?
8. In what month were you born?

Months of the Year **119**

Page 120

Abbreviations 4

The titles that come before or after people's names are usually abbreviated. Start the title with a capital letter and end it with a period.

Title	Abbreviation
married or unmarried man/mister	Mr.
married woman/missus	Mrs.
married or unmarried woman	Ms.
Doctor	Dr.
Junior	Jr.
Senior	Sr.

Read Eugene's letter to a pen pal in France. Circle six titles that could be written correctly as abbreviations. Write the abbreviations on the lines below.

Dear Henri,

You asked me to describe my family. My father is (Mister) Eugene S. Louis. (Senior) He works in real estate, so we're never sure when he'll be home or when he'll have to run out. My mother is (Mistress) Karen Louis. She teaches at my elementary school. She doesn't teach my class, though. My teacher is Ms. Cora Simpson. She is a very tough grader, but we all like her because we learn so much from her.

My aunt is (Doctor) Lila Louis. She is a pediatrician. That means her patients are children. She is so busy that we don't get to see her very much.

My grandfather, (Doctor) Jacob Louis, is a retired veterinarian, which is what we call an animal doctor. He lives on a farm out in the country. I love to visit him because he has all kinds of animals, including horses we can ride!

Now I want to hear about your family!

Your pal,
Eugene S. Louis (Junior)

1. **Mr.**
2. **Sr.**
3. **Mrs.**
4. **Dr.**
5. **Dr.**
6. **Jr.**

120 Titles of People

Page 121

Abbreviations Review 1

Fill in the bubble next to the correct answer.

1. In which sentence is the abbreviation written correctly?
   - ● Mr. Li teaches math.
   - Ⓑ His assistant is Mrs Stevens.
   - Ⓒ Doctor. P. K. Matthews wrote the book.
   - Ⓓ Robert. Smith is the tutor.

2. In which sentence is the abbreviation written correctly?
   - Ⓐ School starts in Sep.
   - ● School starts in Sept.
   - Ⓒ School ends in Jun.
   - Ⓓ School ends in june.

3. In which sentence is the abbreviation written correctly?
   - Ⓐ Mrs Smith teaches science.
   - Ⓑ Her hero is Dctr Albert Einstein.
   - Ⓒ Carl Fox, Jur is my lab partner.
   - ● His dad is Dr. Fox.

4. In which sentence is the abbreviation written correctly?
   - Ⓐ On Mon, I have piano.
   - Ⓑ On Tues., I have karate.
   - Ⓒ On Thu., I have Girl Scouts.
   - ● On Fri, I have tennis.

5. In which sentence is the abbreviation written correctly?
   - Ⓐ The answer is on page 6.
   - Ⓑ I live on Central ave.
   - ● Mom drove me to the ER when I broke my arm.
   - Ⓓ My dad drives an S.U.V.

Abbreviations: Review 1 **121**

Page 122

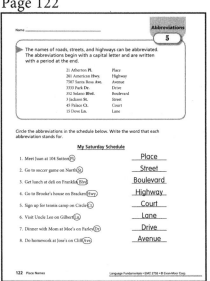

Abbreviations 5

The names of roads, streets, and highways can be abbreviated. The abbreviations begin with a capital letter and are written with a period at the end.

21 Atherton **Pl.**	Place
201 American **Hwy.**	Highway
7507 Santa Rosa **Ave.**	Avenue
3333 Park **Dr.**	Drive
352 Solano **Blvd.**	Boulevard
3 Jackson **St.**	Street
45 Palace **Ct.**	Court
15 Dove **Ln.**	Lane

Circle the abbreviations in the schedule below. Write the word that each abbreviation stands for.

My Saturday Schedule

1. Meet Juan at 104 Sutton (Pl.) **Place**
2. Go to soccer game on North (St.) **Street**
3. Get lunch at deli on Franklin (Blvd.) **Boulevard**
4. Go to Brooke's house on Bracken (Hwy.) **Highway**
5. Sign up for tennis camp on Circle (Ct.) **Court**
6. Visit Uncle Leo on Gilbert (Ln.) **Lane**
7. Dinner with Mom at Moe's on Farley (Dr.) **Drive**
8. Do homework at Jose's on Cliff (Ave.) **Avenue**

122 Place Names

Page 123

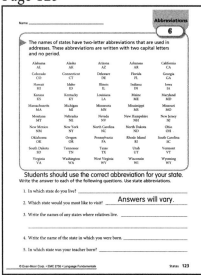

Abbreviations 6

The names of states have two-letter abbreviations that are used in addresses. These abbreviations are written with two capital letters and no period.

Alabama AL	Alaska AK	Arizona AZ	Arkansas AR	California CA
Colorado CO	Connecticut CT	Delaware DE	Florida FL	Georgia GA
Hawaii HI	Idaho ID	Illinois IL	Indiana IN	Iowa IA
Kansas KS	Kentucky KY	Louisiana LA	Maine ME	Maryland MD
Massachusetts MA	Michigan MI	Minnesota MN	Mississippi MS	Missouri MO
Montana MT	Nebraska NE	Nevada NV	New Hampshire NH	New Jersey NJ
New Mexico NM	New York NY	North Carolina NC	North Dakota ND	Ohio OH
Oklahoma OK	Oregon OR	Pennsylvania PA	Rhode Island RI	South Carolina SC
South Dakota SD	Tennessee TN	Texas TX	Utah UT	Vermont VT
Virginia VA	Washington WA	West Virginia WV	Wisconsin WI	Wyoming WY

Students should use the correct abbreviation for your state.

Write the answer to each of the following questions. Use state abbreviations.

1. In which state do you live?
2. Which state would you most like to visit? **Answers will vary.**
3. Write the names of any states where relatives live.
4. Write the name of the state in which you were born?
5. In which state was your teacher born?

States **123**

Page 124

Abbreviations 7

Most measurements can be abbreviated. The abbreviation is the same for the singular and plural form of the measurement. For example, the abbreviation *ft.* can stand for both *foot* and *feet*.

inch	**in.**
foot	**ft.**
yard	**yd.**
mile	**mi.**

Abbreviations for measurements in the metric system are <u>not</u> written with periods.

meter	**m**
centimeter	**cm**
millimeter	**mm**
kilometer	**km**

Write the letter of the correct abbreviation next to each of the following words.

1. millimeter **b.**   a. yd.
2. inch **d.**   b. mm
3. centimeter **c.**   c. cm
4. yard **a.**   d. in.

Rewrite the following sentences using abbreviations for the measurement words.

7. There are 5,280 feet in a mile. **There are 5,280 ft. in a mi.**

8. In a kilometer, there are 1,000 meters. **In a km, there are 1,000 m.**

124 Measurements of Length

Page 125

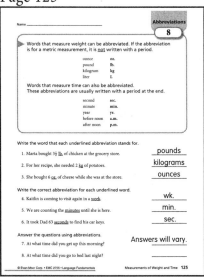

Abbreviations 8

Words that measure weight can be abbreviated. If the abbreviation is for a metric measurement, it is <u>not</u> written with a period.

ounce	**oz.**
pound	**lb.**
kilogram	**kg**
liter	**L**

Words that measure time can also be abbreviated. These abbreviations are usually written with a period at the end.

second	**sec.**
minute	**min.**
year	**yr.**
before noon	**a.m.**
after noon	**p.m.**

Write the word that each underlined abbreviation stands for.

1. Marta bought 3½ <u>lb.</u> of chicken at the grocery store. **pounds**
2. For her recipe, she needed 2 <u>kg</u> of potatoes. **kilograms**
3. She bought 6 <u>oz.</u> of cheese while she was at the store. **ounces**

Write the correct abbreviation for each underlined word.

4. Kaitlin is coming to visit again in a <u>week</u>. **wk.**
5. We are counting the <u>minutes</u> until she is here. **min.**
6. It took Dad 63 <u>seconds</u> to find his car keys. **sec.**

Answer the questions using abbreviations.

7. At what time did you get up this morning? **Answers will vary.**
8. At what time did you go to bed last night?

Measurements of Weight and Time **125**

Page 126

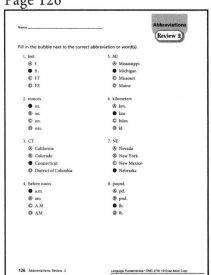

Abbreviations Review 2

Fill in the bubble next to the correct abbreviation or word(s).

1. feet
   - Ⓐ f.
   - ● ft.
   - Ⓒ FT
   - Ⓓ FE

2. ounces
   - ● oz.
   - Ⓑ os.
   - Ⓒ on.
   - Ⓓ ozs.

3. CT
   - Ⓐ California
   - Ⓑ Colorado
   - ● Connecticut
   - Ⓓ District of Columbia

4. before noon
   - ● a.m.
   - Ⓑ am
   - Ⓒ A.M.
   - Ⓓ AM

5. MI
   - Ⓐ Mississippi
   - ● Michigan
   - Ⓒ Missouri
   - Ⓓ Maine

6. kilometers
   - Ⓐ km.
   - ● km
   - Ⓒ kilos
   - Ⓓ kl

7. NE
   - Ⓐ Nevada
   - Ⓑ New York
   - Ⓒ New Mexico
   - ● Nebraska

8. pound
   - Ⓐ pd.
   - Ⓑ pnd.
   - ● lb.
   - Ⓓ lb

126 Abbreviations: Review 2

Page 127

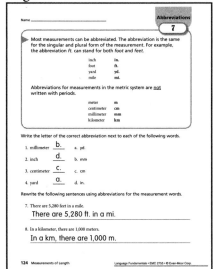

Punctuation 1

Statements and most commands end with a period (.).
It is very important to eat a good breakfast.
Please bring me some cereal.

Interrogative sentences end with a question mark (?).
What did you have for breakfast?

Exclamatory sentences and strong commands end with an exclamation point (!).
This oatmeal is the best I have ever tasted!
Run for your life!

Write the name of the punctuation mark needed for each sentence.

1. You may have eggs or cereal for breakfast **period**
2. Do we have any bacon **question mark**
3. No, but we do have sausage **period**
4. That's my favorite **exclamation point**
5. Please give me two fried eggs **period**
6. Will you have eggs, Olivia **question mark**
7. I hate eggs **exclamation point**
8. Fix me a bowl of granola, please **period**
9. Am I late for school **question mark**
10. No, sit down and eat **exclamation point**

End of Sentences **127**

Page 128
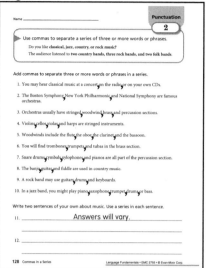

Page 129
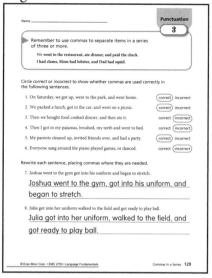

Page 130

Page 131
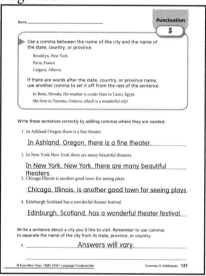

Page 132
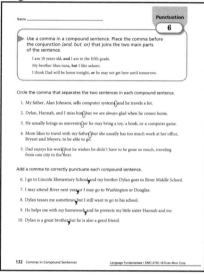

Page 133
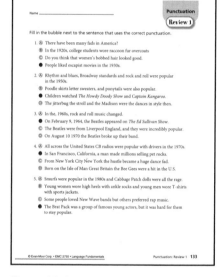

Page 134
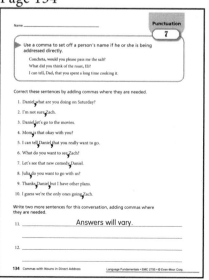

Page 135
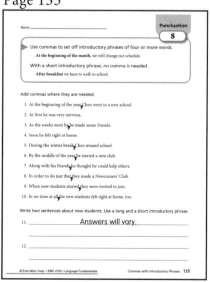

Page 136
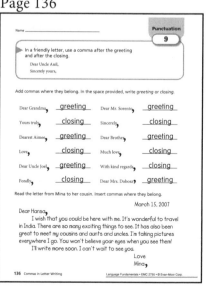

Page 137

When you write the exact words that someone says, use commas to set off the quotation from the rest of the sentence.

Earl said, "I wish that we could go to a restaurant tonight."
"You can help me cook a delicious meal instead," said Earl's sister.

If the quotation already ends in a question mark or an exclamation point, you don't need the comma.

"Do you want to make pizza or spaghetti?" Earl asked.
"Neither!" his sister said laughingly.

Add commas where they are necessary.

1. Jared asked, "Who is the greatest basketball player ever?"
2. Mrs. Young said that Jerry West was the best.
3. "I think Shaquille O'Neal is better," Pedro said.
4. "Michael Jordan rules!" Betty exclaimed.
5. "I don't know," Maria said.
6. "Ann Meyers is the best," Lydia said.
7. Hector said, "No, it's Wilt Chamberlain."
8. Mr. Perez thought that Bill Russell was incredible.
9. "I don't know any of the players," Will admitted.
10. "Rebecca Lobo changed the game," Neka said.

Page 138

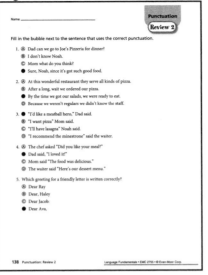

Fill in the bubble next to the sentence that uses the correct punctuation.

1. Ⓐ Dad can we go to Joe's Pizzeria for dinner?
   Ⓑ I don't know Noah.
   Ⓒ Mom what do you recommend?
   ● Sure, Noah, since it's got such good food.

2. Ⓐ At this wonderful restaurant they serve all kinds of pizza.
   Ⓑ After a long, wait we ordered our pizza.
   ● By the time we got our salads, we were ready to eat.
   Ⓓ Because we weren't regulars we didn't know the staff.

3. ● "I'd like a meatball hero," Dad said.
   Ⓑ "I want pizza" Mom said.
   Ⓒ "I'll have lasagna" Noah said.
   Ⓓ "I recommend the minestrone" said the waiter.

4. ● The chef asked "Did you like your meal?"
   Ⓑ Dad said, "I loved it!"
   Ⓒ Mom said "The food was delicious."
   Ⓓ The waiter here "Here's our dessert menu."

5. Which greeting for a friendly letter is written correctly?
   Ⓐ Dear Ray
   Ⓑ Dear, Haley
   Ⓒ Dear Jacob:
   ● Dear Ava,

Page 139

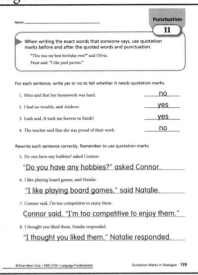

When writing the exact words that someone says, use quotation marks before and after the quoted words and punctuation.

"This was my best birthday ever!" said Olivia.
Payat said, "I like pool parties."

For each sentence, write yes or no to tell whether it needs quotation marks.

1. Mira said that her homework was hard. ___no___
2. I had no trouble, said Andrew. ___yes___
3. Leah said, It took me forever to finish! ___yes___
4. The teacher said that she was proud of their work. ___no___

Rewrite each sentence correctly. Remember to use quotation marks.

5. Do you have any hobbies? asked Connor.
   "Do you have any hobbies?" asked Connor.

6. I like playing board games, said Natalie.
   "I like playing board games," said Natalie.

7. Connor said, I'm too competitive to enjoy them.
   Connor said, "I'm too competitive to enjoy them."

8. I thought you liked them, Natalie responded.
   "I thought you liked them," Natalie responded.

Page 140

Use quotation marks to set off a quotation from other words in a sentence. If a quotation is interrupted by words indicating who is speaking, use quotation marks to set off each part of the speaker's words.

"It's a close game," said Jose, "and I can't say who'll win."

Add quotation marks to the sentences where they are needed.

1. "I like watching movies on TV," said Anna, "but I don't like going to the movies."
2. "Going to the movies is fun," Mrs. Ramos said, "when you have someone to go with."
3. "I don't like people talking," Anna said, "because it makes it hard for me to hear."
4. "I like seeing movies at big theaters," said Nate, "where the screens are huge."
5. "I know what you mean," said Anna, "but I'd rather wait for the DVDs."
6. "I don't watch many movies," said Tyler, "because Mom thinks they're a waste of time."
7. "I know what she means," said Mrs. Ramos, "because I've seen a lot of junk out there."
8. "Tyler," said Anna, "does she let you play video games?"
9. "No, Tyler," she thinks that they're a waste of time, too."
10. "My mother lets me play only 30 minutes a day," said Luke, "if I finish my homework."
11. "Maybe my mother would agree to that," Tyler said thoughtfully.
12. "It's worth a try," Mrs. Ramos said, "if you're sure it won't affect your grades."

Page 141

Use quotation marks around the titles of short stories, poems, and songs.

My mom loves the story "Bernice Bobs Her Hair" by F. Scott Fitzgerald.
"How Not to Have to Dry the Dishes" is my favorite Shel Silverstein story.
"We Shall Overcome" is a powerful song from the civil rights movement.

Rewrite these sentences using the correct punctuation for each title.

1. One of my favorite stories is The Circuit by Francisco Jiménez.
   One of my favorite stories is "The Circuit" by Francisco Jiménez.

2. My favorite song is Who Let the Dogs Out?
   My favorite song is "Who Let the Dogs Out?"

3. I like the poem If I Had a Brontosaurus by Shel Silverstein.
   I like the poem "If I Had a Brontosaurus" by Shel Silverstein.

4. Have you ever read the story The Captain's Story by Mark Twain?
   Have you ever read the story "The Captain's Story" by Mark Twain?

5. The Gardener is a great poem by Robert Louis Stevenson.
   "The Gardener" is a great poem by Robert Louis Stevenson.

Page 142

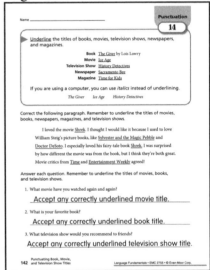

Underline the titles of books, movies, television shows, newspapers, and magazines.

Book   The Giver by Lois Lowry
Movie   Ice Age
Television Show   History Detectives
Newspaper   Sacramento Bee
Magazine   Time for Kids

If you are using a computer, you can use *italics* instead of underlining.

The Giver   Ice Age   History Detectives

Correct the following paragraph. Remember to underline the titles of movies, books, newspapers, magazines, and television shows.

I loved the movie Shrek. I thought I would like it because I used to love William Steig's picture books, like Sylvester and the Magic Pebble and Doctor DeSoto. I especially loved his fairy-tale epic Shrek. I was surprised by how different the movie was from the book, but I think they're both great. Movie critics from Time and Entertainment Weekly agreed!

Answer each question. Remember to underline the titles of movies, books, and television shows.

1. What movie have you watched again and again?
   Accept any correctly underlined movie title.

2. What is your favorite book?
   Accept any correctly underlined book title.

3. What television show would you recommend to friends?
   Accept any correctly underlined television show title.

Page 143

Fill in the bubble next to the correct answer.

1. Which sentence is punctuated correctly?
   Ⓐ Mika said "I want to be on the soccer team."
   ● Her mother said, "I don't think that's such a good idea."
   Ⓒ Mika asked "But why?"
   Ⓓ "You've never played" said her mother.

2. Which sentence is punctuated correctly?
   Ⓐ Nicholas said that "he likes to read sports magazines."
   ● Abigail said, "I like to watch sports on television."
   Ⓒ Julia said that, "she likes playing sports."
   Ⓓ Will said, I just like sports.

3. Which sentence is punctuated correctly?
   Ⓐ "Did you know," said Hailey "that I want to be an actress when I grow up?"
   Ⓑ "The trouble with that plan" said Hailey's mother "is that so few are successful."
   ● "I don't care," said Hailey, "because I have real talent."
   Ⓓ "Of course you do" said Hailey's mother, "because you're my daughter."

4. Which poem title is written correctly?
   Ⓐ The Magic Eraser
   Ⓑ The "Magic" Eraser
   Ⓒ The Magic Eraser (underlined)
   ● "The Magic Eraser"

5. Which book title is written correctly?
   ● Where the Sidewalk Ends (underlined)
   Ⓑ "Where the Sidewalk Ends"
   Ⓒ Where the Sidewalk Ends
   Ⓓ Where the Sidewalk Ends (underlined)

Page 144

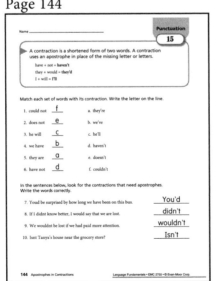

A contraction is a shortened form of two words. A contraction uses an apostrophe in place of the missing letter or letters.

have + not = haven't
they + would = they'd
I + will = I'll

Match each set of words with its contraction. Write the letter on the line.

1. could not ___f___   a. they're
2. does not ___e___   b. we've
3. he will ___c___   c. he'll
4. we have ___b___   d. haven't
5. they are ___a___   e. doesn't
6. have not ___d___   f. couldn't

In the sentences below, look for the contractions that need apostrophes. Write the words correctly.

7. Youd be surprised by how long we have been on this bus. ___You'd___
8. If I didnt know better, I would say that we are lost. ___didn't___
9. We wouldnt be lost if we had paid more attention. ___wouldn't___
10. Isnt Tanya's house near the grocery store? ___Isn't___

Page 145

Possessive nouns show ownership.

Singular = Add 's	Plural Ending in s = Add '	Plural Not Ending in s = Add 's
Tino's temperature	the Johnsons' pool	the children's story hour
the dog's tail	the animals' habitats	the women's group

Rewrite the following sentences correctly.

1. The Campbells pictures were ready for pickup.
   The Campbells' pictures were ready for pickup.

2. Coreys photograph of the sunset was beautiful.
   Corey's photograph of the sunset was beautiful.

3. The pictures of the mens barbecue were hilarious.
   The pictures of the men's barbecue were hilarious.

4. The Garcias photographs were ready at the same time.
   The Garcias' photographs were ready at the same time.

5. Talita and Juans photographs of their classmates were good.
   Talita's and Juan's photographs of their classmates were good.

6. The colors of the childrens clothing were vivid.
   The colors of the children's clothing were vivid.

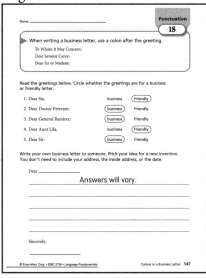
Page 147

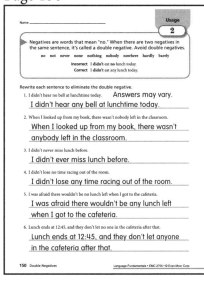

Name _____

Punctuation 18

When writing a business letter, use a colon after the greeting.

To Whom It May Concern:
Dear Senator Carey:
Dear Sir or Madam:

Read the greetings below. Circle whether the greetings are for a business or friendly letter.

1. Dear Sis, — business — (friendly)
2. Dear Doctor Petersen: — (business) — friendly
3. Dear General Ramirez: — (business) — friendly
4. Dear Aunt Lila, — business — (friendly)
5. Dear Sir: — (business) — friendly

Write your own business letter to someone. Pitch your idea for a new invention. You don't need to include your address, the inside address, or the date.

Dear _____

Answers will vary.

Sincerely,

Colons in a Business Letter 147

Page 148

Name _____

Punctuation Review 4

Fill in the bubble next to the correct answer.

1. Which contraction is written correctly?
   ● couldn't
   Ⓑ havent
   Ⓒ weve
   Ⓓ wouldnt

2. Which singular possessive is written correctly?
   Ⓐ Claras' present
   Ⓑ Sadies toy
   ● Ethan's lunch
   Ⓓ Connors snack

3. Which plural possessive is written correctly?
   Ⓐ girl's hobbies
   ● the boys' collections
   Ⓒ the dogs kennel
   Ⓓ the birds feeder

4. Which time is written correctly?
   Ⓐ 945
   ● 9:45
   Ⓒ nine:45
   Ⓓ 9:forty-five

5. Which greeting is written correctly for a business letter?
   Ⓐ Dear Sarah,
   Ⓑ Dear Madam
   ● To Whom It May Concern,
   Ⓓ Dear Mr. Gomez:

148 Punctuation: Review 4

Page 149

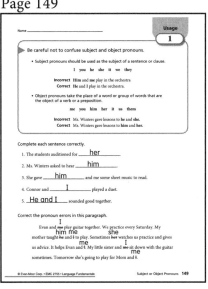

Name _____

Usage 1

Be careful not to confuse subject and object pronouns.

• Subject pronouns should be used as the subject of a sentence or clause.

I you he she it we they

Incorrect **Him** and **me** play in the orchestra.
Correct **He** and **I** play in the orchestra.

• Object pronouns take the place of a word or group of words that are the object of a verb or a preposition.

me you him her it us them

Incorrect Ms. Winters gave lessons to **he** and **she**.
Correct Ms. Winters gave lessons to **him** and **her**.

Complete each sentence correctly.

1. The students auditioned for __her__.
2. Ms. Winters asked to hear __him__.
3. She gave __him__ and me some sheet music to read.
4. Connor and __I__ played a duet.
5. __He and I__ sounded good together.

Correct the pronoun errors in this paragraph.

Evan and ~~me~~ **I** play guitar together. We practice every Saturday. My mother taught ~~he~~ **him** and ~~I~~ **me** to play. Sometimes ~~her~~ **she** watches us practice and gives us advice. It helps Evan and ~~I~~ **me**. My little sister and ~~me~~ **me** sit down with the guitar sometimes. Tomorrow she's going to play for Mom and ~~I~~ **me**.

Subject or Object Pronouns 149

Page 150

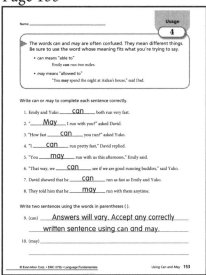

Name _____

Usage 2

Negatives are words that mean "no." When there are two negatives in the same sentence, it's called a double negative. Avoid double negatives.

no not never none nothing nobody nowhere hardly barely

Incorrect I **didn't** eat no lunch today.
Correct I **didn't** eat any lunch today.

Rewrite each sentence to eliminate the double negative.

1. I didn't hear no bell at lunchtime today. **Answers may vary.**
   I didn't hear any bell at lunchtime today.

2. When I looked up from my book, there wasn't nobody left in the classroom.
   When I looked up from my book, there wasn't anybody left in the classroom.

3. I didn't never miss lunch before.
   I didn't ever miss lunch before.

4. I didn't lose no time racing out of the room.
   I didn't lose any time racing out of the room.

5. I was afraid there wouldn't be no lunch left when I got to the cafeteria.
   I was afraid there wouldn't be any lunch left when I got to the cafeteria.

6. Lunch ends at 12:45, and they don't let no one in the cafeteria after that.
   Lunch ends at 12:45, and they don't let anyone in the cafeteria after that.

150 Double Negatives

Page 151

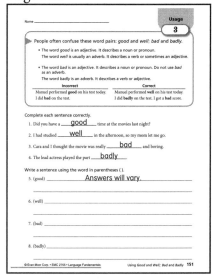

Name _____

Usage 3

People often confuse these word pairs: *good* and *well; bad* and *badly*.

• The word *good* is an adjective. It describes a noun or pronoun.
  The word *well* is usually an adverb. It describes a verb or sometimes an adjective.

• The word *bad* is an adjective. It describes a noun or pronoun. Do not use *bad* as an adverb.
  The word *badly* is an adverb. It describes a verb or adjective.

Incorrect	Correct
Manuel performed **good** on his test today.	Manuel performed **well** on his test today.
I did **bad** on the test.	I did **badly** on the test. I got a **bad** score.

Complete each sentence correctly.

1. Did you have a __good__ time at the movies last night?
2. I had studied __well__ in the afternoon, so my mom let me go.
3. Cara and I thought the movie was really __bad__ and boring.
4. The lead actress played the part __badly__.

Write a sentence using the word in parentheses ( ).

5. (good) __Answers will vary.__
6. (well) _____
7. (bad) _____
8. (badly) _____

Using Good and Well; Bad and Badly 151

Page 152

Name _____

Usage Review 1

Fill in the bubble next to the correct answer.

1. Which sentence is written correctly?
   Ⓐ Sandra likes to walk to school with Tami and I.
   Ⓑ What did they give Ashley and she?
   ● They gave Ashanti and me a round of applause.
   Ⓓ Her and I sang our favorite Beatles song.

2. Which sentence is written correctly?
   ● Tony and I play soccer after school.
   Ⓑ Tony and me are good players.
   Ⓒ The other players kick the ball to him or I.
   Ⓓ The other team doesn't want to play against him or I.

3. Which sentence is written correctly?
   Ⓐ Ekram didn't see no bicycles on the path.
   ● There wasn't anyone in sight.
   Ⓒ Nobody was doing nothing in the park that early.
   Ⓓ Ekram hadn't never seen the park so empty.

4. Which sentence is written correctly?
   ● We danced good at our recital.
   Ⓑ Ms. Weiss said I danced well in my solo.
   Ⓒ It was a well performance for everyone.
   Ⓓ Even my little brother did good.

5. Which sentence is written correctly?
   Ⓐ My brother Roberto cooks good.
   Ⓑ The dinner he made last night was really well.
   Ⓒ Roberto learned our grandmother's lessons good.
   ● She taught him to be a good cook.

152 Usage: Review 1

Page 153

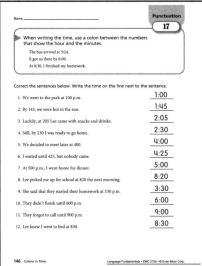

Name _____

Usage 4

The words *can* and *may* are often confused. They mean different things. Be sure to use the word whose meaning fits what you're trying to say.

• *can* means "able to"
  Emily **can** run two miles.

• *may* means "allowed to"
  "You **may** spend the night at Aidan's house," said Dad.

Write *can* or *may* to complete each sentence correctly.

1. Emily and Yuko __can__ both run very fast.
2. "__May__ I run with you?" asked David.
3. "How fast __can__ you run?" asked Yuko.
4. "I __can__ run pretty fast," David replied.
5. "You __may__ run with us this afternoon," Emily said.
6. "That way, we __can__ see if we are good running buddies," said Yuko.
7. David showed that he __can__ run as fast as Emily and Yuko.
8. They told him that he __may__ run with them anytime.

Write two sentences using the words in parentheses ( ).

9. (can) __Answers will vary. Accept any correctly written sentence using can and may.__
10. (may) _____

Using Can and May 153

Page 154

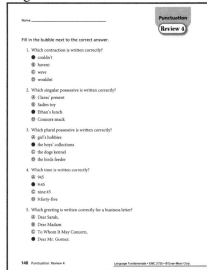

Name _____

Usage 5

The words *lie* and *lay* are often confused.

• Use *lie* to mean "to rest or recline."
• Use *lay* to mean "to put or place."

	lie	lay
Present	I **lie** down when I'm tired.	I **lay** my books on the table.
Past	I will **lie** down tomorrow.	I will **lay** them on the table tomorrow.

Write *lie* or *lay* on the line to complete each sentence.

1. My father likes to __lie__ down for a nap after Sunday dinner.
2. He will __lay__ the paper down on the floor and stretch out on the couch.
3. Our cat likes to __lie__ next to him.
4. She will __lay__ her toy mouse next to Dad's head.

Write four sentences using the form of *lie* or *lay*.

5. lie—present tense: __Answers will vary. Accept any sentence that uses the form correctly.__
6. lay—present tense: _____
7. lie—future tense: _____
8. lay—future tense: _____

154 Using Lie or Lay

Page 155

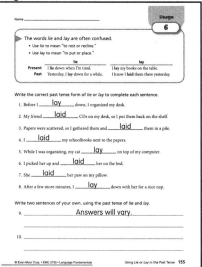

Name _____

Usage 6

The words *lie* and *lay* are often confused.
- Use *lie* to mean "to rest or recline."
- Use *lay* to mean "to put or place."

	lie	*lay*
Present	I lie down when I'm tired.	I lay my books on the table.
Past	Yesterday, I lay down for a while.	I know I laid them there yesterday.

Write the correct past tense form of *lie* or *lay* to complete each sentence.

1. Before I **lay** down, I organized my desk.
2. My friend **laid** CDs on my desk, so I put them back on the shelf.
3. Papers were scattered, so I gathered them and **laid** them in a pile.
4. I **laid** my schoolbooks next to the papers.
5. While I was organizing, my cat **lay** on top of my computer.
6. I picked him up and **laid** her on the bed.
7. She **laid** her paw on my pillow.
8. After a few more minutes, I **lay** down with her for a nice nap.

Write two sentences of your own, using the past tense of *lie* and *lay*.

9. _____ **Answers will vary.** _____

10. _____

Page 156

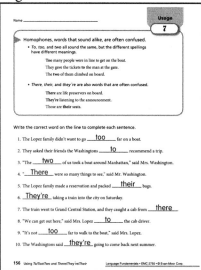

Name _____

Usage 7

Homophones, words that sound alike, are often confused.
- *To, too,* and *two* all sound alike, but the different spellings have different meanings.
  - **Too** many people were in line to get on the boat.
  - They gave the tickets to the man at the gate.
  - The **two** of them climbed on board.
- *There, their,* and *they're* are also words that are often confused.
  - **There** are life preservers on board.
  - **They're** listening to the announcement.
  - Those are **their** seats.

Write the correct word on the line to complete each sentence.

1. The Lopez family didn't want to go **too** far on a boat.
2. They asked their friends the Washingtons **to** recommend a trip.
3. "The **two** of us took a boat around Manhattan," said Mrs. Washington.
4. "**There** were so many things to see," said Mr. Washington.
5. The Lopez family made a reservation and packed **their** bags.
6. **They're** taking a train into the city on Saturday.
7. The train went to Grand Central Station, and they caught a cab from **there**
8. "We can get out here," said Mrs. Lopez **to** the cab driver.
9. "It's not **too** far to walk to the boat," said Mrs. Lopez.
10. The Washingtons said **they're** going to come back next summer.

Page 157

Name _____

Usage Review 2

Fill in the bubble next to the correct answer.

1. Which sentence is written correctly?
   - Ⓐ Thuy asked, "Can I stay up tonight?"
   - Ⓑ "Please, can Maria stay with us tonight, Mom?" asked Ella.
   - Ⓒ My mom said I can stay for dinner.
   - ● My mom said I may stay for dinner.

2. Which sentence is written correctly?
   - Ⓐ Jin Hoon told his dog to lay down.
   - ● Would you please lay those placemats on the table?
   - Ⓒ Benita wanted to lay down for a nap.
   - Ⓓ Isaac will lie the cloth on the table.

3. Which sentence is written correctly?
   - ● Denitra went to the store to get a newspaper.
   - Ⓑ There were only too papers left.
   - Ⓒ Denitra thought, "That's two bad."
   - Ⓓ "I wanted something too read," she said.

4. Which sentence is written correctly?
   - Ⓐ Their not sitting over there.
   - Ⓑ There not sitting over their.
   - Ⓒ They're not sitting over their.
   - ● They're not sitting over there.

5. Which sentence is written correctly?
   - ● It's too bad you two didn't get to meet.
   - Ⓑ It's two bad you to didn't get to meet.
   - Ⓒ It's to bad you two didn't get to meet.
   - Ⓓ It's too bad you two didn't get two meet.

Page 158

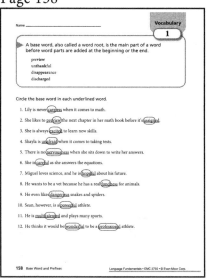

Name _____

Vocabulary 1

A base word, also called a word root, is the main part of a word before word parts are added at the beginning or the end.

preview
unthankful
disappearance
discharged

Circle the base word in each underlined word.

1. Lily is never (care)less when it comes to math.
2. She likes to pre(view) the next chapter in her math book before it's (assign)ed.
3. She is always (excite)d to learn new skills.
4. Shayla is un(afraid) when it comes to taking tests.
5. There is no (nervous)ness when she sits down to write her answers.
6. She is (care)ful as she answers the equations.
7. Miguel loves science, and he is (hope)ful about his future.
8. He wants to be a vet because he has a real (fond)ness for animals.
9. He even likes (danger)ous snakes and spiders.
10. Sean, however, is a (power)ful athlete.
11. He is multi(talent)ed and plays many sports.
12. He thinks it would be (wonder)ful to be a (profession)al athlete.

Page 159

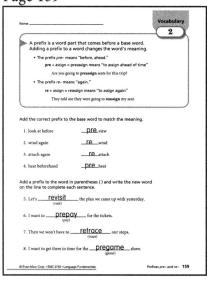

Name _____

Vocabulary 2

A prefix is a word part that comes before a base word. Adding a prefix to a word changes the word's meaning.
- The prefix *pre-* means "before, ahead."
  - **pre** + assign = preassign means "to assign ahead of time"
  - Are you going to preassign seats for this trip?
- The prefix *re-* means "again."
  - **re** + assign = reassign means "to assign again"
  - They told me they were going to reassign my seat.

Add the correct prefix to the base word to match the meaning.

1. look at before **pre** view
2. wind again **re** wind
3. attach again **re** attach
4. heat beforehand **pre** heat

Add a prefix to the word in parentheses ( ) and write the new word on the line to complete each sentence.

5. Let's **revisit** the plan we came up with yesterday. (visit)
6. I want to **prepay** for the tickets. (pay)
7. Then we won't have to **retrace** our steps. (trace)
8. I want to get there in time for the **pregame** show. (game)

Page 160

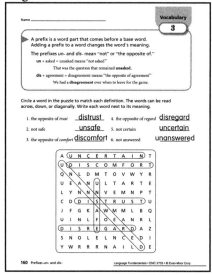

Name _____

Vocabulary 3

A prefix is a word part that comes before a base word. Adding a prefix to a word changes the word's meaning.

The prefixes *un-* and *dis-* mean "not" or "the opposite of."
- **un** + asked = unasked means "not asked"
  - That was the question that remained **unasked**.
- **dis** + agreement = disagreement means "the opposite of agreement"
  - We had a **disagreement** over when to leave for the game.

Circle a word in the puzzle to match each definition. The words can be read across, down, or diagonally. Write each word next to its meaning.

1. the opposite of *trust* **distrust**
2. not safe **unsafe**
3. the opposite of *comfort* **discomfort**
4. the opposite of *regard* **disregard**
5. not certain **uncertain**
6. not answered **unanswered**

A	U	N	C	E	R	T	A	I	N	T
U	D	I	S	C	O	M	F	O	R	T
Q	N	L	D	M	T	O	V	W	Y	R
U	E	A	N	U	L	T	A	R	T	E
L	Y	N	N	V	E	M	N	P	T	
C	D	D	I	S	T	R	U	S	T	U
J	F	G	K	A	W	M	M	L	O	D
U	I	N	L	F	O	E	A	N	R	L
D	I	S	R	E	G	A	R	D	A	Z
S	N	O	L	E	L	N	C	E	D	I
Y	W	R	R	R	N	A	I	L	D	E

Page 161

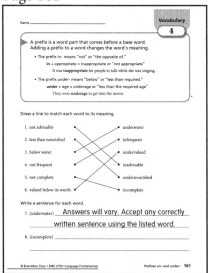

Name _____

Vocabulary 4

A prefix is a word part that comes before a base word. Adding a prefix to a word changes the word's meaning.
- The prefix *in-* means "not" or "the opposite of."
  - **in** + appropriate = inappropriate or "not appropriate"
  - It was **inappropriate** for people to talk while she was singing.
- The prefix *under-* means "below" or "less than required."
  - **under** + age = underage or "less than the required age"
  - They were **underage** to get into the movie.

Draw a line to match each word to its meaning.

1. not advisable — underwater
2. less than nourished — infrequent
3. below water — undervalued
4. not frequent — inadvisable
5. not complete — undernourished
6. valued below its worth — incomplete

Write a sentence for each word.

7. (underwater) **Answers will vary. Accept any correctly written sentence using the listed word.**

8. (incomplete) _____

Page 162

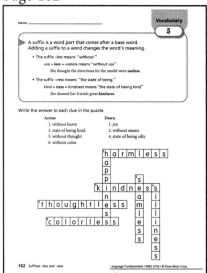

Name _____

Vocabulary 5

A suffix is a word part that comes after a base word. Adding a suffix to a word changes the word's meaning.
- The suffix *-less* means "without."
  - use + less = useless means "without use"
  - She thought the directions for the model were **useless**.
- The suffix *-ness* means "the state of being."
  - kind + ness = kindness means "the state of being kind"
  - She showed her friends great **kindness**.

Write the answer to each clue in the puzzle.

Across
1. without harm
3. state of being kind
5. without thought
6. without color

Down
1. joy
2. without seams
4. without being silly

```
 ¹h a r m l e s s
   a
   p
   p         ²s
 ³k i n d n e s s
   n         a
 ⁴t h o u g h t l e s s
   s         l
             e
 ⁵c o l o r l e s s
             s
             s
```

Page 163

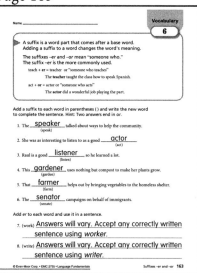

Name _____

Vocabulary 6

A suffix is a word part that comes after a base word. Adding a suffix to a word changes the word's meaning.

The suffixes *-er* and *-or* mean "someone who." The suffix *-er* is the more commonly used.
- teach + er = teacher or "someone who teaches"
  - The **teacher** taught the class how to speak Spanish.
- act + or = actor or "someone who acts"
  - The **actor** did a wonderful job playing the part.

Add a suffix to each word in parentheses ( ) and write the new word to complete the sentence. Hint: Two answers end in *or*.

1. The **speaker** talked about ways to help the community. (speak)
2. She was as interesting to listen to as a good **actor** (act)
3. Raul is a good **listener** so he learned a lot. (listen)
4. This **gardener** uses nothing but compost to make her plants grow. (garden)
5. That **farmer** helps out by bringing vegetables to the homeless shelter. (farm)
6. The **senator** campaigns on behalf of immigrants. (senate)

Add *er* to each word and use it in a sentence.

7. (work) **Answers will vary. Accept any correctly written sentence using *worker*.**

8. (write) **Answers will vary. Accept any correctly written sentence using *writer*.**

Page 164

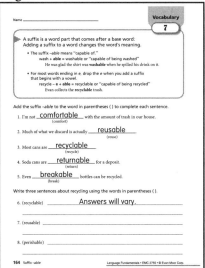

Vocabulary 7

A suffix is a word part that comes after a base word. Adding a suffix to a word changes the word's meaning.

- The suffix *–able* means "capable of."
  wash + able = washable or "capable of being washed"
  He was glad the shirt was **washable** when he spilled his drink on it.
- For most words ending in *e*, drop the *e* when you add a suffix that begins with a vowel.
  recycle – e + able = recyclable or "capable of being recycled"
  Evan collects the **recyclable** trash.

Add the suffix *–able* to the word in parentheses ( ) to complete each sentence.

1. I'm not **comfortable** with the amount of trash in our house.
   (comfort)
2. Much of what we discard is actually **reusable**
   (reuse)
3. Most cans are **recyclable**
   (recycle)
4. Soda cans are **returnable** for a deposit.
   (return)
5. Even **breakable** bottles can be recycled.
   (break)

Write three sentences about recycling using the words in parentheses ( ).

6. (recyclable) **Answers will vary.**

7. (reusable) _____

8. (perishable) _____

164 Suffix –able · Language Fundamentals · EMC 2755 · © Evan-Moor Corp.

Page 165

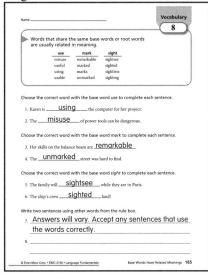

Vocabulary 8

Words that share the same base words or root words are usually related in meaning.

use	mark	sight
misuse	remarkable	sightsee
useful	marked	sighted
using	marks	sightless
usable	unmarked	sighting

Choose the correct word with the base word *use* to complete each sentence.

1. Karen is **using** the computer for her project.
2. The **misuse** of power tools can be dangerous.

Choose the correct word with the base word *mark* to complete each sentence.

3. Her skills on the balance beam are **remarkable**
4. The **unmarked** street was hard to find.

Choose the correct word with the base word *sight* to complete each sentence.

5. The family will **sightsee** while they are in Paris.
6. The ship's crew **sighted** land!

Write two sentences using other words from the rule box.

7. **Answers will vary. Accept any sentences that use the words correctly.**

8. _____

© Evan-Moor Corp. · EMC 2755 · Language Fundamentals   Base Words Have Related Meanings 165

Page 166

Vocabulary Review 1

Fill in the bubble next to the correct answer.

1. Which one is the base word in *disappear*?
   Ⓐ pear
   ● appear
   Ⓒ dis
   Ⓓ ear

2. Which one is the correct meaning of the word *preview*?
   Ⓐ look after
   Ⓑ look through
   Ⓒ look out
   ● look at ahead of time

3. Which sentence uses a form of the base word *sight* correctly?
   ● The latest sighting of Bigfoot was faked.
   Ⓑ A man without sightsee said he met the creature.
   Ⓒ If I sighting Bigfoot, I wouldn't tell anyone.
   Ⓓ People would think I was sightful!

4. Which sentence uses a form of the word *nervous* correctly?
   Ⓐ "The recital is next week," Lucy said nervousor.
   Ⓑ Lucy is nervousless about her next recital.
   ● Lucy's nervousness disappeared as soon as she heard the applause.
   Ⓓ The applause sounded nervously.

5. Which sentence uses a form of the word *comfort* correctly?
   Ⓐ Alice thought that the couch was very uncomfort.
   Ⓑ Alice thought the couch was very comfortness.
   Ⓒ Alice thought the couch was very uncomfortless.
   ● Alice thought the couch was very uncomfortable.

166 Vocabulary: Review 1   Language Fundamentals · EMC 2755 · © Evan-Moor Corp.

Page 167

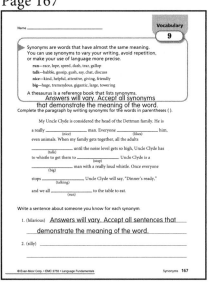

Vocabulary 9

Synonyms are words that have almost the same meaning. You can use synonyms to vary your writing, avoid repetition, or make your use of language more precise.

run—race, lope, speed, dash, tear, gallop
talk—babble, gossip, gush, say, chat, discuss
nice—kind, helpful, attentive, giving, friendly
big—huge, tremendous, gigantic, large, towering

A thesaurus is a reference book that lists synonyms.
Answers will vary. Accept all synonyms that demonstrate the meaning of the word.

Complete the paragraph by writing synonyms for the words in parentheses ( ).

My Uncle Clyde is considered the head of the Dettman family. He is a really _____ man. Everyone _____ him,
(nice)   (likes)
even animals. When my family gets together, all the adults _____ until the noise level gets so high, Uncle Clyde has
(talk)
to whistle to get them to _____ Uncle Clyde is a
(stop)
_____ man with a really loud whistle. Once everyone
(big)
stops _____ Uncle Clyde will say, "Dinner's ready,"
(talking)
and we all _____ to the table to eat.
(run)

Write a sentence about someone you know for each synonym.

1. (hilarious) **Answers will vary. Accept all sentences that demonstrate the meaning of the word.**

2. (silly) _____

© Evan-Moor Corp. · EMC 2755 · Language Fundamentals   Synonyms 167

Page 168

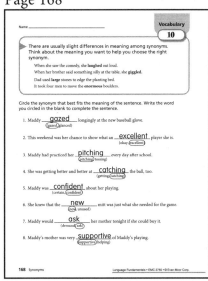

Vocabulary 10

There are usually slight differences in meaning among synonyms. Think about the meaning you want to help you choose the right synonym.

When she saw the comedy, she **laughed** out loud.
When her brother said something silly at the table, she **giggled.**
Dad used **large** stones to edge the planting bed.
It took four men to move the **enormous** boulders.

Circle the synonym that best fits the meaning of the sentence. Write the word you circled in the blank to complete the sentence.

1. Maddy **gazed** longingly at the new baseball glove.
   (gazed / glanced)
2. This weekend was her chance to show what an **excellent** player she is.
   (okay / excellent)
3. Maddy had practiced her **pitching** every day after school.
   (pitching / tossing)
4. She was getting better and better at **catching** the ball, too.
   (getting / catching)
5. Maddy was **confident** about her playing.
   (certain / confident)
6. She knew that the **new** mitt was just what she needed for the game.
   (new / unused)
7. Maddy would **ask** her mother tonight if she could buy it.
   (demand / ask)
8. Maddy's mother was very **supportive** of Maddy's playing.
   (supportive / helping)

168 Synonyms   Language Fundamentals · EMC 2755 · © Evan-Moor Corp.

Page 169

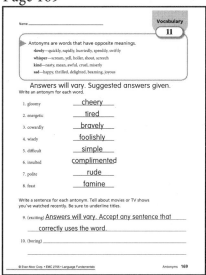

Vocabulary 11

Antonyms are words that have opposite meanings.

slowly—quickly, rapidly, hurriedly, speedily, swiftly
whisper—scream, yell, holler, shout, screech
kind—nasty, mean, awful, cruel, miserly
sad—happy, thrilled, delighted, beaming, joyous

Answers will vary. Suggested answers given.

Write an antonym for each word.

1. gloomy — **cheery**
2. energetic — **tired**
3. cowardly — **bravely**
4. wisely — **foolishly**
5. difficult — **simple**
6. insulted — **complimented**
7. polite — **rude**
8. feast — **famine**

Write a sentence for each antonym. Tell about movies or TV shows you've watched recently. Be sure to underline titles.

9. (exciting) **Answers will vary. Accept any sentence that correctly uses the word.**

10. (boring) _____

© Evan-Moor Corp. · EMC 2755 · Language Fundamentals   Antonyms 169

Page 170

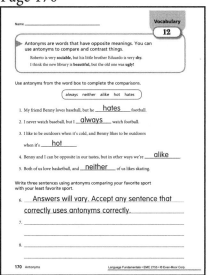

Vocabulary 12

Antonyms are words that have opposite meanings. You can use antonyms to compare and contrast things.

Roberto is very **sociable**, but his little brother Eduardo is very **shy.**
I think the new library is **beautiful**, but the old one was **ugly!**

Use antonyms from the word box to complete the comparisons.

always	neither	alike	hot	hates

1. My friend Benny loves baseball, but he **hates** football.
2. I never watch baseball, but I **always** watch football.
3. I like to be outdoors when it's cold, and Benny likes to be outdoors when it's **hot**
4. Benny and I can be opposite in our tastes, but in other ways we're **alike**
5. Both of us love basketball, and **neither** of us likes skating.

Write three sentences using antonyms comparing your favorite sport with your least favorite sport.

6. **Answers will vary. Accept any sentence that correctly uses antonyms correctly.**

7. _____

8. _____

170 Antonyms   Language Fundamentals · EMC 2755 · © Evan-Moor Corp.

Page 171

Vocabulary 13

Homophones are words that sound alike but have different spellings and meanings.

My sister and I are so **different**.
She can make a pair of pants, and I can't even **sew** on a button!
There is **no** obstacle to our success with this.
I **know** we will come up with a great science project.

Circle the correct homophone to match the meaning.

1. also — (too) / two
2. put down on paper — right / (write)
3. belonging to them — they're / (their)
4. in that place — (there) / they're
5. in this place — (here) / hear
6. 3 minus 2 — won / (one)

Write a sentence for each of these homophones. Make sure that you use the correct meaning for the word's spelling in your sentence.

7. (through) **Answers will vary.**

8. (threw) _____

© Evan-Moor Corp. · EMC 2755 · Language Fundamentals   Homophones 171

Page 172

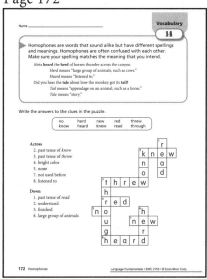

Vocabulary 14

Homophones are words that sound alike but have different spellings and meanings. Homophones are often confused with each other. Make sure your spelling matches the meaning that you intend.

Aleta **heard** the **herd** of horses thunder across the canyon.
Herd means "large group of animals, such as cows."
Heard means "listened to."
Did you hear the **tale** about how the monkey got its **tail**?
Tail means "appendage on an animal, such as a horse."
Tale means "story."

Write the answers to the clues in the puzzle.

no	herd	new	red	threw
know	heard	knew	read	through

Across
2. past tense of *know*
3. past tense of *throw*
4. bright color
5. none
7. not used before
8. listened to

Down
1. past tense of *read*
2. understand
3. finished
6. large group of animals

172 Homophones   Language Fundamentals · EMC 2755 · © Evan-Moor Corp.

Page 173

Fill in the bubble next to the correct answer.

1. Which word is a synonym for *happiness*?
   - ● joy
   - Ⓑ sadness
   - Ⓒ happy
   - Ⓓ joyful

2. Which word is an antonym for *sharp*?
   - Ⓐ knife
   - Ⓑ sharpness
   - Ⓒ pointy
   - ● dull

3. What does the word *they're* mean?
   - Ⓐ that place
   - Ⓑ belonging to them
   - ● they are
   - Ⓓ they will

4. Which words are synonyms?
   - Ⓐ *hear* and *here*
   - ● *kind* and *nice*
   - Ⓒ *sick* and *well*
   - Ⓓ *wrong* and *right*

5. Which words are homophones?
   - Ⓐ *happy* and *sad*
   - ● *know* and *no*
   - Ⓒ *glad* and *joyful*
   - Ⓓ *no* and *never*

© Evan-Moor Corp. • EMC 2755 • Language Fundamentals   Vocabulary: Review 2   173

Page 174

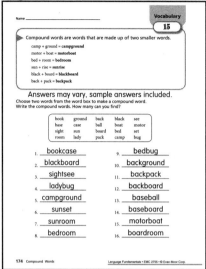

Compound words are words that are made up of two smaller words.

camp + ground = **campground**
motor + boat = **motorboat**
bed + room = **bedroom**
sun + rise = **sunrise**
black + board = **blackboard**
back + pack = **backpack**

Answers may vary, sample answers included.
Choose two words from the word box to make a compound word.
Write the compound words. How many can you find?

book	ground	back	black	see
base	case	ball	boat	motor
sight	sun	board	bed	set
room	lady	pack	camp	bug

1. bookcase
2. blackboard
3. sightsee
4. ladybug
5. campground
6. sunset
7. sunroom
8. bedroom
9. bedbug
10. background
11. backpack
12. backboard
13. baseball
14. baseboard
15. motorboat
16. boardroom

174   Compound Words   Language Fundamentals • EMC 2755 • © Evan-Moor Corp.

Page 175

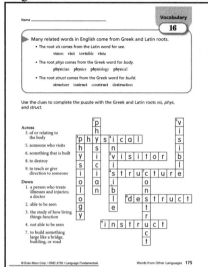

Many related words in English come from Greek and Latin roots.
• The root *vis* comes from the Latin word for *see*.
   vision   visit   invisible   vista
• The root *phys* comes from the Greek word for *body*.
   physician   physics   physiology   physical
• The root *struct* comes from the Greek word for *build*.
   structure   instruct   construct   destruction

Use the clues to complete the puzzle with the Greek and Latin roots *vis*, *phys*, and *struct*.

Across
3. of or relating to the body
5. someone who visits
6. something that is built
8. to destroy
9. to teach or give direction to someone

Down
1. a person who treats illnesses and injuries; a doctor
2. able to be seen
3. the study of how living things function
4. not able to be seen
7. to build something large like a bridge, building, or road

(crossword: physical, visitor, structure, destruct, instruct, physiology, physician, invisible, construct)

© Evan-Moor Corp. • EMC 2755 • Language Fundamentals   Words from Other Languages   175

Page 176

Many words in English come from other languages, such as Arabic, Spanish, or Hindi.

The word *giraffe* comes from the Arabic word *zaraafah*.
The word *canyon* comes from the Spanish word *cañón*.
The word *bandana* comes from the Hindi word *bāndhnū*.

Use your understanding of word meanings to match each word with its language of origin. Write the letter of the origin next to the English word.

1. absurd — g — a. from the Hungarian *gulyás*
2. goulash — a — b. from Hawaiian for a type of instrument
3. knapsack — f — c. from Persian meaning "market"
4. ukulele — b — d. from the French word *liberté* meaning "freedom"
5. moccasin — e — e. from an Algonquin word for *shoe*
6. bazaar — c — f. from the Dutch *knapzak*
7. cookie — h — g. from the French *absurde*
8. liberty — d — h. from the Dutch word *koekje* meaning "little cake"

Read each word and its origin. Write a sentence using the word in English.

9. *hurricane*, from the Spanish word *huracán*   **Answers will vary.**

10. *parka*, from the Russian word for *jacket*   **Answers will vary.**

176   Words from Other Languages   Language Fundamentals • EMC 2755 • © Evan-Moor Corp.

Page 177

Fill in the bubble next to the correct answer.

1. Which word is a compound word?
   - Ⓐ camping
   - ● campground
   - Ⓒ grounded
   - Ⓓ camper

2. Which word does **not** come from the Greek word for *build*?
   - ● instrument
   - Ⓑ instruct
   - Ⓒ structure
   - Ⓓ deconstruction

3. Which word comes from the Latin root *vis*, meaning "see"?
   - Ⓐ divide
   - Ⓑ valley
   - Ⓒ very
   - ● visible

4. Which word comes from the Spanish word *cañón*, meaning "deep valley"?
   - Ⓐ can't
   - Ⓑ cannon
   - Ⓒ carrot
   - ● canyon

5. Which word comes from the Italian word *mascera*, meaning "something you wear to cover your face"?
   - Ⓐ me
   - Ⓑ match
   - ● mask
   - Ⓓ marble

© Evan-Moor Corp. • EMC 2755 • Language Fundamentals   Vocabulary: Review 3   177

Page 178

You can add word endings, such as *–s*, *–ed*, *–ing*, *–er*, and *–est*, to base words to make new words.

Manuel stops training today.
Yesterday he stopped running after school.
He is pacing himself because tomorrow is the 10K race.

Add *–s*, *–ed*, *–ing*, *–er*, or *–est* to each word to complete the sentence.

1. Sonya wait**s** for the bus every morning with her friends Ashanti and Kevin.
2. They don't mind wait**ing** as long as they can do it together.
3. The bus stop**s** at the corner of Olive and Elm.
4. It take**s** the bus fifteen minutes to get them to school.
5. It takes long**er** to get there when the weather is bad.
6. The long**est** it ever took to get to school was one hour!
7. It had started snow**ing** that morning, and the roads hadn't been cleared.
8. The snowplows clear**ed** the roads later, so the ride home was quicker.

Write a sentence for each form of the word *rain*.

9. (rains)   **Answers will vary.**

10. (raining)

178   Word Meaning   Language Fundamentals • EMC 2755 • © Evan-Moor Corp.

Page 179

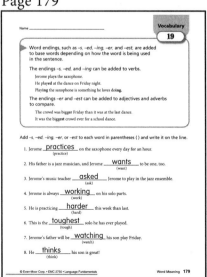

Word endings, such as *–s*, *–ed*, *–ing*, *–er*, and *–est*, are added to base words depending on how the word is being used in the sentence.

The endings *–s*, *–ed*, and *–ing* can be added to verbs.
   Jerome plays the saxophone.
   He played at the dance on Friday night.
   Playing the saxophone is something he loves doing.
The endings *–er* and *–est* can be added to adjectives and adverbs to compare.
   The crowd was bigger Friday than it was at the last dance.
   It was the biggest crowd ever for a school dance.

Add *–s*, *–ed*, *–ing*, *–er*, or *–est* to each word in parentheses ( ) and write it on the line.

1. Jerome **practices** on the saxophone every day for an hour. (practice)
2. His father is a jazz musician, and Jerome **wants** to be one, too. (want)
3. Jerome's music teacher **asked** Jerome to play in the jazz ensemble. (ask)
4. Jerome is always **working** on his solo parts. (work)
5. He is practicing **harder** this week than last. (hard)
6. This is the **toughest** solo he has ever played. (tough)
7. Jerome's father will be **watching** his son play Friday. (watch)
8. He **thinks** his son is great! (think)

© Evan-Moor Corp. • EMC 2755 • Language Fundamentals   Word Meaning   179

Page 180

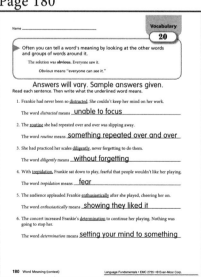

Often you can tell a word's meaning by looking at the other words and groups of words around it.

The solution was **obvious**. Everyone saw it.
Obvious means "everyone can see it."

Answers will vary. Sample answers given.
Read each sentence. Then write what the underlined word means.

1. Frankie had never been so underlined. She couldn't keep her mind on her work.
   The word *distracted* means **unable to focus**

2. The routine she had repeated over and over was slipping away.
   The word *routine* means **something repeated over and over**

3. She had practiced her scales diligently, never forgetting to do them.
   The word *diligently* means **without forgetting**

4. With trepidation, Frankie sat down to play, fearful that people wouldn't like her playing.
   The word *trepidation* means **fear**

5. The audience applauded Frankie enthusiastically after she played, cheering her on.
   The word *enthusiastically* means **showing they liked it**

6. The concert increased Frankie's determination to continue her playing. Nothing was going to stop her.
   The word *determination* means **setting your mind to something**

180   Word Meaning (context)   Language Fundamentals • EMC 2755 • © Evan-Moor Corp.

Page 181

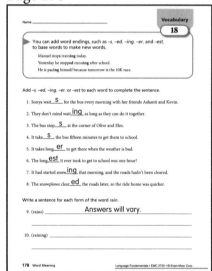

Often you can tell a word's meaning by looking at the other words and groups of words around it.

The panther's body was **sleek** and muscular. There wasn't an ounce of fat on him.
The word sleek means "lean" or "trim."

Read the paragraph. Then answer the questions.

There was a scavenger hunt at school. Everyone was anticipating the fun to come. Last year, they had had a great time searching high and low for the things on the list. They couldn't wait! Everyone congregated in the gym as the rules were explained and the lists were passed out. Then the group dispersed, and the search began. After hours of poring over the clues, trying to figure out what they meant, and then scrambling to find the things on the list, everyone began to head back to the school. Andy Lopez's team triumphed because they found everything on the list first. They won a free lunch at Sundae's.

Answers will vary. Sample answers given.

1. *scavenger hunt* means **a game where you look for things**
2. *anticipating* means **waiting for**
3. *congregated* means **gathered**
4. *dispersed* means **broke up**
5. *poring* means **studying carefully**
6. *triumphed* means **won**

© Evan-Moor Corp. • EMC 2755 • Language Fundamentals   Word Meaning (context)   181

Page 182

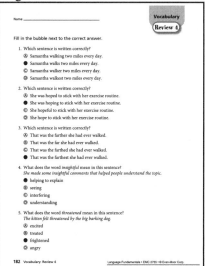

Name _____

Vocabulary
Review 4

Fill in the bubble next to the correct answer.

1. Which sentence is written correctly?
   Ⓐ Samantha walking two miles every day.
   ● Samantha walks two miles every day.
   Ⓒ Samantha walker two miles every day.
   Ⓓ Samantha walkest two miles every day.

2. Which sentence is written correctly?
   Ⓐ She was hoped to stick with her exercise routine.
   ● She was hoping to stick with her exercise routine.
   Ⓒ She hopeful to stick with her exercise routine.
   Ⓓ She hope to stick with her exercise routine.

3. Which sentence is written correctly?
   Ⓐ That was the farther she had ever walked.
   Ⓑ That was the far she had ever walked.
   Ⓒ That was the farthed she had ever walked.
   ● That was the farthest she had ever walked.

4. What does the word *insightful* mean in this sentence?
   She made some insightful comments that helped people understand the topic.
   ● helping to explain
   Ⓑ seeing
   Ⓒ interfering
   Ⓓ understanding

5. What does the word *threatened* mean in this sentence?
   The kitten felt threatened by the big barking dog.
   Ⓐ excited
   Ⓑ treated
   ● frightened
   Ⓓ angry

182 Vocabulary: Review 4   Language Fundamentals • EMC 2755 • © Evan-Moor Corp.

Page 184

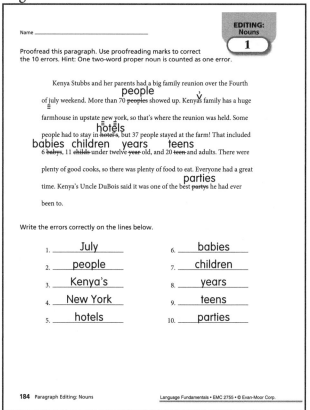

Name _____

EDITING:
Nouns
1

Proofread this paragraph. Use proofreading marks to correct
the 10 errors. Hint: One two-word proper noun is counted as one error.

Kenya Stubbs and her parents had a big family reunion over the Fourth
of july weekend. More than 70 ~~peoples~~ **people** showed up. Kenya's family has a huge
farmhouse in upstate new york, so that's where the reunion was held. Some
people had to stay in ~~hotel's~~ **hotels**, but 37 people stayed at the farm! That included
6 ~~babys~~ **babies**, 11 ~~childs~~ **children** under twelve ~~year~~ **years** old, and 20 ~~teen~~ **teens** and adults. There were
plenty of good cooks, so there was plenty of food to eat. Everyone had a great
time. Kenya's Uncle DuBois said it was one of the best ~~partys~~ **parties** he had ever
been to.

Write the errors correctly on the lines below.

1. July
2. people
3. Kenya's
4. New York
5. hotels

6. babies
7. children
8. years
9. teens
10. parties

184 Paragraph Editing: Nouns   Language Fundamentals • EMC 2755 • © Evan-Moor Corp.

Page 185

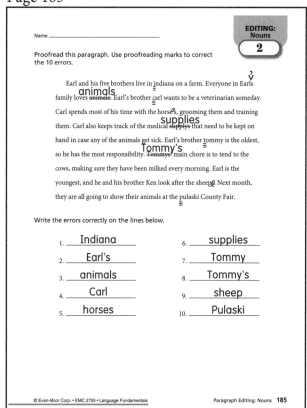

Name _____

EDITING:
Nouns
2

Proofread this paragraph. Use proofreading marks to correct
the 10 errors.

Earl and his five brothers live in indiana on a farm. Everyone in Earls
family loves ~~animale~~ **animals**. Earl's brother carl wants to be a veterinarian someday.
Carl spends most of his time with the horses, grooming them and training
them. Carl also keeps track of the medical ~~supplys~~ **supplies** that need to be kept on
hand in case any of the animals get sick. Earl's brother tommy is the oldest,
so he has the most responsibility. ~~Tommys~~ **Tommy's** main chore is to tend to the
cows, making sure they have been milked every morning. Earl is the
youngest, and he and his brother Ken look after the sheep. Next month,
they are all going to show their animals at the pulaski County Fair.

Write the errors correctly on the lines below.

1. Indiana
2. Earl's
3. animals
4. Carl
5. horses

6. supplies
7. Tommy
8. Tommy's
9. sheep
10. Pulaski

© Evan-Moor Corp. • EMC 2755 • Language Fundamentals   Paragraph Editing: Nouns 185

Page 186

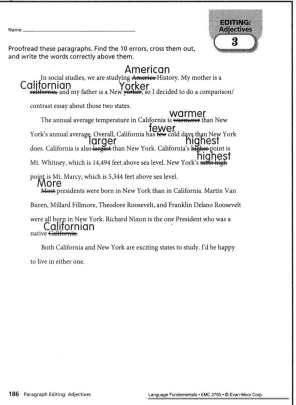

Name _____

EDITING: Adjectives 3

Proofread these paragraphs. Find the 10 errors, cross them out, and write the words correctly above them.

In social studies, we are studying ~~America~~ **American** History. My mother is a ~~California~~ **Californian**, and my father is a New ~~yorker~~ **Yorker**, so I decided to do a comparison/contrast essay about those two states.

The annual average temperature in California is ~~warmerer~~ **warmer** than New York's annual average. Overall, California has ~~few~~ **fewer** cold days than New York does. California is also ~~largest~~ **larger** than New York. California's ~~higher~~ **highest** point is Mt. Whitney, which is 14,494 feet above sea level. New York's ~~most high~~ **highest** point is Mt. Marcy, which is 5,344 feet above sea level.

~~Most~~ **More** presidents were born in New York than in California. Martin Van Buren, Millard Fillmore, Theodore Roosevelt, and Franklin Delano Roosevelt were all born in New York. Richard Nixon is the one President who was a native ~~California~~ **Californian**.

Both California and New York are exciting states to study. I'd be happy to live in either one.

Page 187

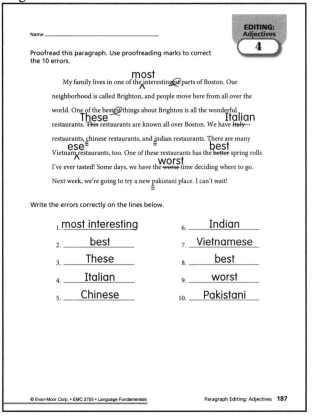

Name _____

EDITING: Adjectives 4

Proofread this paragraph. Use proofreading marks to correct the 10 errors.

My family lives in one of the interestinger **most** parts of Boston. Our neighborhood is called Brighton, and people move here from all over the world. One of the bestest **best** things about Brighton is all the wonderful restaurants. ~~This~~ **These** restaurants are known all over Boston. We have ~~Italy~~ **Italian** restaurants, chinese restaurants, and indian restaurants. There are many Vietnam **ese** restaurants, too. One of these restaurants has the ~~better~~ **best** spring rolls I've ever tasted! Some days, we have the ~~worse~~ **worst** time deciding where to go. Next week, we're going to try a new pakistani place. I can't wait!

Write the errors correctly on the lines below.

1. most interesting
2. best
3. These
4. Italian
5. Chinese
6. Indian
7. Vietnamese
8. best
9. worst
10. Pakistani

Page 188

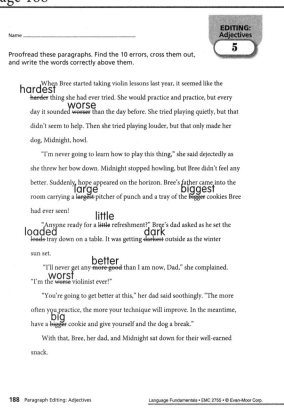

Name _____

EDITING: Adjectives 5

Proofread these paragraphs. Find the 10 errors, cross them out, and write the words correctly above them.

When Bree started taking violin lessons last year, it seemed like the ~~harder~~ **hardest** thing she had ever tried. She would practice and practice, but every day it sounded ~~worser~~ **worse** than the day before. She tried playing quietly, but that didn't seem to help. Then she tried playing louder, but that only made her dog, Midnight, howl.

"I'm never going to learn how to play this thing," she said dejectedly as she threw her bow down. Midnight stopped howling, but Bree didn't feel any better. Suddenly, hope appeared on the horizon. Bree's father came into the room carrying a ~~largest~~ **large** pitcher of punch and a tray of the ~~bigger~~ **biggest** cookies Bree had ever seen!

"Anyone ready for a ~~little~~ **little** refreshment?" Bree's dad asked as he set the ~~loads~~ **loaded** tray down on a table. It was getting ~~darkest~~ **dark** outside as the winter sun set.

"I'll never get any ~~more good~~ **better** than I am now, Dad," she complained. "I'm the ~~worse~~ **worst** violinist ever!"

"You're going to get better at this," her dad said soothingly. "The more often you practice, the more your technique will improve. In the meantime, have a ~~bigger~~ **big** cookie and give yourself and the dog a break."

With that, Bree, her dad, and Midnight sat down for their well-earned snack.

Page 189

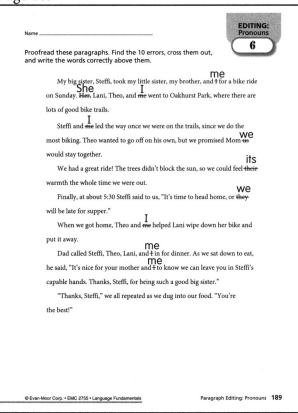

Name _____

EDITING: Pronouns 6

Proofread these paragraphs. Find the 10 errors, cross them out, and write the words correctly above them.

My big sister, Steffi, took my little sister, my brother, and ~~I~~ **me** for a bike ride on Sunday. ~~Her~~ **She**, Lani, Theo, and ~~me~~ **I** went to Oakhurst Park, where there are lots of good bike trails.

Steffi and ~~me~~ **I** led the way once we were on the trails, since we do the most biking. Theo wanted to go off on his own, but we promised Mom ~~us~~ **we** would stay together.

We had a great ride! The trees didn't block the sun, so we could feel ~~their~~ **its** warmth the whole time we were out.

Finally, at about 5:30 Steffi said to us, "It's time to head home, or ~~they~~ **we** will be late for supper."

When we got home, Theo and ~~me~~ **I** helped Lani wipe down her bike and put it away.

Dad called Steffi, Theo, Lani, and ~~I~~ **me** in for dinner. As we sat down to eat, he said, "It's nice for your mother and ~~I~~ **me** to know we can leave you in Steffi's capable hands. Thanks, Steffi, for being such a good big sister."

"Thanks, Steffi," we all repeated as we dug into our food. "You're the best!"

Page 190

EDITING:
Pronouns
7

Proofread these paragraphs. Find the 10 errors, cross them out,
and write the words correctly above them.

Whenever my family goes to the beach, ~~you~~ [we] have a great time. The hard

part of the trip comes when it's time for ~~we~~ [us] to gather our belongings, load the

car, and head home.

"Is this ~~my~~ [mine] or yours?" my brother asks as he holds up a shoe.

"It's not ~~mines~~ [mine]," I reply, "so ~~they~~ [it] must be yours."

My father always loses ~~his~~ [his] towel. He turns to my mom and ~~I~~ [me] and says,

"Has anyone seen my towel?"

Then my mom and ~~me~~ [I] go searching for it. It's usually half-buried in the

sand somewhere.

"Here it is," one of us will say while pulling the towel out from the sand.

"I believe this is ~~your~~ [yours]."

Every family has traditions, and I guess this is one of ~~ours~~ [ours].

Page 191

EDITING:
Pronouns
8

Proofread these paragraphs. Find the 10 errors, cross them out,
and write the words correctly above them.

My friends and ~~me~~ [I] belong to a hiking club. We go hiking once a month

in the hills near where ~~us~~ [we] live. We have a guide who takes ~~them~~ [us] on these

hikes. Her name is Andrea, and she knows a lot about the animals, birds,

and flowers we find on our hikes.

We have to wear special clothes when we hike. Ginnie and ~~me~~ [I] have the

same kind of hiking boots. The shoes are very comfortable, but ~~their~~ [they're] very

sturdy, too. Lourdes's boots are also very sturdy and comfortable, plus ~~it's~~ [they're]

really cool looking. They have green stripes on the sides.

Andrea tells us about the birds ~~they~~ [we] see on our hikes. She knows just

about every bird there is! One time, we saw a bald eagle sitting high up in

a tree. When we looked through binoculars, we could see ~~it's~~ [its] nest. We see

quail all the time. They are so cute ~~with~~ [their] they little crests that look like a

big teardrop!

When we're old enough, Lourdes and ~~me~~ [I] want to become guides like

Andrea. It must be great to spend all that time outdoors!

Page 192

EDITING:
Verbs
9

Proofread these paragraphs. Find the 10 errors, cross them out,
and write the words correctly above them.

Last weekend, our school ~~putted~~ [put] on its first ever Dog Wash and Bake Sale

to raise money for our school music program. We ~~studyed~~ [studied] different types

of school fundraisers, and ~~it come~~ [came] down to two: a dog wash and a bake sale.

We couldn't decide which one, so instead we went ahead with plans for both.

The fifth-grade class ~~were~~ [was] in charge of organizing the baked goods, and

the sixth-graders were in charge of the dog wash. The other classes ~~drawed~~ [drew]

pictures for posters and decorated the playground.

On Saturday morning, people ~~brang~~ [brought] their dogs and ~~line~~ [lined] up in the dog

wash area. We had huge tubs and hoses, as well as plenty of dog shampoo.

It got very wet in the dog wash area, and a couple of kids ~~slided~~ [slid] on the

soapsuds and fell. They got back up and kept washing dogs, so we knew

they were okay.

Everyone, including some of the dogs, ~~eat~~ [ate] lots of cookies and cupcakes.

We ~~selled~~ [sold] all the baked goods and made $475. The dog wash raised another

$263. That meant we raised $738 to help the school buy sheet music for our

music program.

Page 193

EDITING:
Verbs
10

Proofread these paragraphs. Use proofreading marks to correct
the 10 errors.

Tanya has a big test tomorrow, and she is studying for it tonight. She

~~studyed~~ [studied] all last weekend and every night this week, but it's an important test,

so she want to make sure she's ready. She be reviewing every chapter in her

social studies book, and her brothers is taking turns quizzing her on the

material covered. Tanya answers the questions, and sometimes she writes

down special things she need to remember.

Tanya's mother will call her when dinner is ready. Tanya's mother

believe that you can't learn anything if you don't eat properly. Tanya's

family knows that Tanya will do well on the test. She always ~~do~~ [does].

Write the errors correctly on the lines below.

1. studied
2. wants
3. is
4. are
5. writes
6. needs
7. call
8. believes
9. eat
10. does

Page 194

EDITING: Verbs 11

Proofread these paragraphs. Use proofreading marks to correct the 10 errors.

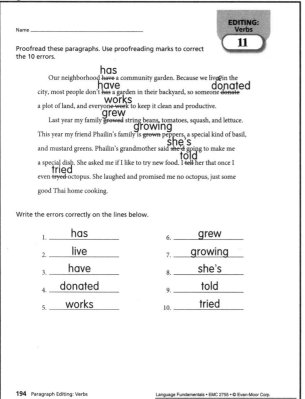

  Our neighborhood ~~have~~ **has** a community garden. Because we live in the city, most people don't ~~has~~ **have** a garden in their backyard, so someone ~~donate~~ **donated** a plot of land, and everyone ~~work~~ **works** to keep it clean and productive.

  Last year my family ~~growed~~ **grew** string beans, tomatoes, squash, and lettuce. This year my friend Phailin's family is ~~grown~~ **growing** peppers, a special kind of basil, and mustard greens. Phailin's grandmother said ~~she'd~~ **she's** going to make me a special dish. She asked me if I like to try new food. I ~~tell~~ **told** her that once I even ~~tryed~~ **tried** octopus. She laughed and promised me no octopus, just some good Thai home cooking.

Write the errors correctly on the lines below.

1.   has   6.   grew
2.   live   7.   growing
3.   have   8.   she's
4.   donated   9.   told
5.   works   10.   tried

Page 195

EDITING: Verbs 12

Proofread these paragraphs. Find the 10 errors, cross them out, and write the words correctly above them.

  Shane's birthday was coming up, and his father ~~ask~~ **asked** him what he wanted to do.

  "I want to go bowling," Shane ~~replyed~~ **replied**, as he finished loading his dishes into the dishwasher.

  "Bowling!" his father said in complete surprise. "Where did you get that idea?"

  "From Makayla's Grandma Lucy," Shane answered. "She has ~~bin~~ **been** bowling since she was a teenager, and she ~~teached~~ **taught** Makayla to bowl. I went with them once, and it's pretty cool."

  "Okay," Shane's father said doubtfully. "It's your birthday."

  Shane ~~sended~~ **sent** out invitations to ten friends. Some of them laughed when they ~~heared~~ **heard** what they were going to do, but they all said yes.

  Makayla's Grandma Lucy was there, and she ~~give~~ **gave** everyone pointers on how to stand and how to move their arms slowly so that ~~they~~ **have** has the most control over the ball.

  Once Shane's friends got into it, they ~~have~~ **had** a great time. As a matter of fact, two of Shane's friends decided to have their next birthday parties at the bowling alley.

  "Well, Shane," his father said with a smile, "it looks as if ~~you'd~~ **you've** started a trend. I might even take up bowling myself!"

Page 196

EDITING: Adverbs 13

Proofread these paragraphs. Find the 10 errors, cross them out, and write the words correctly above them.

  Rachel felt ready for her soccer game. She had played ~~bad~~ **badly** in her last game, but that's because she had hurt her ankle. As soon as she twisted it, it hurt ~~terrible~~ **terribly**, and it continued to throb painfully through the rest of the game.

  Rachel sat out the next three games reluctantly, but she knew her ankle would throb ~~worst~~ **worse** if she didn't listen to Coach's advice. She watched the team play worse in each game. Rachel was their best kicker, and she could run ~~quicklier~~ **more quickly** than anyone except Nina, who was as fast as the wind.

  Last week, Coach had finally said that Rachel was ready to get back into the game. Today, as soon as the game started Rachel knew she was going to play ~~best~~ **better** than she ever had before. Soccer was something she loved more than anything, and she had missed it ~~bad~~ **badly**.

  As the game progressed, Rachel's kicks went right where she meant them to go. Her team showed what they could do, playing ~~more good~~ **better** and ~~more~~ **better** good as the end of the game drew nearer. In the final minutes of the game, someone ~~sudden~~ **suddenly** kicked the ball to Rachel. As she slammed it past the other team's goalie, she heard voices roar ~~loud~~ **loudly** from the stands. They'd won! That's when Rachel knew that she wanted to play soccer forever! There was nothing like it.

Page 197

EDITING: Sentences 14

Proofread this paragraph.
Correct the incomplete sentences by adding words to make them complete. Then rewrite the paragraph on the lines.

  Do you Like to camp? So my family. We **does** every summer for two weeks. Our favorite place to camp **is** Lake of the Ozarks. **There are** Many great campgrounds there. **We** Camped at one last year that had a playground for kids, with swings and a seesaw. My little brothers and sisters **really liked that**. My sister Anika and I love to swim, so **is nice to be** it near the lake. This summer **we're going to camp** for three weeks. **I** Get to bring a friend this time.

_____

  Answers may vary. Sample answers are given.

_____
_____
_____
_____
_____
_____
_____

Page 198

EDITING: Sentences 15

Find each run-on sentence in these paragraphs and correct it. You can create two sentences or make the run-on sentence into a compound or complex sentence using conjunctions.

The famous Pullman porters were African-American men who worked on sleeping-car trains during the 19th and 20th centuries⊙they carried luggage, made up beds, and served food and drinks. African-American men weren't allowed to work at many steady, good-paying jobs, being a Pullman ∧ *so* porter was a desirable job.

People used to travel long distances by train, the old Pullman cars had ∧ *and* sleeping berths so people could sleep on their long journeys. The Pullman porters saw to the passengers' needs, the quality of their service was ∧ *,and* well-known among frequent travelers. Up until the 1920s though, the porters worked many hours for very little money, they had been trying to organize to ∧ *so* change their working conditions for years. In 1925, A. Philip Randolph joined with a large number of porters⊙they founded the Brotherhood of Sleeping Car Porters, the first African-American-controlled union in U.S. history. The strength of the union was behind them, Pullman porters' *With* working conditions and pay improved. In 1978, the Brotherhood of Sleeping Car Porters ceased to be an independent organization, it merged with the *when* Brotherhood of Railway and Airline Clerks.

Answers may vary. Sample answers are given.

Page 199

EDITING: Sentences 16

Read this paragraph and rewrite it to make it read more smoothly. Combine sentences to avoid choppiness and unnecessary repetition. Use compound sentences, complex sentences, and other sentence-combining techniques.
Rewrites will vary. A sample rewrite is given.

My grandparents are baseball fans. They love to watch baseball games all during baseball season. There's only one problem. The problem is that Nana is a Red Sox fan. Grandpa is a Yankee fan. There has been a rivalry for years. The rivalry is between Red Sox fans and Yankee fans. The Red Sox are the Boston baseball team. The Yankees are a New York baseball team. The Red Sox fans have never forgotten the great baseball player. His name was Babe Ruth. Babe Ruth left the Boston Red Sox. Babe Ruth went to play for the Yankees. This happened way back in 1920. The Red Sox fans still talk about it.

My grandparents are baseball fans, and they love to watch the games all during baseball season. There's only one problem. Nana is a Red Sox fan, and Grandpa is a Yankee fan. There has been a rivalry for years between Boston Red Sox fans and New York Yankee fans. The Red Sox fans have never forgotten the great baseball player, Babe Ruth. Babe Ruth left the Boston Red Sox and went to play for the Yankees. This happened way back in 1920, but the Red Sox fans still talk about it.

Page 200

EDITING: Sentences 17

Read these paragraphs and then rewrite them to make them read more smoothly. Combine sentences to avoid choppiness and unnecessary repetition. Use compound sentences, complex sentences, and other sentence-combining techniques. **Rewrites will vary. A sample rewrite is given.**

One of Lupe's family's favorite things to do is invite friends over. The family invites them over for a taco feast.

Everyone in the family helps. They help get ready for the party. Lupe's older brother chops onions. He chops chiles. He chops tomatoes. He puts them in bowls. The bowls are special bowls. They are used only when company comes.

Lupe's mother makes guacamole. Guacamole is a dip. The dip is wonderful. It is made from avocados. Lupe's Abuela taught Lupe's mother how to make this dip. This dip is very popular with everyone. Abuela also taught Lupe how to make tortillas. Abuela's are better.

One of Lupe's family's favorite things to do is invite friends over for a taco feast.

Everyone in the family helps get ready for the party. Lupe's older brother chops onions, chiles, and tomatoes. He puts them in special bowls that are used only when company comes.

Lupe's mother makes a wonderful dip called guacamole. It is made from avocados. Lupe's Abuela taught Lupe's mother how to make this very popular dip. Abuela also taught Lupe how to make tortillas, but Abuela's are better.

Page 201

EDITING: Capitalization 18

Proofread this paragraph. Use proofreading marks to correct the 10 errors. Hint: Two two-word proper nouns and one four-word proper noun count as one error each.

My Uncle Jason lives in new jersey. he works in New York City. I like to visit him there on school vacations. my parents let me fly by myself from chicago because Uncle jason meets me at the airport in newark. sometimes, Uncle Jason lets me go to work with him at his law office. then we go to lunch together at the museum of modern art. Later we go to central park and watch people sail miniature boats on this really cool pond.

Rewrite the paragraph on the lines below. Remember to use capital letters where they belong.

My Uncle Jason lives in New Jersey. He works in New York City. I like to visit him there on school vacations. My parents let me fly by myself from Chicago because Uncle Jason meets me at the airport in Newark. Sometimes, Uncle Jason lets me go to work with him at his law office. Then we go to lunch together at the Museum of Modern Art. Later we go to Central Park and watch people sail miniature boats on this really cool pond.

Page 202

EDITING: Capitalization 19

Proofread this paragraph. Use proofreading marks to correct the 10 errors. Hint: Two two-word holiday names and one three-word holiday name count as one error each.

What's your favorite holiday? I love the <u>f</u>ourth of <u>j</u>uly. I'm a big fan of fireworks, patriotic songs, and cookouts. Other people prefer the winter holidays, such as <u>h</u>anukkah, <u>k</u>wanzaa, or <u>c</u>hristmas. There's something about a <u>d</u>ecember holiday that breaks up the long stretch of dreary weather. My mom likes any holiday that involves a <u>m</u>onday off from work. We always do something special on <u>p</u>residents' <u>d</u>ay, <u>l</u>abor day, and Memorial Day. Sometimes, Mom can get <u>f</u>riday off, too, so we can leave as soon as school lets out and head to the beach or the woods to go camping. <u>L</u>ast september, we went to the beach for five days. It was great!

Rewrite the paragraph on the lines below. Remember to use capital letters where they belong.

What's your favorite holiday? I love the Fourth of July. I'm a big fan of fireworks, patriotic songs, and cookouts. Other people prefer the winter holidays, such as Hanukkah, Kwanzaa, or Christmas. There's something about a December holiday that breaks up the long stretch of dreary weather. My mom likes any holiday that involves a Monday off from work. We always do something special on Presidents' Day, Labor Day, and Memorial Day. Sometimes, Mom can get Friday off, too, so we can leave as soon as school lets out and head to the beach or the woods to go camping. Last September, we went to the beach for five days. It was great!

Page 203

EDITING: Capitalization 20

Write the titles correctly.

1. Folk Tales
   "beauty and the beast" **"Beauty and the Beast"**
   "why opossum has a bare tail" **"Why Opossum Has a Bare Tail"**
   "anansi and turtle" **"Anansi and Turtle"**

2. Magazines
   ranger rick **Ranger Rick**
   time for kids **Time for Kids**

3. Books
   maniac magee **Maniac Magee**
   bridge to terabithia **Bridge to Terabithia**

4. Songs
   "swing low, sweet chariot" **"Swing Low, Sweet Chariot"**
   "my favorite things" **"My Favorite Things"**

5. Poem
   "eletelephony" **"Eletelephony"**

Answer the following questions.

6. What is your favorite book?
   Answers will vary.

7. What is your favorite song?

Page 204

EDITING: Punctuation 21

Proofread this paragraph. Use proofreading marks to correct the 10 errors.

Do you like roller-coaster rides? I used to be scared of them, but now I ride on one every time I go to an amusement park. My brother, Jeb, likes to ride on them, too. Last summer, we went to Coney Island with my parents. Jeb and I rode on the Cyclone, which some people think is the best roller coaster ever. The ride was so cool. We screamed like maniacs the whole way down. Do you know what Jeb said as soon as we got off the ride? "Let's go again," he said. So we did. My mom thinks we're nuts to want to ride on roller coasters all the time. My dad is pretty cool about it. He used to like to go on roller coasters himself, but now he says he's too old and too smart to do it again.

Page 205

EDITING: Punctuation 22

Proofread this paragraph. Use proofreading marks to correct the 10 errors.

What's your favorite season? Is it fall, when the leaves turn colors, and the air gets that nice crisp feeling to it? Or is winter your favorite? Winter brings snow to the mountains and the smell of burning wood as people use their fireplaces to make their houses all nice and cozy. Spring is the favorite season for many people. That sound of the first returning robin is just amazing. The buds appear on the trees, and the flowers begin to poke through the ground. Before you know it, it's summer. The days get longer and warmer, and the smell of barbecue fills the summer evening air. That has to make summer the best season of all.

Page 206

EDITING: Punctuation 23

Proofread these paragraphs. Use proofreading marks to correct the 10 errors.

"What time do you have? Ella asked her friend Luis. My watch broke, so I'm wearing Susans, but I dont think it's working either."

Its 2:45," Luis said. "Why? Do you have to be somewhere this afternoon?"

"I'm supposed to be home by 3:15," Ella responded. My mom's taking me shopping for a new bike.

"Get a move on Ella," Luis said. "What's more important than shopping for a new bike?"

Write the corrected paragraphs on the lines below. Remember to include the correct punctuation.

"What time do you have?" Ella asked her friend Luis. "My watch broke, so I'm wearing Susan's, but I don't think it's working either."

"It's 2:45," Luis said. "Why? Do you have to be somewhere this afternoon?"

"I'm supposed to be home by 3:15," Ella responded. "My mom's taking me shopping for a new bike."

"Get a move on, Ella," Luis said. "What's more important than shopping for a new bike?"

Page 207

EDITING: Punctuation 24

Proofread these paragraphs. Use proofreading marks to correct the 10 errors.

Liam's great-grandmother, Gigi, was born on April 16 1914. When Gigi was a little girl automobiles were a new invention. People traveled on streetcars and trains or they walked long distances to get to where they wanted to go.

Most families didnt have cars but Gigi's family had one. They would go for long Sunday rides and theyd have a picnic somewhere along the way. They would always bring sandwiches fruit punch and cookies that Gigi's mother had made. After they had eaten they would pile back into the car and head home for a nice long nap!

Write the corrected first paragraph on the lines below. Remember to include the correct punctuation.

Liam's great-grandmother, Gigi, was born on April 16, 1914. When Gigi was a little girl, automobiles were a new invention. People traveled on streetcars and trains, or they walked long distances to get to where they wanted to go.

Page 208

EDITING: Punctuation 25

Proofread these paragraphs. Use proofreading marks to correct the 10 errors.

Terrys family was going river rafting on Saturday and they said he could bring one friend along.

"Terry why don't you invite that boy who moved in across the street last month? his mother asked.

"Mom I hardly know him! He could turn out to be a total freak," Terry objected. Terry wasn't crazy about the idea of being the first one to try out the new kid.

Just remember, Terry, that being new feels pretty rotten until someone makes you feel like you belong," his mother pointed out.

"Yeah, you're right," Terry said as he picked up the phone.

"That would be great, said Jorge when Terry asked him to go river rafting.

And thats exactly what the trip turned out to be—great! Jorge was funny and fun, and best of all, he loved to paddle!

Page 209

EDITING: Punctuation 26

Proofread these paragraphs. Use proofreading marks to correct the 10 errors.

Zachs school newspaper took a survey of students and teachers to find out peoples (people's) favorite books, poems, stories movies, songs, and television shows.

The fifth-grade students favorite book was Harry Potter and the Goblet of Fire. The third-grade students (student's) favorite book was Charlotte's Web.

The favorite movie for first-graders was Shrek. The favorite story for fourth-graders was On Board the Titanic.

The big surprise was the teachers choice for best song. The majority of the teachers chose On Top of Spaghetti as their favorite song!

Page 210

Name _____

EDITING: Punctuation 27

Proofread this friendly letter. Use proofreading marks to correct the 10 errors.

June 3⌄2006

Dear Tío Roberto⌄

Thank you so much for the birthday present. I've wanted my own tent for ages⌄and the one you bought me is perfect!

Two weeks from now⌄Dr⌄and Mrs⌄Marquez are coming with their son Jaime to stay with us for ten days. Dad said that Jaime and I can camp out in the backyard. Since the tent sleeps two⌄Jaime and I will be able to stay in it.

Thanks again for the gift⌄Tío Roberto. You're the best!

Love⌄

José

210 Paragraph Editing: Punctuation   Language Fundamentals • EMC 2755 • © Evan-Moor Corp.

Page 211

Name _____

EDITING: Punctuation 28

Proofread this business letter. Use proofreading marks to correct the 10 errors.

November 1⌄2007

Who Are You Costume Company

17 Lowell Av⌄e

New Rochelle⌄Ny⌄10952

To Whom It May Concern⌄:

On September 18⌄2007⌄I purchased a pirate costume made by your company to wear to a Halloween party.

The party began at 7⌄00. By 8:30, the costume began to fall apart. I had to leave the party early before the costume was completely destroyed.

I am returning the costume to you⌄and I would appreciate a full refund. My receipt is enclosed.

Sincerely⌄

Jeremy Nyack

© Evan-Moor Corp. • EMC 2755 • Language Fundamentals   Paragraph Editing: Punctuation 211

Page 212

Name _____

EDITING: Usage 29

Proofread these paragraphs. Find the 10 errors, cross them out, and write the words correctly above them.

My friends and I like to play baseball, but we don't have ~~no~~ **any** baseball fields in our neighborhood. Jenette's backyard is huge though, and it works really ~~good~~ **well** as a baseball diamond.

First, we measure out the distances between the bases, and then we ~~lie~~ **lay** the bases down where they belong. There isn't ~~nobody~~ **anybody** who can ~~lie~~ **lay** out bases like Jenette. We ~~may~~ **can** count on those bases to be exactly where they're supposed to be.

Julia is our star batter. There isn't ~~no one~~ **anyone** who can hit a ball as far as she can. She bats so ~~good~~ **well** that hardly anyone wants to be in the outfield when she hits the ball. Once during practice, she hit it to Chen and ~~I~~ **me**. Instead of trying to catch the ball, we both ran away from it. We didn't want ~~no~~ **any** part of that fast fly ball. Good thing we're on her team!

Answers may vary in students' corrections of the double negatives. Sample answers given.

212 Paragraph Editing: Usage   Language Fundamentals • EMC 2755 • © Evan-Moor Corp.

Page 213

Name _____

EDITING: Usage 30

Proofread these paragraphs. Find the 10 errors, cross them out, and write the words correctly above them.

"Mom, ~~can~~ **may** I go to Mary Catherine's house to play video games?" Tanja asked her mother. "Her parents invited me for dinner, ~~to~~ **too**. ~~There~~ **They're** making jambalaya tonight."

"Have you finished your homework?" Mom asked.

"I plan ~~too~~ **to** do the last of it when I get home," Tanja said. "~~Their~~ **There** isn't that much left to do."

"Okay, sweetie," Mom replied, "as long as you're sure you can finish up by bedtime. Say hi to Mary Catherine's parents for me. ~~Their~~ **They're** nice people. We should have them over for dinner sometime. Before you go, Tanja, would you please wake your father? He went ~~to~~ **lie** lay down for a nap before supper."

"I'd be only ~~two~~ **too** happy to wake him," Tanja said with a grin.

"On second thought, you don't have ~~too~~ **to**. You go on ahead and have fun with Mary Catherine," Mom said as Tanja left. "I'm glad you ~~to~~ **two** are such great friends!"

© Evan-Moor Corp. • EMC 2755 • Language Fundamentals   Paragraph Editing: Usage 213

Language Fundamentals • EMC 2755 • © Evan-Moor Corp.